Law of the Jungle

Law of the Jungle

**THE $19 BILLION LEGAL BATTLE OVER OIL
IN THE RAIN FOREST AND THE LAWYER
WHO'D STOP AT NOTHING TO WIN**

Paul M. Barrett

CROWN PUBLISHERS
NEW YORK

Library of Congress Cataloging-in-Publication Data
Barrett, Paul (Paul M.) author.
Law of the jungle: the $19 billion legal battle over oil in the rain forest and the
lawyer who'd stop at nothing to win / by Paul M. Barrett.—First edition.
     pages cm
Includes bibliographical references and index.
1. Donziger, Steven R. 2. Environmental lawyers—United States—Biography.
3. Liability for oil pollution damages—Ecuador. 4. Chevron Corporation—
Trials, litigation, etc. I. Title.

KF373.D595B37 2014
344.7304'6332—dc23   2013038226

ISBN 978-0-7704-3634-6
Ebook ISBN 978-0-7704-3635-3

PRINTED IN THE UNITED STATES OF AMERICA

Map by Fred Haynes
Jacket design by Eric White
Jacket photograph Sacramento Bee/ZUMApress.com

10 9 8 7 6 5 4 3 2 1

First Edition

For Julie, as always

Contents

Contents

COLOMBIA

Balao Terminal

PACIFIC
OCEAN

Pipeline

Rio Esmeraldas

EQUATOR

Quito ★

Rio
Guayllabamba

▲ Cotopaxi
(19,347 ft.)

Chimborazo
(20,702 ft.) ▲

ECUADOR

Guayaquil

Gulf of
Guayaquil

• Lago Agrio

Rio Aguarico

Rio Napo

TEXACO
OIL ZONE

Rio Curaray

AMAZON
RAIN FOREST

Rio Pastaza

A N D E S   M O U N T A I N S

N

PERU

Lago Agrio

San Carlos
•

Cofán

Coca
•

(Francisco de Orellana)

Rio Aguarico

Rio Napo

Secoya

TEXACO
OIL ZONE

ECUADOR

Huaorani

ORIENTE REGION

The meek shall inherit the earth, but not its mineral rights.

—J. Paul Getty

Law of the Jungle

Chapter One

SURVEILLANCE

The lawyer Steven Donziger stepped out onto 104th Street. He looked west toward Riverside Park and east toward Broadway. The dark sedans had been tailing him for at least a month now. They followed him for blocks at a time, slowing when he slowed, stopping when he stopped, their passengers watching his every move.

Donziger lived on a quiet block on the Upper West Side of Manhattan. He worked from home, a two-bedroom apartment he shared with his wife, their five-year-old son, and a cocker spaniel. Photographs and artwork from Latin America adorned the apartment. Documents in cardboard boxes surrounded the dining table. In the narrow foyer, stacks of stapled legal filings competed for space with a mud-spattered mountain bike.

On this morning in the spring of 2012, Donziger had wheeled the bicycle down the hall to the elevator and across the marble-floored lobby. Fifty years old, he dressed like a graduate student, in jeans, unironed button-down shirt, and tattered jacket.

"Cómo estás?" he asked the doorman as they bumped fists.

"Bien, muy bien, señor."

Then Donziger had emerged from the building and, as was his habit, searched for the dark sedans. Six-foot-four and powerfully built, he would not have been difficult to track. Sometimes, in addition to the cars, he thought he saw men on foot, pretending to peer into store windows if he looked their way.

Donziger began pedaling toward Ocean Grill, a seafood restaurant where he did business over lunch. As he approached the corner, he glanced over his shoulder in time to see the large car pull out of its parking space and fall in behind him. He didn't fear actual physical harm. The company was too smart, he thought, to turn him into a martyr. It wanted to distract him, intimidate him.

He despised his corporate foes: their money, their influence, their cynical disrespect for his clients in the Amazonian rain forest of northeastern Ecuador. The company would never willingly pay what it owed. Its lawyers and lobbyists had said as much. Now they were coming after him, making it personal. He'd written down license plate numbers, but the police weren't interested. Every day people killed each other in New York. What did he expect the police to do about cars that might or might not have been following him?

The surveillance wasn't his main worry. A year earlier, in February 2011, the company had sued him. The 193-page suit, filed under the federal antiracketeering statute, alleged that he had ginned up fraudulent evidence as part of a conspiracy to extort the company. A federal judge had taken the accusations seriously. The judge forced him to turn over his hard drives, e-mail, and boxes of documents. Donziger had said some truly dumb things—he admitted that much—and now they were public. His bravado sounded incriminating, he also acknowledged, especially if it was taken out of context. He'd cut a few corners, used tactics they didn't teach back at Harvard Law School. He could lose his law license. Conceivably, the U.S. Attorney's Office could bring criminal charges.

The company, as Donziger saw it, fought dirty; he fought back in kind. Slugging it out, he'd pulled off something amazing. His ragtag team had gone to a provincial Ecuadorian courtroom and won a judgment that mighty Texaco had ruined the lives of thousands of farmers and Amazon tribesmen. Because of him, a tiny third-world nation had spoken truth to power. Donziger had pressed the case for nearly twenty years now, beginning as the most junior member of the plaintiffs' legal team and ultimately rising to field commander. Before going after Texaco (which was acquired in 2001 by Chevron), he'd never brought even a slip-and-fall suit. That he'd survived this long must have shocked the oil company and its lawyers. No wonder they were branding him a racketeer and prying into his personal life.

He was not alone, though. Impressed by the potential for gargantuan legal fees, Patton Boggs, a tough corporate law firm, had joined Donziger. Together, they were seeking liens against refineries, terminals, and tankers worldwide. He'd retained a famous white-collar defense attorney to represent him in the racketeering suit. The Amazon pollution case had been featured on *60 Minutes* and in the *New York Times, Vanity Fair, The New Yorker,* and *Bloomberg Businessweek.* In 2009, it was the subject of an acclaimed documentary that played at the Sundance Film Festival. A rock star in green-activism circles, Donziger had received support from Bianca Jagger, Sting, and Sting's wife, the actress Trudie Styler. He had given Brad Pitt and Angelina Jolie a private tour of the oil zone in Ecuador.

"I cannot believe what we have accomplished," Donziger had written in private notes several years earlier, during a flight to Ecuador. "I cannot wait to get off the plane and see my fellow soldiers—often the only people I feel who get me. I want to look in their eyes and see if they understand the enormity of what this team has accomplished." He had gone toe-to-toe with one of the most powerful multinationals in the world and won the largest pollution verdict in history: $19 billion. That was billion with a "b," real money by anyone's standard. If he could survive the vengeful countersuit and collect the judgment, the Ecuador case would, in Donziger's expansive estimation, create a precedent benefitting "millions of persons victimized by human rights abuses committed by multinational corporations pursuing economic gain." And it would make him a very wealthy man.

Arriving at the Ocean Grill, he slowed his bicycle. The surveillance sedan—*Wait, were there two of them?*—kept cruising south. Donziger chained his bike to a NO PARKING sign and shrugged off his backpack. The spy cars disappeared in traffic. He knew they would circle back. They always did.

Chapter Two

PRESSURE

Six years before he played cat-and-mouse in Manhattan with oil company private eyes, Donziger was headed one cool morning to the Palacio de Justicia in Quito, Ecuador. "We are going down to have a little chat with the judge," he told the documentary film crew he had invited to follow him. He emphasized the word "chat" in a way that sounded menacing. "This is something you would never do in the United States," he continued. "But in Ecuador, this is how the game is played. It's dirty. We have to—occasionally—use pressure tactics to neutralize their corruption, and today is one of those examples."

Donziger was not an ordinary lawyer. Just out of Harvard Law School, he had worked briefly in a conventional job as a public defender, representing teenagers accused of street crime. But that was a long time ago. The Ecuador oil pollution case had allowed him to grow into what he wanted to be—a human-rights advocate, a rabble-rouser, a performance artist with a law degree. Clarence Darrow meets Martin Luther King Jr. meets Abbie Hoffman.

On this day, he aimed to convince an Ecuadorian judge to block Chevron's attempt to inspect a laboratory Donziger's team was using to analyze pollution evidence. The company alleged that the lab was incompetent and crooked. Donziger countered that the lab was fine; it was the oil company, he said, that was dishonestly harassing the plaintiffs. As he told the American film crew scrambling to keep up with him, justice in Ecuador often resembled a back-alley brawl.

Donziger and his entourage entered the courthouse and walked down a narrow hallway toward the judge's office. He had arranged for Ecuadorian television news stations to cover the confrontation. Donziger ushered several cameramen into the judge's chamber, a cubbyhole space that got so crowded there was no room to turn around. The judge, an elderly bald man, cowered at his desk, blinking behind large eyeglasses. "I sat down in the chair directly in front of the judge," Donziger later recalled, "where he could smell my breath."

"I am part of the plaintiffs' legal team," Donziger told the judge. The American lawyer wore a charcoal suit with a blue shirt and muted red tie. As a non-Ecuadorian, he did not have the right to speak in court as a lawyer, but technicalities did not deter Donziger. He rose to his feet, drew himself to his full height, and with piercing brown eyes peered down at the judge. "You have to be very careful with the Texaco lawyers," he began in American-accented Spanish. "They play dirty. They are trying to corrupt a legal process that thirty thousand Ecuadorians are carrying out. They are fighting for their lives." He repeated: "For their lives."

The judge was breathing heavily, as if he might have a heart attack.

Donziger cited no Ecuadorian statute or precedent. He invoked only his own ferocious indignation. "They are trying to use you, Your Honor, to do an inspection that is not legal," he lectured. "Please be careful. Please be very careful."

The trembling judge announced on the spot that he would suspend the laboratory inspection "in order to study the issue further." He placed a feeble hand on the sheaf of legal papers on his desk and added, "That's what I have to offer you."

At that moment, Diego Larrea, one of the oil company's lawyers, entered the judge's office. Larrea had learned belatedly of Donziger's preemptive strike.

"You've suspended the order?" Larrea asked the judge, incredulous. "Your Honor, it must be clear, this is another maneuver."

Donziger, towering over Larrea, who stood a good six inches shorter, assumed an expression of unrestrained wrath. "This is a corrupt Texaco lawyer!" he bellowed, pointing a long finger at Larrea. In fact, Chevron had subsumed Texaco five years earlier. Chevron paid Larrea's fees and was the defendant in the litigation. But Texaco had been the oil company active in Ecuador years earlier, and it was Texaco (pronounced locally *"Tek-ZAH-ko"*) that would resonate with Ecuadorian television viewers.

"Sir," Larrea said, turning to Donziger and pointing back at him, "you are going to be held responsible for what you say."

"I take responsibility, sir. You are a corrupt lawyer." His voice rising theatrically, Donziger repeated the epithet with relish, *abogado Tek-ZAH-ko corrupto*: "You are a corrupt Texaco lawyer! You are a corrupt lawyer!"

The TV cameras swiveled from combatant to combatant. The judge, unwilling or unable to restore order, reared back from his desk, but there was no place to escape. Finally, a flustered secretary took it upon herself to announce, "This is becoming personal! Step out, please!" The verbal rumble moved to the hallway, TV news and documentary cameras rolling.

Later, Donziger coolly assessed his performance. "Very effective," he wrote in his notes. "Talk about corruption, talk about how they try to use innocent and good people as vehicles for their own corruption." He had accomplished his purpose, both in the judge's office and with Ecuadorian television viewers.

Chapter Three

ARRIVAL

The righteous fury Donziger could summon seemingly at will on be-half of his rain forest clients flowed in equal parts from deeply felt empathy with their plight and his acute thespian instincts. One can genuinely care for the powerless while relishing the role of their protector.

In the personal notes he kept on a laptop computer, Donziger recalled his first visit to a tribe called the Cofán along the Aguarico River: "When I arrived in the village, I could see the desperation and hope that was being projected onto my presence." He won-dered whether he "could deliver any tangible benefit" to the Indi-ans, "either then or ever." He hated what he saw as "the desperation in the eyes of the children, and the hollow resignation in the eyes of their parents."

To honor him, the Cofán children sang traditional story songs for Donziger. Performing without musical accompaniment, the shabbily dressed choir described a time long before their birth when the forest was unspoiled, a common theme of the tribal rep-ertoire. The children performed a dance in Donziger's honor, dip-ping their hands in symbolic oil to illustrate what had befallen their culture and the rain forest they lived in and depended on. An elderly woman who sang with the children wore a colorful toucan feather through her nose, the sharpened tip penetrating one nostril, passing through the cartilage, and exiting the other nostril.

Emergildo Criollo, the leader of the Cofán community, initially had mixed feelings about Donziger. He appreciated that the American lawyer had trekked to the remote enclave but found the outsider overwhelming. Donziger spoke too loudly and waved his arms in a manner that made the Indians uneasy. The intricacies of the court proceedings he described eluded the Cofán. But Criollo came to trust him. "He spent time with us," the tribal leader said. "We saw this gringo lawyer had great passion."

The chain of events that had brought Donziger to Criollo's village began more than four decades before the lawyer's first visit. One day, when Criollo was a boy of six, a helicopter appeared above the treetops. "We were all amazed at the noise it made," he told me, remembering the remarkable 1964 encounter. "Which type of animal is this that comes flying from so high in the sky?"

Criollo saw the bulbous metal bird disgorge a number of white men in trousers and wide-brimmed hats. At the time, his father was teaching him to use a blow pipe and poison-tipped darts to hunt howler monkeys. The Cofán spoke a local language called *A'ingae*. A few knew Spanish because of earlier interaction with missionaries and rubber traders, but none of them knew the language spoken by the men from the sky. "We were scared," Criollo said, "so we hid."*

---

* Criollo told me the oilmen were the first Americans he ever encountered. In fact, an American missionary family named Borman had had extensive contact with the Cofán as early as 1955, nine years before Texaco arrived. Given Criollo's young age at the time of these events, it is not surprising that his chronology is slightly inaccurate.

The helicopters continued to arrive, delivering other strange machines. "Day and night, they cut the trees. There were explosions and fires. The white men were digging holes." Criollo and other members of the tribe wondered what they were looking for. He and his father crept to the edge of a clearing the outsiders had carved. "They were eating lunch. They gave us rice. It was the first time we tasted rice, and it was delicious." The yellow cheese the Indians were given smelled terrible to them, so they threw it into the jungle.

The Cofán lived a relatively isolated existence. They hunted, fished, and grew vegetables, mostly without interference from Hispanic Ecuador. In the late nineteenth century, rubber harvesters and traders had invaded the area and subjected several generations of Indians to brutal debt servitude. The intruders receded and then disappeared during the global depression of the 1930s, giving the Cofán and other tribes several decades of respite before the arrival of the new outsiders seeking oil and sowing fresh disruption. During all this time, the Indians also encountered American Protestant missionaries and Spanish Catholics. The foreign Christians provided machetes, mirrors, and clothing, in addition to Bible lessons. Some Indians went to live at missionary settlements, abandoning villages and straining clan ties.

In the songs and myths Donziger heard, the Cofán recalled an idyllic pastoral history before the appearance of the oil industry. What the Indians glossed over was their more complicated actual history, including serial intrusions they were ill-equipped to resist. They had barely endured encroaching modernity, clinging to a shrinking array of traditions. As a little boy, Criollo wore an old-fashioned Cofán tunic. The workers from the helicopters lifted his garment to see whether the six-year-old was male or female. Humiliated, he resolved to wear pants given out by the missionaries.

The white men at first drilled holes and made the earth shake. Later, they built towers as high as the tallest jungle trees. And some time after that, the Cofán noticed the men were bringing up from beneath the jungle floor a black viscous substance, which they stored in large pits. Before long, a multicolored sheen appeared on the surface of the streams where the Cofán fished and bathed and gathered drinking water. The underside of Cofán canoes acquired a greasy veneer. The firewood Cofán women gathered at the river's edge became covered in black goo. Freshly caught fish emitted a strange odor. The Cofán did not have words for "industrial pollution" or "contamination." They carried on as they always had.

Eventually, the Cofán shaman said he was troubled by the appearance of the gummy black fluid. He speculated that it was the blood of a sacred underground race that protected the people and animals of the rain forest. According to legend, the subterranean beings lived in a beautiful parallel world reached by means of a magical passageway. Were the white men killing the hallowed underground people? Would the monkey and wild pig the Cofán hunted soon disappear as a result? To his people's amazement, the shaman lacked answers.

Cofán children began to suffer from unfamiliar stomach ailments that neither the shaman's roots, nor the missionaries' medicine, could cure, Criollo said. "We had skin rashes. Children cried with pain in their limbs." Women had miscarriages, which he insisted "was something new." In fact, the Cofán had endured illness before the oil men arrived. Residents of the rain forest were not immune to miscarriage or disease. During the decades of rubber harvesting and Christian evangelizing, Indians suffered from ailments imported by outsiders. Still, Criollo and other Cofán felt certain that the oil had brought new and more severe afflictions.

More than a decade after the helicopters first arrived, Criollo was eighteen and married. His wife bore their second son. Something was wrong with the boy: At six months old, he remained tiny and fragile, like a newborn. With the assistance of Protestant missionaries, Criollo took the child to a hospital in Quito, but they couldn't help him. "He died there," Criollo said. "We were very sad, and we did not understand."

Then, Criollo's older son fell ill. "I had taken him to the river. Even the little children swam in the river and bathed there. The water had oil in it." The three-year-old child swallowed contaminated water. "When we got back home, he became sick in his stomach and started vomiting." He threw up blood. Lago Agrio, the oil town nearby, had no doctors in residence. Without an airplane or helicopter, there was no way to get quickly to the closest evangelical settlement. "My son died twenty-four hours later," Criollo said. Two children were now dead. As Criollo recounted these stories, his demeanor was flat, unemotional.

After the death of his children, Criollo was sent by his community to Lago Agrio to learn the cause of the illnesses. The frontier outpost was little more than a collection of oil camps surrounded by tumbledown taverns, whorehouses, and shacks inhabited by newly arrived mestizo settlers. More outgoing Cofán men, especially those who learned some Spanish, could get work clearing brush or guarding equipment. But when they earned a little cash from an oil job, the Cofán tended to spend it on whiskey and prostitutes, Criollo said. Even the beloved shaman, once known for his ascetic ways, became a heavy drinker and died of alcohol poisoning.

As for the ailing children, evangelicals in town explained to Criollo that they, too, were being poisoned. "Our water was no longer safe because of the drilling," he told me. His wife got sick. Doctors said she had cancer of the uterus. "She had her insides removed [by means of a hysterectomy]. The pain did not go away. . . . She was never the same woman after that."

The Cofán lost faith in shamans who could not cure the new illnesses. Young people lost their native language and spoke only Spanish. Girls drifted off to the brothels catering to Ecuadorian oil-field laborers. The Cofán lost territory to homesteaders arriving from Quito on the road national authorities had ordered the oil company to build. Steel pipes snaked through the forest; streams glistened with unnatural colors. "We lost our land," said Criollo. "We lost our life."

Chapter Four

PRODUCTION

In the early 1960s, Texaco Inc. retained ambitions for the Ecuadorian rain forest long since abandoned by rival oil companies. Standard Oil of New Jersey, a spin-off of the old Rockefeller monopoly, had poked around for decades with little to show for its investment. Shell packed up in 1950, the last of the majors to leave. Since then, the Ecuadorian jungle east of the Andes, known as the Oriente, had "remained virtually abandoned," according to an internal Texaco memo. As far as oil riches were concerned, Ecuadorian president Galo Plaza Lasso famously declared during this period, *"el Oriente es un mito,"* a myth.

Texaco disagreed. Headquartered in the gleaming Art Deco Chrysler Building in New York City, the company had a defiant reputation inherited from its founder, Joseph "Buckskin Joe" Cullinan. A refugee from Standard Oil who struck it rich on the Gulf Coast of Texas at the turn of the twentieth century, Cullinan started the Texas Company to take advantage of a legendary gusher called Spindletop. Plentiful crude sold for just three cents a barrel; unregulated extraction spewed so much contamination that drinkable water commanded five cents a cup. With financial backing from New York's Lapham brothers and a steel magnate named John "Bet-a-Million" Gates, Cullinan built a network of pipelines, refineries, and train connections that transported cheap Gulf Coast oil to customers up north. The Texas Company thrived on expanding demand for gasoline to power a new phenomenon called the automobile.

To Cullinan's great displeasure, his financiers shifted management activities to New York. An Irish immigrant, he lectured that the company's "attitude and activities were branded with the name *Texas* and Texas ideals"—but to no avail. Cullinan eventually lost the power struggle and was ousted. In his later years, he flew a skull-and-crossbones flag over the Petroleum Building in Houston "as a warning to privilege and oppression."

The Texas Company, which changed its name to Texaco in the 1950s, became a creature of New York. An aloof outsider in its own industry, it was the only oil major that did not participate in a trade group called the All-American Wildcatters Association. Rival executives of the good ol' boy persuasion referred to Texaco as "the meanest company in the world." The buttoned-down men in the Chrysler Building could afford to be arrogant. By mid-century, they ran the largest oil producer in the United States and claimed to have the rights to more oil in the ground than any competitor.

Texaco management didn't care that others had given up on Ecuador. The company had discovered crude in southeastern Colombia, and there seemed no logical reason why the political demarcation running invisibly beneath the rain forest canopy should preclude additional finds in northeastern Ecuador. Based on this hope, Texaco representatives signed a contract in March 1964 with the military junta that ruled in Quito. The deal awarded the American company the right to search for oil on more than 3.5 million acres, later augmented by an additional 4 million acres. This territory, larger than the state of Maryland, turned out to contain the choicest oil reserves in the Oriente.

In the mid-1960s, the region lacked roads, towns, and airfields, making it difficult to develop. The jungle had reclaimed mule paths and work camps from the rubber-trading era. After descending via rope ladders dangling from helicopters, workers used machetes and chain saws to clear brush and trees. It was these aerial arrivals that brought Texaco employees into contact with rain forest residents like young Emergildo Criollo of the Cofán.

The cross-cultural encounters did not always proceed amicably. Other tribes, such as the Huaorani, who lived to the south, greeted oil explorers at spear point. In response, Texaco subcontractors sent fixed-wing planes over contested areas and occasionally tossed down sticks of lighted dynamite, according to Giovanni Rosanía Schiavone, an Ecuadorian geologist who worked in the industry for thirty years. Decades later, he described the dynamite drops in a credible, confessional tone. "These were bombs to scare away the *indígenas*," he said, "so they would not interfere with the seismic surveys." In retrospect, Rosanía recognized the callousness of this conduct. At the time, terrorizing Indians seemed of no consequence.*

Working by hand, industry "doodlebugging" teams cut miles of three-yard-wide trails through the jungle. They drilled hundred-foot holes to bury their charges. Carefully sequenced explosions were charted by field seismographs, which confirmed subsurface formations containing oil. Improved drilling technology allowed Texaco to explore deeper and more effectively than Shell had in the 1940s.

On March 29, 1967, Texaco's exertions paid off. "In a remote wildcat in the jungle country of northern Ecuador," the trade publication *Oil & Gas Journal* reported, the company "hit the jackpot." In its internal history, Texaco recounted: "5,000,000 Ecuadorians heard with enormous jubilation the expected and sensational news: OIL HAD GUSHED IN THE EAST!"

---

* I couldn't independently confirm Rosanía's account of dynamite attacks.

It seems unlikely that the nation's entire population, much of which in the 1960s was beyond the reach of radio and television, received instantaneous word of the Lago Agrio breakthrough. Nevertheless, for Ecuador, it was an event of historic proportion. On its inaugural day, the Lago Agrio No. 1 well "tossed" 2,730 barrels. By the end of the year, Texaco had drilled four wells roughly twenty miles south of the border with Colombia. Together they produced 8,000 barrels a day, and there was hope that the Oriente reserves held far more.

Two decades after the Oriente had been written off as devoid of accessible oil, Ecuador's leading conservative newspaper, *El Universo,* applauded Texaco's success. FABULOUS OIL PROSPECTS IN EASTERN ECUADOR, the paper announced. "The spreading highways will bring civilization, the land will be better cultivated, the virgin pastures will enable domesticated livestock to graze, and primitive man will in one way or another be integrated into the life of today." Soon after Lago Agrio No. 1 began producing, the country's president, Otto Arosemena Gómez, arrived for an official visit. Max E. Crawford, the president and chief executive officer of Texaco's Latin American subsidiary, hosted the head of state and his son, Otto Jr., for an inspection of the four-story Lago Agrio derrick in a clearing surrounded by thick vegetation. The men wore white short-sleeved shirts and Indian-style necklaces woven from bird feathers, although photographs of the occasion reveal no actual Indians in attendance.

Ecuador, Arosemena recognized, could not get at its valuable oil without the help of multinationals and their money. On April 7, 1968, the president's picture appeared in an eight-page advertising supplement in the *New York Times*: "Welcome to Ecuador! The Country That Makes Business a Pleasure." For his color portrait, Arosemena wore a dark business suit with pink pin stripes and matching polka-dot tie and pocket square. "Ecuadorians know the rich potential of their land," he wrote in an open letter. "But as men devoted to work and orderly processes, they also see the possibilities of tapping the potential limited by the scarcity of capital. Hence the extension of the invitation to the foreign businessman and investor to place his faith, invest, work, and construct for Ecuador." The invitation might as well have been addressed directly to Texaco's boardroom in the Chrysler Building.

And the oil company RSVP'd enthusiastically in the affirmative. "Wherever a wheel turns or an engine throbs, we must have energy," the narrator of a 1970 Texaco promotional film intoned. The corporate documentary showed a car pulling into a suburban Texaco station. "Petroleum," the narrator continued, "where do they find it? How do they go?" The answer, illustrated by images of lush Ecuadorian foliage: "Anywhere and everywhere, and always with a gamble."

In 1972, when oil began to flow through a newly constructed pipeline from Lago Agrio to the Pacific coast, the tiny republic celebrated. A symbolic first barrel of crude, contained in a traditional wooden cask, was paraded through the streets of Quito atop a small army tank. Soldiers in ceremonial nineteenth-century uniforms marched with troops in modern camouflage. An open military truck near the rear of the procession bore a group of stone-faced Indians (who showed no sign of enjoying the occasion). The city's Catholic bishop sprinkled the first barrel with holy water. Spectators surged forward, seeking to touch the hallowed cask. Parents held out cups to receive a drop or two, which they daubed on their children's foreheads. After all the hoopla and speeches, the government placed the first barrel on an altar at the National Military Academy.

Beyond contributing to the national treasury, oil served other Ecuadorian aims. Beginning in 1963, a year before Texaco received permission to explore in the rain forest, the government developed plans for "colonizing" the region, which in Quito was commonly referred to as "empty territory." Eager to increase agricultural production, the government offered poor people from the highlands free property if they agreed to plant crops or raise cattle. Hundreds of homesteaders responded—eventually tens of thousands—each family cutting down a patch of jungle. Colonization addressed other goals, as well. Ecuador had lost a large portion of the eastern jungle in 1941 to an invading Peruvian army. Settlement of the Oriente helped secure Ecuadorian sovereignty. The army saw homesteaders as forming a "living border" with Peru and Colombia, and for years, the military provided colonists with free air travel to the region.

The lure of land drew so many campesinos from draught-prone Loja Province in the south that the government officially named Texaco's burgeoning rain forest oil camp Nueva Loja (New Loja). Locally, however, everyone called the town Lago Agrio, or Sour Lake, the name Texaco explorers gave it in the 1960s. It was named after a town in south Texas where Buckskin Joe Cullinan had made one of his early finds.

José Antonio Bricerio Castillo, a farmer who migrated in 1970 from Loja, knew nothing about petroleum before he arrived. "I wanted land of my own," he said, "enough land to feed my family and make some money to live." He sold most of his belongings and loaded his wife and four children (and a few caged chickens) onto a propeller plane. The journey took them into the lush rain forest, where they landed on an isolated airstrip built by Texaco. Bricerio cleared his swampy share of the forest to grow cacao, bananas, manioc, yucca, and beans. His children had children of their own. Into his seventies, Bricerio still tended his crops with a simple machete, in a never-ending battle against the encroaching jungle. He lived with his wife in a ramshackle one-story wooden house with a dirt floor and no plumbing.

Times had been even tougher when he first arrived. He struggled then to get crops to market. There were no stores, and basic supplies were scarce. It was the oil company, Bricerio told me, that in 1972 finished the paved road from Quito, making commerce easier. "Many more settlers arrived, and there were more jobs," he recounted in an even tone, neither grateful to nor resentful of "*Tek-ZAH-ko.*"

Unlike the Cofán and other indigenous people, men like Bricerio lacked a spiritual tie to the ancient forest. The colonists unsentimentally razed trees to grow fruit and graze cattle. Government-sponsored agricultural settlement resulted in vastly more deforestation than did oil development. Farmers like Bricerio felt no affection for the Indians, whose land the government gave them. Some homesteaders supplemented their farming with temporary work as oil field laborers. They resented what they saw as the company's favoritism toward the Indians, who knew the jungle terrain better than the new arrivals and would accept lower wages. The Indians, in turn, hated the homesteaders. Violence between them was not uncommon.

The colonists thought little, at least at first, of Texaco's prolific spraying of waste oil on unpaved roads to keep down the dust and create an asphalt-like coating. Barefoot children found themselves covered in black gunk which could only be removed with rags dipped in gasoline. When it rained, the oil on the roads became slippery. Tankers sometimes slid into ditches, disgorging their contents, or crashed into roadside pipelines, causing spills that could last for days. But in the early years, unless people or livestock were killed, such events received little attention. Oil had no special stigma. After long days of work in the fields or cleaning storage tanks at a Texaco facility, Bricerio and many others would rub hot petroleum on their aching knees and elbows to relieve the pain.

*   *   *

Long before the modern settlement of the Oriente, and even before the Spanish arrived in the 1530s looking for gold, natives of what would become Ecuador found naturally occurring surface pools of oil, which they used for tarring canoes. The country achieved independence in 1830 and took its modern name from the equatorial line that runs through it. Ecuador covers 108,623 square miles, roughly the size of the state of Colorado. It is bounded by Colombia to the north, Peru on the east and south, and the Pacific Ocean on the west. Six hundred miles west of the mainland are Ecuador's Galapagos Islands, visited by Charles Darwin in the 1830s and, in more recent years, by tourists eager to see giant tortoises and blue-footed boobies.

Ecuador's extreme geography and history of foreign incursion have contributed to a fragmented culture. For eons, the snow-capped mountains separated people in the highlands, or Sierra, from those on the coast. The jungle walled off the Oriente and its tribes. In Quito, which sits in a Sierra valley nine thousand feet above sea level, a Spanish-descended landowning class presided over haciendas worked by the indebted poor. Highland valleys were home to the majority of the native Ecuadorian population, whose subjugation by the Incas had occurred only a few decades before the Spaniards invaded.

The Oriente made up nearly half of Ecuador's territory but had only a tiny percentage of the population. One of the earth's richest biological zones, it teemed with leaf-cutting ants and psychedelically hued butterflies; boas, tapirs, and tree sloths. In addition to the Cofán and the Huaorani, the region's indigenous people included the Kichwa, the Secoya, the Siona, and the Shuar. Short in stature, the Huaorani (pronounced *"Wow-RAH-nee"*) were the most violence-prone, pursuing animal prey and human foe with equal vigor. Their rain forest neighbors called them *aucas,* or savages. The Huaorani referred to all non-Huaorani as *cowode,* meaning "cannibals." Huaorani men traditionally wrapped a cord made of wild cotton around their hips and positioned so that it kept the penis upright, a presentation representing power and energy.

A few years after the defeat of the Spanish, an independent Ecuadorian republic constituted itself in Quito. Its founding convention named one of Simón Bolívar's generals as head of state and enacted a constitution that assured the dominance of white landowners. This model of ethnic hierarchy and military influence would persist. Most mixed-race mestizos lived on the margins economically and socially, with the native Indians and people of African descent faring even worse. A conservative Catholic Church legitimized the caste system.

The economy assumed its basic shape early in the nation's independent life, with heavy reliance on a single export. In the late nineteenth century, a growing global appetite for chocolate spurred cacao cultivation. Levies on cacao exports financed construction of roads, bridges, and a railroad from Quito to Guayaquil. The cacao boom collapsed after 1920, as plant diseases took a toll and increased production in other countries drove down prices. Rarely stable, the Ecuadorian political system slipped into a period of chaos. Twenty-three chiefs of state held power in the twenty-two years between 1925 and 1947. This boom-bust pattern, accented by political pandemonium, would repeat itself with the rise of the banana industry in the late 1940s, followed by its decline in the 1960s. The powerful generals viewed Texaco's interest in jungle crude as a fresh opportunity for economic salvation. But while oil produced wealth for some Ecuadorians, it did not calm the society's volatile nature or cure its severe economic inequality.

Seeking oil in the rain forest, Texaco engineers asked for assistance from both the Ecuadorian military and the Christian missionaries. In the 1950s, evangelicals affiliated with the Summer Institute of Linguistics, an organization based at the University of Oklahoma, had decided to spread the Gospel to the people of the northern Oriente. A troop of SIL missionaries flew small airplanes over Huaorani settlements, dropping trinkets and broadcasting words of friendship. Some of the Indians were not persuaded. In January 1956, five evangelicals landed on a river sandbar and set up camp. Several days later, all five were speared to death. The evocatively named Rachel Saint, the sister of one of those slain, toured the United States in 1957 with a Huaorani woman who, under Saint's tutelage, had accepted Christ. After the pair appeared onstage with Billy Graham and on the popular television show *This Is Your Life,* contributions for Latin American evangelism skyrocketed.

Saint eventually returned to the northern Oriente. In the late 1960s, the Ecuadorian government paid her and the SIL to create a Huaorani "reservation," which attracted hundreds of tribe members. In exchange for relocating, the Huaorani received food, protection from rivals, and Christian education. Texaco invested in Saint's entrepreneurial evangelism, providing transportation, supplies, and cash. The Christians helped appease what the company referred to in one internal document as "savage indigenous tribes." It was from the missionaries that company employees learned the art of aerial gift-giving, according to American contract helicopter pilot Walt Snyder. Texaco, he said, dropped boxes of machetes "to pacify" the Huaorani (an odd choice to encourage nonviolence). Missionaries using Texaco-supplied aircraft removed some two hundred Huaorani from the path of oil crews, taking them to live in Saint's settlement.

With the natives more or less under control, Texaco expanded its operations rapidly. Giovanni Rosanía, later an Ecuadorian oil industry executive, had a job at the time overseeing aerial transport for a Texaco subcontractor. "We had more helicopters flying continuously in Ecuador than anyplace else in the world, other than Vietnam and Cambodia," he told me. Bell choppers ferried thousands of workers to construct landing strips made of hardwood palm trunks. Cargo planes designed for short takeoffs and landings brought in tractors, trucks, and steel pipe. In 1970, twenty-seven subcontractors were working for Texaco, employing thirty-six hundred people, 90 percent of whom were Ecuadorian.

To bring oil out of the jungle, Texaco paid for the construction of a pipeline that began in Lago Agrio, rose as high as thirteen thousand feet as it crossed the Andes, and descended to a port on the Pacific. Completed in June 1972, the $150 million, 312-mile Trans-Ecuadorian Pipeline was one of the boldest engineering achievements in Latin America. Texaco could have exported oil by means of a safer, less lofty route through Colombia, but Ecuadorian authorities demanded that the pipeline remain within their borders. Texaco would operate the pipeline for two decades before turning it over to Ecuador. The government also compelled the company to spend more than $55 million on roads and bridges that provided an eastward path for homesteaders.

As oil began to flow to tankers bound for California, Ecuador enjoyed an export-driven economic boom more pronounced than those spurred by cacao and bananas. The timing could not have been better. An embargo imposed in 1973 by the Organization of Petroleum Exporting Countries, or OPEC, drove up global prices. Barrels of Ecuadorian crude that initially sold for several dollars apiece soon brought $14. Traditionally viewed as an economic backwater, Ecuador joined OPEC and hosted the organization's international conference in Quito in 1974.

While Texaco dominated Ecuador's oil fields, the country's leadership looked out for itself. As early as 1969, President José María Velasco Ibarra, a durable populist, announced a series of changes in the country's deal with Texaco. He increased from 6 percent to 11.5 percent the royalty rate on oil Texaco shipped, and demanded that Texaco return two-thirds of its territorial concession so that other foreign companies could bid on access to the oil fields. Velasco Ibarra seized dictatorial powers in 1970 and two years later was ousted by a military junta; the generals were motivated in part by their desire to control the oil proceeds, which they spent on roads and schools, as well as tanks and planes. The junta also forced Texaco to hand over one-quarter ownership of its venture to a newly created state oil company, later renamed Petroecuador. Then the government raised royalty rates again and, over a period of five years, pushed up the tax rate on Texaco's earnings from 44.4 percent to 87.3 percent. "We dictated terms to Texaco, and the company accepted," explained Luis Alberto Aráuz, the Quito lawyer who negotiated the revisions on behalf of the junta.

Because of the rising government levies, Gulf Oil, which had been a passive investor alongside Texaco, decided to pull out of Ecuador. Petroecuador bought Gulf's shares. As a result, as of 1977, the government held a majority 62.5 percent stake in the Texaco-led consortium and controlled nearly two-thirds of the oil Texaco pumped. Ecuador refined some of the oil domestically and sold the rest abroad. Citing high taxes and royalties, seven other foreign companies followed Gulf's example and returned jungle concessions to the military government in the mid-1970s.

Ecuador as a whole profited handsomely from Texaco's activities. In the twenty-year period from 1972 through 1992, when Texaco gave up ownership and left the country, the "actual government take" from the consortium amounted to $23.5 billion, according to Aráuz's 616-page book, *Ecuadorian Oil Law*. His calculation included royalties, taxes, and sales of the government's share of the oil from the Oriente. In contrast, according to the Aráuz book, Texaco received $1.6 billion. Assuming that's accurate, it suggests a 93-to-7 percent split, favoring Ecuador. Chevron retrospectively has estimated Texaco's profits at just $490 million. Different accounting methods may explain the conflicting figures.

Regardless of the precise breakdown, Ecuador kept something in the neighborhood of nine-tenths of the Oriente oil money generated during the 1970s and 1980s. The perception that multinationals routinely fleece developing countries such as Ecuador from which they extract natural resources isn't always true. Many poor nations have suffered what's known as the "resource curse": the tendency of governments endowed with rich mineral deposits or petroleum reserves to squander their wealth by means of corruption and waste, while ordinary people endure minimal wages and environmental degradation. But at least since the 1970s, the oil industry generally has had to channel the majority of petroleum revenue to host governments and their national oil companies. Whether the Ecuadorian generals and their civilian successors in this case used petroleum profits wisely is another question.

The industry generating all of those billions of dollars for Ecuador was far from pristine. Drilling and refining oil is a dirty business, especially when the company doing the work operates without regulatory oversight.

Texaco bulldozed hundreds of jungle clearings of several acres each, usually on elevated ground that drained into one of the streams threading the Amazon watershed. Getting petroleum up from more than a mile beneath the surface involved several stages of work. First, drillers explored whether there was enough oil to make it worth going after. They used fluids known as drilling muds to cool and lubricate the drill bit, carry out cuttings, and exert downward pressure on the well. Drilling muds may contain acids, corrosion inhibitors, biocides, and fungicides—chemical compounds you would not want in your drinking water.

The preliminary process of creating a well brought oil to the surface, combined with natural gas and "formation water." The briny formation water had coexisted underground with the oil for millions of years and might contain naturally occurring trace amounts of arsenic, cadmium, cyanide, lead, and mercury. In the oil itself were yet more ingredients that if ingested could cause serious illness to humans and animals. Among these were benzene, toluene, and xylene. During the drilling and early testing process, Texaco poured a mixture of drilling muds, formation water, and oil into earthen pits dug near each platform. While it would have been possible to line the pits with concrete or metal to prevent leaching, Texaco left the holes unlined. The company created hundreds of pits—exactly how many is a matter of dispute—each the size of a large swimming pool. Many were outfitted with "gooseneck" piping systems that siphoned tainted rainwater runoff into adjacent streams.

Before moving to the main pipeline across the Andes, the oil had to be separated from formation water and natural gas. Lacking a feasible way to get the gas to market, Texaco burned it off via flares, which became a common feature of the jungle landscape. Engineers connected successful wells to feeder lines that brought the remaining combination of oil and formation water to separation stations. When the combination was stored in large tanks, the oil naturally floated on top of the water. This allowed crude to be removed and routed over the Andes for eventual export. The tainted water, known at this stage as "produced water," was piped to another series of open pits. Workers were supposed to skim off residual petroleum and treat the water with detoxifying compounds. The produced water then was simply released. Texaco discharged billions of gallons of petroleum-exposed water into streams, rivers, and lagoons.

The monograph-length contract Luis Aráuz negotiated with Texaco in 1973 contained four lines of text addressing "Conservation of Natural Resources." The contract instructed the oil company to "adopt the advisable measures for the protection of the flora, fauna, and other natural resources" and "avoid the contamination of waters, atmosphere, and land, under the control of the pertinent agencies of the State."

But what were the pertinent agencies designated to enforce this provision?

"In truth, there were none," Aráuz told me. The environment, he explained, was not a central consideration in his contract with Texaco.

The Ecuadorian Constitution guaranteed its citizens a "right to live in an environment free of contamination." A separate statute, the Hydrocarbon Law of 1971, required "the protection of the flora and fauna and other natural resources" and prohibited "contamination of waters, atmosphere, and lands." But these obligations were not fleshed out with specific regulations until the 1990s, after Texaco had left the country, Aráuz noted. For decades, they were empty platitudes.

In a 1976 letter, a Texaco manager based in Quito informed the company's board of directors that the Ecuadorian government had requested that Texaco drain and cover its waste-oil pits. Ecuadorians in positions of authority in Quito normally did not pay much attention to Texaco's cleanup methods, but in this instance, the government had been made aware of a "contamination problem" attributed to "excessive rains and, in some cases . . . improper drainage of the pits," according to the letter. Texaco, however, rejected the Ecuadorian proposal, noting that draining and covering the pits would be "significantly more expensive."

In 1980, Texaco debated internally whether to line its waste pits to cut down on contamination of the surrounding countryside. For a decade, most states in the United States had required the lining of waste pits, subject to permit, according to the Environmental Protection Agency. Texas prohibited unlined pits beginning in 1969. In an internal communication, however, Texaco's district superintendent explained to a company engineer why in Ecuador the company would not follow the industry trend toward lining its waste pits. "First," he said, "the current pits are necessary for efficient and economical operation." The alternative to the existing unlined pits, the superintendent added, "is to use steel pits at a prohibitive cost." Another option would be "to fill the old pits, dig new pits, and line the new pits. . . . The total cost of eliminating the old pits and lining new pits would be $4,197,968."

That amount—less than $12 million in 2013 inflation-adjusted dollars—was more than Texaco was willing to pay to protect the rain forest and its inhabitants. The term "corporate responsibility" was not yet part of the business lexicon. Nor had the Amazon yet penetrated the American consciousness as a symbol of the earth's vulnerability to man-made pollution. "It is recommended," the Texaco supervisor concluded, "that the pits neither be fenced, lined, nor filled." His recommendation prevailed, and the pits were left unlined and exposed.

A full record of Texaco's "contamination problems" in the jungle will never be assembled, because, at least for some time, it was company policy to conceal evidence of pollution. On July 17, 1972, the head of the Texaco office in Coral Gables, Florida, which oversaw Latin America, sent a one-page memorandum to company personnel in Quito. R. C. Shields, the senior executive, entitled the memo "Reporting of Environmental Incidents" and marked it "Personal and Confidential." Shields instructed Texaco employees in Ecuador not to disclose accidents or, for that matter, standard company practices that might result in ecological damage. "Only major events as per Oil Spill Response Plan instructions are to be reported," the memo stated. It defined a "major event" as "one which attracts the attention of the press and/or regulatory authorities or in your judgment merits reporting." Since there were no regulatory authorities to speak of, and journalists rarely ventured to the lowland oil fields, this instruction reasonably could have been interpreted as an order to cover up contamination. It's difficult to see how else it would have been read.

Years later, oil company lawyers and public relations special-ists would offer a more benign interpretation of the Shields memo. They insisted that it merely established "guidelines and priorities" for internal record-keeping. Headquarters, they contended, didn't need to know about every minor mishap. One spokesman, Kent Robertson, told me that subsequent verbal instructions super-seded the memo and required Texaco workers to report pollution "as promptly as possible."

Chevron's retrospective attempts to minimize the Shields direc-tive were not very convincing, especially in light of the memo's em-phatic tone. Without a hint of ambiguity, it concluded: "No reports are to be kept on a routine basis and all previous reports are to be removed from Field and Division Offices and destroyed." Texaco wanted no record of the impact of its drilling on the environment.

Chapter Five

LITIGATION

In 1993, the year after Texaco surrendered ownership of its Oriente operations to Ecuador's state-owned oil company, Steven Donziger invited American journalists to the United States Courthouse for the Southern District of New York for what promised to be a most unusual event. A press release carried a four-deck headline in front-page newspaper style:

RAINFOREST INDIANS LAUNCH
BILLION-DOLLAR LAWSUIT AGAINST TEXACO

Claim Oil Company Ruined Their Rivers and Land
in Amazon Basin of Ecuador

Tribal Leaders to Arrive in New York Today
to File Class Action Papers at US Courthouse

"CATASTROPHE WORSE THAN THE
***EXXON VALDEZ,"* LAWYERS SAY**

The body of the release promised "tribal leaders in traditional dress" would attend on November 3. Stripped in across the top of the breathless announcement were Donziger's name and phone number. The media, he predicted, would be more curious about costumed Indians than the less exotic migrant farmers who were the majority of the plaintiffs in the case.

Emergildo Criollo, by now a Cofán elder, was in New York on November 3. He wore on his stoic face the tribe's distinctive geometric red-paint markings. Elias Piyaguaje, a leader of the Secoya people, appeared in a bright pink tunic. "Our rivers have been poisoned," Piyaguaje told a battery of television cameras. "We cannot drink," he added. "We cannot bathe. We cannot believe in the future of our existence."

The photo op received lively coverage around the world. Donziger was elated. ECUADORIAN INDIANS SUING TEXACO, announced the headline above a *New York Times* article highlighting the plaintiffs' "traditional garb." The legal spectacular hadn't been Donziger's doing alone. The research and financial resources driving the litigation were supplied by other, more experienced attorneys. But it was Donziger's name at the top of the press release and, included with others, on the first page of the class-action complaint: *Aguinda v. Texaco Inc.* He may have been the most junior member of the plaintiffs' legal team, but he was a counsel of record on his first civil lawsuit. Most lawyers would have started with something more modest—maybe a simple breach-of-contract dispute. "Steve," said Chris Jochnick, a friend from Harvard Law School, "always wanted to do things big."

Donziger grew up in upper-middle-class comfort in Jacksonville, Florida, the son of a successful businessman. His father, Michael, a Brooklyn native, ran a family-owned electronics company. He and his wife, Karin, had two daughters in addition to their outgoing son. The Donzigers donated time and money to the River Garden

Hebrew Home for the Aged and the Jewish National Fund. Karin Donziger enjoyed fund-raising dinners and did volunteer work for poor north Florida fruit pickers. A smart, garrulous, sports-crazy boy, Steven did well enough in school, if not quite as well as his ambitious parents hoped. His maternal grandfather had been politically prominent, serving as the elected district attorney of Brooklyn, New York, and later as a state court judge. Steven's parents wanted their son to build on that tradition, go to an Ivy League law school, get a job with a good firm, and involve himself in public affairs. When it was time for him to go off to college, they had hoped he would do better than American University in Washington, D.C.

For most liberal-minded undergraduates in the early 1980s, the fervent activism of the movements for civil rights and against the Vietnam War had been replaced by post-Watergate ennui. Donziger rejected this fashionable apathy. Recalling his childhood in Jacksonville, he often mentioned the time his mother took him to a supermarket protest in support of farmworker activist César Chávez. In Washington, where politics is the hometown industry and favorite spectator sport, he lacked a particular cause but developed a love for partisanship, debate, and disagreement. Opposing the sunny conservatism of the Reagan administration came naturally to Donziger. He wrote for the undergraduate newspaper, where he got a kick out of seeing his byline and sounding off on campus controversies. He studied Spanish with the goal of learning about the proxy Cold War struggles roiling Central America. Above all, he had no intention of fulfilling his parents' traditional dreams.

"Most of us went to Daytona Beach for spring break," recalled a classmate. "Steven went to Nicaragua." Upon graduating from American University, Donziger landed a job with United Press International, a slumping wire service willing to send him to Managua as a paid reporter. In retrospect, he perceived a logical progression to his career: "Being a journalist is good preparation for being a human rights lawyer," he said. "You're looking for truth that the corporate and political establishment wants to cover up."

In the early 1980s, Nicaragua's Sandinista government aspired to foment a leftist, anti-Washington movement throughout Central America. The Reagan administration responded by helping to finance shady right-wing "contra" militias, which fought the regime. Donziger gloried in the intrigue. "You wanted to be around the guy because he was gutsy and funny," recalled fellow reporter Michael Allen, a housemate in Managua. When word of a rural skirmish reached the encampment of American journalists, Donziger would often be the first to suggest that they pile into a car and inspect the scene, whether or not this was wise from the standpoint of personal safety. He exuded a combative charisma. "Steve wasn't a dyed-in-the-wool Marxist or anything," Allen said, "but he admired the Sandinistas' bravery" in standing up to the contras and their American backers. Donziger struck Allen as self-aware about "the whole strange situation of our being down there, kids just out of college, in the middle of a foreign civil war. . . . He liked the idea, I think, of being in a risky situation. We were really *living*."

Most American journalists colored their reportage with skepticism toward the Sandinistas. Donziger's dispatches—he wrote more than 150 over four years—allowed the leftists to have their say about Washington. "It is really a shame that a government that represents a people peace-loving and fair-minded should stoop so low as to try to justify its criminal behavior by such infamous sort of lies," Nicaraguan foreign minister Miguel d'Escoto told the young reporter in November 1984. Two years later, when the Sandinistas shot down a U.S. plane bringing supplies to the contras, Donziger covered a ceremony during which coffins containing two fliers' remains were delivered to the American Embassy. "I am embarrassed that they were in this country to bring death to the Nicaraguan people," Jane Williamson, an expat teacher from Maine, told him.

He described abuses by both sides in the civil war. In a valley north of Managua where contras had been active, villagers told him that Sandinista soldiers had torched about sixty houses. "Rubble from the houses stretched for a mile," Donziger wrote. "Pigs, ducks, even a donkey were left behind. A schoolhouse was destroyed, its nine desks thrown haphazardly in a yard."

Donziger was a talented writer and enjoyed the romance of the foreign correspondent's life but ultimately did not choose reporting as a profession. Worried about ever making it to journalism's top ranks, he wanted to do more than wander the hinterlands, observing and chronicling. Donziger saw himself not as an analyst, but as a protagonist.

He returned to the United States and in 1987 went to work for an advocacy group devoted to Cubans who had fled the island in 1980 in what became known as the Mariel boatlift. Many of the immigrants had been released from Cuban jails and asylums. Thousands ended up in U.S. prisons and were threatened with deportation back to their Communist homeland. This led to rioting by some of the Cuban inmates. Drawn instinctively to fight for the unfortunate, Donziger became their strategist and spokesman. He arranged for the *Houston Chronicle* to profile one inmate to whom he assigned the appealing moniker "the Interpreter"—Manuel Monzon. A "Havana-born former engineering student," in Donziger's telling, Monzon had settled in New Jersey, where he took a factory job. With Donziger serving as translator, Monzon's wife described him as "a good father, a good son, a good husband, and above all, a good friend." The article acknowledged in passing that two years after the boatlift, this purportedly model immigrant was convicted of possession of cocaine with intent to distribute and sentenced to four years in prison. The heartwarming narrative Donziger created for Monzon could not transform hard reality, as the Cuban's American sojourn turned sour.

Already functioning as something akin to a lawyer for the

imprisoned Marielistas, Donziger took the next logical step of obtaining a law degree. One of his heroes, consumer-rights crusader Ralph Nader, had gone to Harvard Law School, and that's where he set his sights. Like Nader, he aspired to employ blue-chip credentials to challenge the establishment. His precocious accomplishments as a foreign correspondent and inmate activist set him apart from most other aspirants, and his application was accepted. In the fall of 1988, Donziger, then twenty-seven, arrived in Cambridge, Massachusetts.

Harvard produces many corporate lawyers whose careers fail to fulfill their youthful ideals, generating an anomalous mixture of material success, frustration, and disappointment. Donziger experienced no such inner struggle. He never felt the tug of the richly paid corporate world. In Cambridge, he gravitated toward human rights and criminal law. During one summer break, he worked for lawyers in Atlanta who represented murderers on death row. And he threw himself into campus causes such as opposing the elimination of the school's public-interest career-counseling program. His methods, applauded by some, irritated others. In the fall of 1990, several students distributed flyers objecting that the school's newspaper, the *Harvard Law Record,* had allowed Donziger to write anonymous articles casting his own activist campaigns in a positive light. Donziger would have none of it. "I categorically reject the assumption that somebody needs to be completely removed from something to write about it objectively," he told the *Harvard Crimson,* the undergraduate daily. He dismissed the criticism of his deception and conflict of interest as "the paranoia of conservative activists."

Donziger embraced Critical Legal Studies, a rebellious scholarly movement influenced by Marxism and French literary theory. Prevalent within Harvard's faculty, CLS taught that corporations and the politically privileged systematically manipulated legal concepts—the sanctity of contracts, for example, or "due process"—to maintain hierarchical authority and take advantage of ordinary people. "We learned that you can't rely on law to be a progressive instrument," said Donziger's friend Jochnick. The "law is just one medium and can be harnessed by powerful actors to obstruct progress." Law, in this view, didn't offer neutral principles, let alone a clear path to justice. It provided an alternative to politics: a means to an end.

Critical Legal Studies did not appeal to all liberal law students. Barack Obama, for one, adopted a less jaded perspective. A former Chicago community organizer who had grown up in Hawaii and gone to college at Columbia, Obama had concerns about how Harvard was run, but he preferred to work within the system, demanding that institutions live up to their professed ideals. Conciliatory to his core and wary of CLS's ingrained cynicism, Obama climbed the ladder at the *Harvard Law Review* and went on to become the first black president of the prestigious journal–cum–honor society. Their intellectual differences notwithstanding, Obama and Donziger enjoyed a friendly rivalry on the basketball court at the law school gym. Aspiring attorneys burned off plentiful stores of competitive energy in pickup games heavy on trash talk. "Big Steve" had an advantage in height and muscle; the more slender Obama displayed greater dexterity and a superior left-handed jump shot.

Donziger and Obama were fans of Harvard's most contentious professor: Derrick Bell, a black civil-rights expert who announced in the fall of 1990 that he would take an unpaid leave of absence until the law school appointed a nonwhite woman to its tenured faculty. (Harvard had sixty-two tenured professors, five of whom were white women; three, black men.) As part of his protest, Bell gathered sympathetic students in a basement classroom for a weekly teach-in. The throwback 1960s-style underground sessions drew national attention. When a reporter from the *New York Times* visited, Donziger's classmates were unsurprised that the young law student managed to get himself quoted. "The fact that students are willing to take a class with no credit," he told the *Times,* "sends a strong message to the faculty that we need more diversity, more ferment, more alternatives to the white male perspective." He took the teasing in stride when classmates reminded him that he was noticeably white and male.

Donziger sought ferment far beyond Harvard's tree-shaded campus. In early 1991, he and his buddy Jochnick decided to do something to undermine the conventional view of Operation Desert Storm, the U.S. military response to Iraq's invasion of Kuwait. "We were watching this hail of bombs on television, and everyone is calling it 'the cleanest war ever,'" Jochnick said. "Well, in trying to overthrow Saddam Hussein, the U.S. forces were actually going after civilian infrastructure, and there was a huge human impact." Once the fighting ended, Donziger, Jochnick, and a third student raised money from liberal foundations for an audacious mission to chronicle the plight of Iraqi civilians. The self-appointed fact finders brought along graduate students from the Harvard School of Public Health and a documentary filmmaker.

Donziger called the group "the Harvard Study Team" to give it more credibility and attract the interest of major newspapers. "Steve was very savvy, media-wise," Jochnick said. "He had a real nose for a story, having been a professional journalist in Central America." He even convinced producers with ABC's *Nightline* program to air a segment on the trip. The *Los Angeles Times* headlined its article 170,000 IRAQI CHILDREN FACE DEATH, HEALTH STUDY FINDS. In his promotional efforts, Donziger stressed the 170,000-fatality figure, a thinly supported extrapolation of the number of Iraqi children who might perish from the "delayed effects" of the Gulf crisis. Over the objection of the more-cautious public health scholars, he based the projection on data collected from only four Iraqi hospitals. A United Nations spokesman responded hesitantly, saying that the U.N. had not reviewed the findings but acknowledging that "the situation is critical, especially for women and children."

Despite its dubious statistical grounding, Donziger's agitation illuminated the anguish of war. He showed tremendous audacity in leading an amateur expedition to a still-volatile conflict zone. In the process, though, he obscured the culpability of the drama's central villain, Saddam Hussein, the Iraqi dictator who had started the bloodshed by invading a neighboring country and who for decades had subjugated and slaughtered his own people. Donziger blocked out complicating context, turning a morally murky situation into one defined in black-and-white.

Harvard, meanwhile, reacted angrily to its reputation being appropriated without permission. The university instructed Donziger to stop using its name in connection with the Iraqi venture, which the school had neither sponsored nor overseen. Unchastened by his alma mater's irritation, Donziger saw the Middle East adventure as a model for future activism. Jochnick cofounded a nonprofit group, the Center for Economic and Social Rights, to organize similar missions. The center's first project was supporting a lawsuit put together by a father-son team named Bonifaz.

John Bonifaz, another Harvard friend of Donziger's, was the son of Cristóbal Bonifaz, a lawyer and immigrant from Ecuador who lived in Amherst, Massachusetts. John had interested his father in oil contamination in the Oriente after reading an article on the topic in a newsletter published by the human-rights group Oxfam. "This is your country," John told his father. "Why don't you go do something about it?" The Oxfam report described field research in the rain forest by another American attorney, a woman named Judith Kimerling. In October 1992, Cristóbal Bonifaz sat down to write Kimerling a letter. "I was born in Ecuador," he wrote, "but have lived for the past 35 years in the United States. It is for this reason that I feel profoundly outraged [by] what you describe to be taking place there."

The Bonifazes were a storied Ecuadorian family. Cristóbal's grandfather Neptalí Bonifaz Ascázubi, a wealthy Sierra landowner, had been elected the nation's president in 1931. He never assumed power, however, as his foes in the legislature kept him from office. Rebellious provincial military units clashed with a Quito garrison backing Bonifaz. More than one thousand people died in what became known as the Four Days War, and Neptalí Bonifaz fled the capital.

Cristóbal Bonifaz came to the United States in the 1950s and earned a Ph.D. in chemical engineering at the Massachusetts Institute of Technology. He landed a research job at DuPont but never got over a sense of alienation in his adopted country. Washington and Quito feuded in the late 1960s over fishing rights off Ecuador's coast. The Ecuadorian Navy arrested American fishermen, and the United States cut military aid to Ecuador. "It seems ironic," Bonifaz wrote in a letter published in the *New York Times,* "that profit-making fishing fleets of an industrialized nation, with one-fifteenth of the world's population that consumes more than 50 percent of the world's resources, should flock to fish in these waters under the same umbrella that allows mercury poisoning of fish or the use of napalm." Determined to oppose U.S. government and corporate misdeeds, Bonifaz obtained a law degree in 1984 at the age of forty-nine. In his first case, he sued the U.S. Air Force over fighter-jet noise at a base in Pennsylvania, securing a $1.5 million settlement for nearby homeowners.

Bonifaz explained to Kimerling that in American courts, "class action law permits a group of named plaintiffs to sue as representatives of a plaintiff class, on behalf of a large group." He had in mind a gigantic environmental-damage claim, which would yield, not incidentally, a treasure in legal fees.

A Yale-trained litigator who needed no instruction on class-action law, Kimerling reacted warily. She suspected it would be difficult to meet the burden of proof showing that contamination over a large area caused particular illnesses, especially when the victims were barely educated peasants lacking medical records. She also wondered about Bonifaz's intention to single out Texaco, as Kimerling believed that Petroecuador and the Ecuadorian government shared liability for the ecological harm. She favored a narrower civil action, filed in Ecuador, stressing violation of indigenous land rights. But her approach, if successful, would generate, at best, a modest cash recovery and little attention in the U.S. media.

Kimerling was every bit as unconventional an attorney as Bonifaz. After graduating from Yale Law School, the Alabama native served as an assistant attorney general of the state of New York. She helped sue Occidental Petroleum, the parent of Hooker Chemical & Plastics, a company that buried hazardous waste beneath Love Canal, a small upstate community which became synonymous with corporate irresponsibility. Kimerling's labors ameliorated the damage in Love Canal but took a personal toll. In the late 1980s, she decided to take a sabbatical abroad. Not the sort to lounge in a Parisian cafe, she opted to save the Ecuadorian rain forest. She signed up for Spanish lessons and bought a plane ticket to Quito. In the Oriente she found a grimy industrial zone crisscrossed by rusting pipelines and roads slick with oil. "Hundreds of oil wells generate more than 4.3 million gallons of toxic waste every day," she observed. Virtually all of this produced water is "spilled or discharged into the environment without treatment, contaminating countless streams and rivers—often the only sources of water for surrounding communities."

Slim and unfussy about how she wore her curly brown hair, Kimerling, then in her early thirties, traveled by herself to Lago Agrio and other frontier oil towns. Texaco workers, amused by her pluck and possibly hoping to impress the attractive female adventurer, more often than not answered her questions. She understood technical data, having pored over mounds of it during the Love Canal investigation. In Quito, she dug out government records describing enormous spills from the Trans-Ecuadorian Pipeline. A severe earthquake in 1987 had dumped millions of gallons of oil into the Coca and Napo Rivers, destroying fish and plant life. Since 1972, such accidents had resulted in the release of an astounding 16.8 million gallons of oil, according to Kimerling's analysis.

As a result of her findings, the New York–based Natural Resources Defense Council launched a rain forest campaign focused on Ecuador. The NRDC's on-staff celebrity lawyer, Robert F. Kennedy Jr., toured the Oriente with Kimerling. Measured by sheer volume, the pipeline spills constituted a worse disaster than the 10.8 million gallons released by the stricken *Exxon Valdez* tanker into Alaska's Prince William Sound in 1989. "Judy Kimerling's work," RFK Jr. wrote in an essay in 1990, "has made this tragedy public for the first time." Kimerling took Kennedy to a clinic in Lago Agrio, where he noted "adults and children affected with skin rashes, headaches, dysentery, and respiratory ailments." In 1991, the NRDC published Kimerling's findings as a ninety-page softcover book called *Amazon Crude*. RFK Jr. contributed his impassioned essay as an introduction. The *New York Times* called *Amazon Crude* "the *Silent Spring* of Ecuador's increasingly aggressive environmental movement."

Beyond its ecological analysis, Kimerling's book included a discussion of oil economics, showing the effect of petroleum production on national finances. The benefits, as she made clear, were considerable. Oil fueled a decade-long boom in Ecuador in the 1970s, boosting what had been one of Latin America's poorest economies by an average of 7 percent a year. Average annual per capita income rose from $290 in 1972 to $1,490 in 1982. Oil soon accounted for half of Ecuador's exports. The military regimes of the 1970s earmarked petroleum revenue for improved health care, education, and roads. Infant mortality fell by more than 50 percent between 1967 and 1992. Life expectancy for an Ecuadorian born in 1992 was seventy years, compared to fifty-seven a quarter century earlier. Illiteracy declined, and gross domestic product rose. Small towns gained electricity. The government subsidized domestic fuel, and by the close of the 1970s, auto imports were increasing by 12 percent annually.

While aggregate wealth grew, however, Ecuador's least fortunate fell further behind. In 1975, government figures showed the country had a poverty rate of 47 percent. That level rose to 57 percent in 1987, and 67 percent in 1995. As poverty increased, wealth became more concentrated. In 1988, the World Bank calculated that Ecuador's wealthiest 10 percent enjoyed 47 percent of the income; in 1993, they got 55 percent. The bank found that the bottom 20 percent of the population saw its share of income decline over the same period from 2.6 percent to 1.7 percent. In the Oriente, Kimerling noted, many homesteaders were just as badly off as the indigenous people. "Their poverty," she wrote, "is deepened by oil pollution that can contaminate their water supplies, destroy local fisheries, and kill crops and livestock."

Having illuminated Ecuador's oil dilemma—strong growth and escalating income for some, combined with gross inequity and health-threatening pollution for others—Kimerling did what came naturally: She began researching potential grounds under Ecuadorian law for vindicating the rights of victims. Given the paucity of environmental protections in Ecuador, however, this proved a frustrating inquiry. Then, in October 1992, she received Cristóbal Bonifaz's presumptuous letter. It was Kimerling who had discovered the Oriente oil disaster; she lived for weeks at a time with indigenous tribes while conducting her research. Now this interloper wanted to turn her revelations into his own bells-and-whistles U.S. class-action suit.

Bonifaz told Kimerling in the letter that he knew influential people in Quito, but that they were "either too skittish to pursue these matters, or view these issues as personal attacks," since many of them worked for the oil industry. He didn't trust Ecuadorian environmental organizations, either: "I do not place many in these groups beyond CIA influence."

Kimerling knew the Ecuadorian environmentalists, and they were not CIA dupes. She wondered how Bonifaz, a conspiracy-minded expat who hadn't lived in Ecuador for decades, would make connections in oil field towns and rain forest villages. She declined to join his lawsuit.

That, as it happened, pleased Bonifaz. Nothing prevented him from borrowing Kimerling's published research for litigation purposes. He and his son discussed others who might help. John suggested Steven Donziger, who spoke Spanish and had lived for four years in Central America.

The invitation to work on the Ecuador lawsuit gave Donziger a chance to recalibrate a career he feared had narrowed too quickly. "What gets my metabolism racing," he explained, "is the idea that the law can be used as a weapon to club injustice into submission and create a better world."

He had a lofty sense of his legal pedigree, tracing back to his mother's father, Aaron Koota, who served as the Brooklyn D.A. and then as a trial judge in the 1960s and 1970s. Years later, Donziger recounted to the *New York Times* that he drew inspiration from two Democratic heroes whose photos hung on his grandfather's office wall: Hubert Humphrey and Bobby Kennedy. Koota himself, though a loyal Democrat, was no progressive. He earned "a reputation as a tough crime fighter who was criticized by such groups as the New York Civil Liberties Union for what they said was insensitivity to the rights of the accused and for seeking publicity," the *Times* said in a 1984 obituary. "I know I have been criticized, called a headline-hunter," Koota was quoted as saying, "but I am convinced there are times when a District Attorney must use the newspapers to awaken the community to a menace in its midst, even before he collects enough evidence to prosecute anybody." That affinity for sensationalism got passed down to Koota's grandson.

Upon graduating from Harvard in 1991, Donziger took his legal club to Washington, where he joined the juvenile court division of the public defender's office. The work was not for the faint-hearted. One of his clients, a thirteen-year-old, was convicted of murder and sent to a reform school. Another was shot and killed soon after Donziger got charges against him dismissed. After two years, the young lawyer decided he did not feel fulfilled. "Some of my colleagues called it 'God's work,'" he reflected. "But to me it was simply too limited in scale to effect the kind of broad-based change that I wanted to focus on. I was looking for an outlet in Latin America."

The case against Texaco seemed to Donziger to fit the bill. Unlike the largely anonymous workings of local criminal justice, suing a major oil company seemed likely to draw wide public attention. He liked the idea of a campaign that combined litigation with the promotional tactics at which he excelled. One of the lessons he had learned from observing the Nicaraguan civil war was the potential of "asymmetrical warfare," whether on a battlefield or in a courtroom. "You have to, if you have inferior resources, battle in creative ways," he said years later, "just like Viet Cong did against the Americans in Vietnam ... [or] in Nicaragua, the Sandinistas against Somoza." So Donziger signed on. In 1993, he helped organize an expedition to Ecuador financed by Cristóbal Bonifaz. The trip resembled the Harvard student mission to Iraq two years earlier. Once again, the goal was to demonstrate human collateral damage from American activity overseas.

The journey to Ecuador did not, however, go smoothly. Donziger, alluding to his Nicaraguan experience, gave speeches about the troubles of the rural poor. Cristóbal Bonifaz resented Donziger's know-it-all attitude. "When we went into the local communities," Jochnick recalled, "Steve had a way of dominating the conversation that clearly irritated Cristóbal." Bonifaz did not seem at ease in rain forest oil towns and Indian villages. Unlike Donziger, who enjoyed the local food and relished interaction with peasant Ecuadorians, Bonifaz ate packaged snacks brought from the United States and kept to himself. "In a weird way," Jochnick said, "Steve seemed like he was more in his element than Cristóbal."

Years later, Bonifaz acknowledged the cultural canyon separating his elite family from the workers they once employed: "My father lived like a feudal lord," he said. "He carried a little chest of money, and hundreds of Indians came down out of the mountains to meet him. He would call out their names, one by one, and give them some money. It was their yearly wages." The lawsuit provided Bonifaz a means to compensate for his family's heritage. But that didn't mean the lawyer was comfortable around farmers and tribesmen.

For all the tension, though, members of the Bonifaz group were unified in their reaction to the degradation of the rain forest. "Everywhere I looked," Bonifaz recounted, "there were lakes of oil. Black dust covered everything. I had to put a kerchief over my mouth to breathe. In a little village, I met María Aguinda, a Kichwa Indian, who invited me into her hut. She was barefoot, and she washed her feet in a barrel of gasoline before going inside. I also met her daughter, whose back was covered with some kind of growths. Lots of other people in the village had skin problems. They told me they couldn't drink from the rivers; that they had to collect rainwater instead. Their animals kept drinking from the rivers and dying."

Donziger recalled seeing "the carcass of a cow that had wandered in [to a waste-oil pit], become trapped, and asphyxiated." When he poked a stick into the pit and pulled it out, "the gooey oil sludge dripped slowly back into the pit. It had the same consistency of fudge mix being poured into a baking pan, but this was truly grotesque both in odor and texture."

Eager to sign up potential clients, the Americans got a mixed reception. By the early 1990s, some Ecuadorian Indian tribes had organized themselves into federations. Bonifaz and his retinue met in the town of Coca with an indigenous group known by its initials, FCUNAE. The indigenous leaders were wary of the Americans. It did not help that Bonifaz implied that he had Kimerling's cooperation, when, in fact, she had warned FCUNAE to steer clear of him. Bonifaz bulled ahead, securing the signatures of María Aguinda and several dozen other indigenous villagers and mestizo farmers.

An American doctor accompanying Bonifaz did medical exams of twelve residents; public health grad students collected thirty-three water samples. Using this modest database, the team concluded that water used for drinking, bathing, and fishing in the Oriente contained dangerous levels of oil-related toxic compounds known as polycyclic aromatic hydrocarbons (PAHs). Some samples showed PAH levels ten to one thousand times greater than U.S. Environmental Protection Agency safety guidelines. The medical exams "found cases of dermatitis apparently related to oil contaminants." Extrapolating from those findings, the researchers said in a report: "The presence of high levels of toxic compounds and oil-related injuries indicate that the exposed population faces an increased risk of serious and non-reversible health effects such as cancers and neurological and reproductive problems." Although phrased in tentative terms, this was the sort of evidence Bonifaz had hoped to find.

It fell to Donziger, with his "nose for a story," to figure out how a suit against Texaco ought to be marketed to the American public. The key, he decided, was the Indians' victimhood and their bid for vindication against unfeeling U.S. corporate power. Toward this end, the plaintiffs' team enjoyed a stroke of promotional luck: The

U.S. Agency for International Development, a branch of the State Department, without knowledge of the incipient class action, decided to bring several indigenous Ecuadorians from the Oriente to Boston for political training. Entirely by coincidence, Donziger would have his Indian photo op, and American taxpayers unwittingly would cover the airfare.

The USAID-sponsored trip took place in the fall of 1993. One participant was Emergildo Criollo, the Cofán tribesman who in the 1970s lost his two young boys to illnesses he attributed to oil pollution. He boarded an airplane for the first time in his life to make the long journey to Miami and then Boston. When Bonifaz learned that the indigenous representatives would be in Massachusetts, he arranged to meet with them. "That is when the lawsuit began," Criollo recalled. "The lawyers explained that we would take the fight to the house of Texaco."

Bonifaz helped underwrite a several-day extension of the Indians' U.S. visit and had them transported to New York, so they could participate in the November 1993 Donziger-orchestrated, media-intensive class-action filing. Surprised USAID officials were "aghast" when their attempt at nonpartisan civics education transmogrified into a "billion-dollar lawsuit against Texaco." Criollo did not see himself as a pawn of the plaintiffs' lawyers: "I was glad to meet them," he said. "Steven Donziger said we could make the American company take responsibility."

Chapter Six

REMEDIATION

Popularized as part of the consumer-rights movement of the 1960s, class actions had become common in the United States by the late 1980s. These mass lawsuits offered an alternative to the traditional model of a civil action brought on behalf of a sole victim or small group of victims claiming individualized harm caused by the defendant. Plaintiffs' lawyers used class actions to go after manufacturers of asbestos-laden fireproofing material, defective birth control devices, medicines with dangerous side effects, and other harmful products. Although business interests and judicial conservatives complained, courts gradually accepted class actions on the theory that they allowed people who had suffered common injuries to pool their resources and confront large corporations with consolidated demands for compensation. Facing a mass lawsuit, many companies preferred to cut their losses, avoid potentially catastrophic punitive damages, and settle with an entire class. If aimed at genuine wrongdoing and handled correctly, a class action can provide wholesale justice, as opposed to the arduous case-by-case retail method. Like other legal procedures, of course, the mass suit is also subject to abuse.

Named for María Aguinda, the indigenous tribe member who cleaned oil from her feet with gasoline-soaked rags, *Aguinda v. Texaco Inc.* represented a new kind of class action seeking to hold American corporations responsible for alleged misdeeds overseas. Donziger saw the case in grand terms, as a way to "re-allocate some of the costs of globalization . . . from the most vulnerable rain forest dwellers to the most powerful energy companies on the planet."

Aguinda named seventy-six Indians and migrant farmers suing on behalf of thirty thousand "similarly situated" people living in a Rhode Island–sized portion of the original Texaco concession. The class accused Texaco of "negligent, reckless, intentional, and outrageous acts and omissions." This conduct, the plaintiffs claimed, caused "property damage, personal injuries, increased risks of cancer, and other diseases." As a basis for demanding that Texaco answer in New York for its conduct, the plaintiffs' team cited an obscure law approved by the first Congress of the United States: the Alien Tort Statute of 1789, which allowed foreign nationals to file actions in U.S. courts based on "violations of the laws of nations," a vaguely defined body of principles embodied in treaties and diplomatic customs.

Little legislative history survives to explain what precisely the inaugural Congress had in mind when it approved the statute. Scholars infer that it was intended to assure European merchants and diplomats that they could rely on the infant American judiciary to entertain their complaints. The law gathered dust until the 1980s, at which point activist litigators began invoking it on behalf of groups of foreigners seeking recompense from repressive rulers in their homelands. In the 1990s, the human-rights bar adapted the statute yet again for use against U.S.-based multinational corporations, although "stretched" might be a more accurate word than "adapted," as the drafters of the Alien Tort Statute could not possibly have anticipated it applying to these situations. Both the basic class-action mechanism and its combination with the Alien

Tort Statute to address corporate misconduct abroad illustrate how creative legal minds expand concepts of liability if given latitude to do so by the courts.

Bonifaz, *Aguinda*'s quirky architect, never seriously considered bringing the case in his home country. Ecuador's institutionally weak judiciary did not allow class actions. Moreover, Texaco had operated in the legally unpredictable country since the 1960s and retained connections with the political and military elite. Donziger agreed with the strategy: "The largest judgment [in Ecuador] against an oil company after more than twenty years of oil activity and millions of gallons of spills and dumping," the younger lawyer noted, "was less than one thousand dollars." He had a bigger prize in mind.

But filing a complex case thousands of miles away from the scene of the alleged wrongdoing presented challenges. Bonifaz had little experience with international litigation. Prior to *Aguinda*, Donziger had had no civil courtroom experience whatsoever. After leaving his public defender job, he had become executive director of a criminal justice research project sponsored by a liberal think tank. The Ecuador pollution case did not generate immediate income for either lawyer. Without reinforcement, they would be buried by Texaco's inevitable avalanche of court filings.

The claimants wisely sought additional firepower from the Philadelphia firm of Kohn, Swift & Graf. Bonifaz allied himself with Kohn Swift because its founders had helped pioneer class actions in the United States. In 1986, the firm filed suit on behalf of Filipinos who alleged that deposed dictator Ferdinand Marcos had tortured or executed thousands of his countrymen. The firm eventually secured a $2 billion judgment against the estate of Marcos (who died in 1989), although there was no ready means of collecting the award. Eager to burnish the firm's human-rights reputation, Joseph Kohn, the son of one of the founders, agreed to join the case against Texaco. The oil company, Kohn said in New York on the day the suit was announced to the media, with the traditionally adorned tribesmen appearing beside the legal team, "has essentially ruined what was once one of the most pristine forests in the world, with calamitous results for the inhabitants of the region." He promised that his firm would cover up-front expenses in exchange for half of the 25 percent contingency fee Bonifaz had arranged with the Oriente class representatives.

"It was not taken as a pro-bono case," Kohn later told an interviewer. "A lot of my motivation is, I think, at the end of the day, it will be a lucrative case for the firm, and it may put us in a position to do more of these kinds of cases." *Aguinda,* he added, "could be the largest fee-producing case the firm has ever had."

The suit did not come as a shock to Texaco. As early as 1991, Ecuador was shaping up as a serious public relations problem. That year the Natural Resources Defense Council began promoting Judith Kimerling's book, *Amazon Crude,* as part of its rain forest–preservation campaign. In Alaska, meanwhile, the fallout from the 1989 *Exxon Valdez* spill drew unwelcome attention to the environmental record of the industry as a whole. J. Donald Annett, Texaco's top safety executive, tried to blunt the impact of *Amazon Crude* by contacting activists raising questions about Oriente oil operations. "Texaco has been careful to comply with the laws of Ecuador, oil industry standards of 'good practice,' and Texaco's own Guiding Principles and Objectives," Annett said in a 1991 letter to the NRDC. At the same time, Texaco's lawyers began gearing up for litigation.

Signaling its anxiety, Texaco supplemented its main outside law firm, Kaye, Scholer, Fierman, Hays & Handler, one of the premier corporate-defense outfits in New York, by hiring King & Spalding of Atlanta and its eminence grise, Griffin Bell, a former U.S. attorney general from the Carter administration. After the *Valdez* spill,

Exxon brought in Bell to lead an internal corporate review. Companies paid the courtly Southern lawyer to restore tarnished reputations. Bell and his underlings argued that the *Aguinda* plaintiffs failed to offer specific scientific proof of a connection between oil contamination and illness. The plaintiffs' initial complaint relied on Kimerling's research. But she had never claimed to prove that pollution had caused particular ailments. The Harvard graduate students financed by Bonifaz had warned of an increased risk of cancer, but they hadn't gathered rigorous epidemiological evidence. Plaintiffs in American courts are allowed to initiate cases based on preliminary facts merely suggesting wrongdoing and harm. Detailed evidence typically emerges, if at all, during subsequent depositions, review of corporate documents, and expert investigation.

Texaco's legal team also offered several procedural defenses, the most significant of which was centered on the doctrine of *forum non conveniens*. The company argued that New York was not the appropriate ("convenient") place for the case to be tried. The proper forum was Ecuador, where the alleged wrongs occurred and the supposed victims resided. To reinforce this point, the company sought the backing of the conservative government of Ecuadorian president Sixto Durán Ballén. An internal Texaco memo dated December 3, 1993, shows that a Texaco lobbyist helped draft an official letter sent by Ecuador's ambassador in Washington to the U.S. State Department, warning that an American ruling on the propriety of drilling in the Oriente would discourage American companies from investing in Ecuador. In a brief filed with the federal court in New York, the Durán Ballén administration urged dismissal of the suit: Allowing the action would cause "substantial and unwarranted interference with Ecuador's sovereign right to develop and regulate its own natural resources and may strain friendly relations between the United States and Ecuador."

Reading Texaco's legal papers, Donziger experienced a "depressing, sinking feeling." Bell and his legions knew what they were doing. Texaco's filings, which Donziger studied during a flight to Ecuador in early 1994 to interview potential witnesses, were voluminous and expertly crafted. His side, he wrote in his private notes, "seemed helpless and hopeless." A big corporation "either beat you down so bad that by the end the case is worth a fraction of the damages, or you give up."

Donziger's pessimism turned out to be exaggerated. The judge assigned to hear *Aguinda,* Vincent Broderick, a pipe-smoking former New York City police commissioner, wasn't the sort to be overly impressed by Bell's prestige or Texaco's corporate might. In April 1994, Broderick acknowledged that resolving claims involving tens of thousands of purported victims scattered across the Amazon would present "substantial difficulties." Nevertheless, he declined to dismiss the case and ordered the parties to begin discovery, the pretrial fact-finding process involving the exchange of documents and the deposition of potential witnesses.

Texaco had not left Ecuador in the early 1990s on its own initiative. Profits from its operations in the Oriente contributed only marginally to the company's bottom line, but Wall Street assesses the strength of oil companies in part based on the reserves to which they have access. Texaco wanted to continue to book the millions of barrels of Oriente reserves. Quito, however, refused to extend the consortium. Driven by nationalist and economic imperatives, the Ecuadorian government sought full control of Oriente oil production. Texaco had no choice but to leave.

From a financial perspective, Ecuador had mismanaged its petroleum boom. Oil gave the country access to international credit, and it borrowed heavily. But after national debt ballooned during the 1970s and early 1980s, interest rates rose and oil prices fell, and Ecuador descended into a wrenching recession. Following the pattern established earlier with the export of cocoa and bananas, Quito treated oil as a panacea, failing to diversify into other industries. After the 1987 earthquake, which halted oil exports for months, the country defaulted on its foreign loans, requiring a humiliating debt restructuring. When the national oil company, Petroecuador, assumed operational responsibility for the consortium in 1990, "it was time for Texaco to go," said Giovanni Rosanía, by then a senior Ecuadorian petroleum executive.

Rosanía at various times worked for Petroecuador, the Texaco consortium, and the Ministry of Energy and Mines. He had mixed feelings about the foreigners. Without Texaco, oil wouldn't have modernized Ecuador's economy, providing Rosanía with a comfortable life. But the foreigners could be overbearing and even cruel, in Rosanía's eyes, as illustrated by his allegation that early on, exploration had included the dropping of dynamite from airplanes to scare off inconveniently located Indians. Even in their more routine dealings with Ecuadorians, the foreigners could be excrutiatingly patronizing. "You, the petroleum workers, are the direct beneficiaries of our work together for twenty-eight years," Warren Gillies, a Texaco executive, said in a farewell speech to Petroecuador employees in 1992. "Your country and every one of you have grown doing this labor."

Around the time of Gillies's speech, Rosanía began negotiating with Texaco representatives over one aspect of the company's departure: the waste-oil pits and surface spills at drill sites in the jungle. According to Rosanía, Texaco representatives brought him a plan to "remediate" the mess, saying it would cost only $3 million—a fraction of what he thought was required. "Shove it up your ass," he said he told them, or words to that effect.

Talks continued for more than a year, intensifying after the *Aguinda* suit was filed in New York in November 1993. "Texaco did not say so, but there had to be a connection" between the lawsuit and the company's urgency about doing some sort of cleanup, Rosanía said. "They wanted to finish as fast as they could and get out [of Ecuador]." In 1995, when Rosanía was serving as deputy minister of energy and mines, he signed an agreement with Texaco under which the company agreed to remediate 37.5 percent of the Oriente oil sites. The percentage reflected Texaco's ownership stake from 1977 through the dissolution of the venture. (Years later, the company said it spent $40 million on this work.) Texaco committed to investigate 133 well sites and seven spill areas. At some locations it took no action, however, either because it claimed to find a lack of contamination or because Petroecuador had reworked the sites and layered on new waste.

The cleanup project's main shortcoming was built into its explicit terms: Texaco never had the obligation to address two-thirds of the well and separation sites it had operated since 1972. The company did not promise to clean up any degraded waterways or provide medical treatment to anyone. Yet Ecuador accepted these limitations, and Petroecuador assumed responsibility for the sites that Texaco disregarded. This was a missed opportunity, as Ecuador failed to use the leverage it temporarily enjoyed. Texaco wanted to continue to produce oil in the Oriente. If Ecuador had made the environment a priority, it might have negotiated with the company to clean up the entire concession area in exchange for a limited extension of Texaco's right to produce in the Oriente. But Ecuador did not make the environment much of a priority. (Neither did Texaco, of course, as demonstrated by the rampant contamination it caused in the first place.)

Texaco bought a dubious separate peace with FCUNAE. The company created a $1 million fund which the indigenous federation drew on to buy trucks, office furniture, outboard motors, and a speedboat. The company made a second $1 million payment for rain forest schools and medical dispensaries, although those fa-

cilities were never completed. In the wake of *Aguinda,* Lago Agrio
and four other municipalities sued Texaco in Ecuadorian courts.
To settle the suits, the company doled out another $5 million. In
return, the local governments gave Texaco releases from any pollution liability. How the towns divided and spent the settlement
funds remains something of a mystery.

Even with the best of intentions—which many would claim Texaco
lacked—cleansing a ten- or twenty-year-old oil site in the middle of
a rain forest is not an easy job. The basic protocol called for manu-
ally skimming off the crude oil resting on top of each waste pit or,
in the case of surface spills, the mucky oil puddles remaining on the
ground. Nearly thirty thousand barrels were treated and recycled
via Petroecuador pipelines, according to Texaco. The hydrocarbon-
tainted liquid beneath the oil layer in each pit was supposed to be
tested and, if necessary, treated with stabilizing chemicals. The liquid was then channeled into nearby rivers and streams. Contaminated soil was supposed to be backhoed from the empty pits and
washed with powerful detergents. The pits were then filled, covered
over with fresh dirt, and planted with local vegetation.

Texaco announced that at the sites for which it took responsibility the company met the agreed-upon cleanup standard, as measured by total petroleum hydrocarbons, or TPH. Crude oil contains
so many chemical compounds that technicians commonly measure contamination by TPH on a parts-per-million basis, rather
than by analysis of the individual components. Chemicals that
may occur in TPH include benzene, toluene, and others that are
hazardous to human health. In the United States, soil standards
for an oil cleanup varied at the time from state to state and according to land usage and proximity to groundwater. After an oil spill,
American federal and state authorities imposed cleanup goals as

low as 100 TPH. In Ecuador, Texaco said it would remediate the waste pits to a level of 5,000 TPH.* The Quito government agreed to the more permissive goal, which compared to the most stringent standard used in the United States allowed fifty times as much contamination to be left in the ground in Ecuador. Once again, Quito's failure to strike a better bargain helped undercut the effectiveness of the remediation program.

Whether these efforts were sufficient became an almost-immediate source of controversy. Under the terms of the remediation plan, the Ecuadorian government had to certify site-by-site that Texaco fulfilled its obligations in a scientifically valid manner. Quito, in due course, gave the company its approval. Other observers were more skeptical. Wilma Subra, an American chemist honored by the MacArthur Foundation "genius grant" program for work with oil-patch communities in Louisiana, independently reviewed Texaco's cleanup shortly after it was completed. Subra said that even if Texaco's subcontractors had done what they were supposed to do, "they really did not do much." Judith Kimerling, a diehard Texaco critic, agreed: "At many locations, contaminated liquids were dumped into rivers and streams without proper sampling and treatment," she observed. "Waste pits containing high levels of petroleum were backfilled without removing or treating the oil."

---

* Texaco maintained that focusing exclusively on TPH as a proxy for toxicity exaggerated dangers to human health. The company stressed the need to analyze TPH, a static measurement, with the Toxicity Characteristic Leaching Procedure (TCLP). While TPH indicates the absolute amount of petroleum hydrocarbons in a soil sample, the TCLP predicts the ability of toxicants to move from waste material into groundwater. Using the TCLP, the company claimed that it met its obligations to ensure that residual oil in and near waste pits remained stationary and didn't contaminate water supplies. The company said that it also fulfilled its duties under the static 5,000 ppm TPH soil limit. For the sake of simplicity and consistency, I will refer to TPH levels as a measure of contamination.

Years later, Giovanni Rosanía embodied official Ecuador's equivocal position on the remediation. Chain-smoking and drinking bitter black coffee during a long conversation in his Quito consulting office, Rosanía made a series of excuses. He pointed out that a new government took over in August 1996, forcing him to leave his post at the Ministry of Energy and Mines. As a result, he would not vouch for the execution of the cleanup. "I was responsible for what I did and what I signed," he said, meaning the 1995 agreement under which Texaco launched the project. All through the late 1990s and into the 2000s, he acknowledged, his former employer Petroecuador failed to do its considerable share of the work: "Many pits were left behind." In other words, Rosanía had put his name on a contract, which the national oil company did not fulfill. It was a shame, he seemed to be saying, but what could he have done?

As Rosanía described these events, his sigh and sagging shoulders conveyed a sense of fatalism tinged ever so slightly by guilt. Self-justifying helplessness characterized the recollections of a number of members of the Quito political and technocratic elite to whom I spoke. Life brought unfairness, they observed. The indigent residents of rural areas always seemed to bear the brunt of injustice. It had always been thus, they suggested, and probably always would be.

At the same time, Rosanía admitted that, despite his government's certification, he personally wasn't sure whether the American oil company had completed even the partial cleanup it had promised. "I am not defending Texaco," he said. The entire topic obviously made him uneasy.

In contrast, some Ecuadorians applauded Texaco's cleanup efforts. The company received a letter of appreciation in 1997 from Hugo Gerardo Camacho Naranjo, a leader of a town covered by the $5 million municipal settlement. Camacho, whose opinion may have been shaped by the corporate largesse, wished to express gratitude to Texaco "for the environmental remediation work performed on the creek which has its origin near well SA-89." The cleanup, he said, had "produced such a positive outcome for the local population that it has become a beautiful family visiting place."

Chapter Seven

JURISDICTION

Judge Broderick made no secret of his disquiet over the far-flung *Aguinda* class action. "Effective adjudication in New York," he re-marked, would be "problematic at best." He did not, however, shy from challenges. As police commissioner in the mid-1960s, the for-mer federal prosecutor had led his force through racial integration and the biggest transit strike in city history. Public officials in New York dealt with problematic situations as a matter of course. Not that Broderick assumed *Aguinda* could resolve the social tensions that gave rise to it. "Developing nations such as Ecuador benefit from foreign investment," he noted, "but are injured by environ-mental pollution." He didn't see a simple way to strike a balance. By allowing discovery to begin, he signaled that Texaco would not avoid answering the accusations it faced.

Just as the seventy-four-year-old judge was digging into the case, however, his health faltered. In March 1995, he died of cancer. The plaintiffs had lost a solicitous audience on the bench. The case was reassigned to Jed Rakoff, a new appointee of President Bill Clinton. From the start, Rakoff, then fifty-two, viewed *Aguinda* less sympa-thetically than Broderick had. Like his predecessor, Rakoff was a former prosecutor and law firm partner known for professional accomplishment rather than an ideological agenda. He did have a predisposition on certain forms of regulation, though. In 1991, he had written a law journal essay, entitled "Moral Qualms About Environmental Prosecutions," in which he questioned the punishment of executives for violations committed by subordinates.

The Ecuadorian plaintiffs would not have understood the significance of the judicial changing of the guard. But some did sense that they were being left in the dark—by their own attorneys. "We are concerned about the silence surrounding the lawsuit against Texaco," a Capuchin missionary based in Coca wrote to Judith Kimerling in November 1995. The priest worked with tribe members and lived in their midst. "There is no news from Bonifaz," he wrote. "It is like he has been swallowed up by the earth." Bonifaz had promised the villagers that they would receive medical attention for their various ailments. María Aguinda later told an interviewer that the American lawyers who took her signature in 1993 said they would return to her village, Rumipamba, with doctors in tow. No physicians ever materialized.

Donziger simply couldn't spare the time to visit Ecuador. His think-tank work had evolved into editing a substantial book, entitled *The Real War on Crime,* which Harper Perennial published in 1996. The book decried what it depicted as a manipulative and overly punitive justice system. "A hoax is afoot," the muckraking work warned. "Politicians at every level—federal, state, and local—have measured our obsession, capitalized on our fears, campaigned on 'get tough' platforms, and won." In Donziger's opinion, colored by the cynicism of Critical Legal Studies, those in authority distorted "the system" to get results they wanted. Not even basic crime statistics were trustworthy. Among the few angels in the book's pages were selfless public defenders, who routinely "carry 350 cases or more at a time, and have several different trials scheduled for the same day." Donziger, a former public defender, no longer bore that kind of burden. But in the mid-nineties, *Aguinda* commanded only a portion of his attention. Bonifaz remained in charge of the case. Donziger, though emotionally committed to battling Texaco, felt he had to keep other options open, in case *Aguinda* failed.

In November 1996, the significance of Broderick's death became clear. Judge Rakoff granted Texaco's motion to dismiss the suit without any further discovery. Rakoff lectured the plaintiffs' lawyers that they needed to "face the reality" that the authority of the U.S. judiciary "does not include a general writ to right the world's wrongs." In Rakoff's caution one senses an unease about the very idea of using the American legal process to grapple with another nation's complex social and economic history.

While the Republic of Ecuador, at Texaco's request, had sought this result, the ruling elicited outrage in Quito. Ecuador's politics had undergone another upheaval. The new president, Abdalá Bucaram, reversed his country's position on *Aguinda*. Known widely as *"El Loco,"* or "The Crazy Man," Bucaram had his attorney general accuse Rakoff of "unjustly and illegally" discriminating against Ecuadorians seeking justice. But in 1997, after serving just six months, Bucaram was removed by the Ecuadorian legislature for "mental incapacity."

Ecuador's next president, Fabián Alarcón, made matters in the case even murkier. His administration said that it did not oppose the suit but, at the same time, would not admit to any contributory liability. Quito arrived at this position in response to quiet lobbying by Bonifaz. In November 1996, he promised the Ecuadorian government in writing never to seek damages from Ecuador or Petroecuador. He vowed in a formal three-page agreement that even if Texaco were to obtain a judgment in the United States obliging Ecuador to contribute to a monetary resolution, his clients would "expressly waive the right to collect any amount whatsoever arising from such decision."

This constituted a monumental concession by Bonifaz. By pledging not to go after Ecuador or its national oil company, he reassured the Quito government that it could support the suit against Texaco without risking any liability itself. The arrangement had grave long-term implications. Bonifaz effectively absolved the Ecuadorian state of blame for ecological damage that the country's leaders, at a minimum, had tolerated. Yet during Texaco's two decades of operations, more than 90 percent of the proceeds from oil sales remained in Ecuador. By late 1996, Petroecuador had been running the former Texaco fields for six years. There were indications that, as operators, the Ecuadorians were even less scrupulous than their American predecessors. As Rosanía acknowledged, Petroecuador showed no inclination to clean up the waste-oil pits it agreed to remediate. Bonifaz's motive for letting Ecuador off the hook could not have been more transparent: He sought a colossal payout from Texaco, and he wanted to focus judicial and public animus solely on the wealthy American company. Indicting a malevolent global oil giant had more sex appeal than trying to hold a struggling national government responsible for letting down its people.

After these dizzying developments, the U.S. Court of Appeals for the Second Circuit in New York suggested that Judge Rakoff reconsider the whole situation. A three-judge panel of the appellate court ruled in October 1998 that if Texaco wanted to avoid the American judiciary, it should promise to submit to Ecuadorian jurisdiction (assuming that the plaintiffs had the wherewithal to refile their suit in Ecuador).

Ever on the lookout for media attention, Donziger contacted *Nightline,* the ABC news show, which had chronicled his Iraqi adventure. In the segment that aired that fall, correspondent Dave Marash memorably described the Oriente: "This Amazon paradise," he told viewers, "is as pocked and chipped and scratched as dinnerware at a greasy spoon." The strong implication was that American greed had wrecked a Garden of Eden.

Upbraided by the appellate court for being too hasty in his dismissal, Rakoff scheduled a hearing for February 1, 1999. It had been five years since the original filing of the class action, and more than eight years since Texaco passed operational control of the Oriente oil fields to Petroecuador. In anticipation of the hearing, Texaco filed court papers making a significant concession: If Rakoff dismissed the case for a second time, the company would submit to Ecuadorian jurisdiction. "If that's what it took to get Rakoff to dismiss the case, and the Second Circuit to affirm, then okay," recalled one former Texaco executive.

Texaco's senior officials felt unthreatened by the Ecuadorian judiciary for the same reason that the plaintiffs didn't trust it: Mass litigation was alien to Ecuadorian jurisprudence. Moreover, on September 30, 1998, the latest Quito government had certified in writing that Texaco fully performed the oil-field remediation and would be "released, absolved, and discharged forever" from any ecological liability claim by the republic. The release did not refer to claims by private parties. But without the backing of the Ecuadorian executive branch, the plaintiffs seemed to have little chance of prevailing in that country's courts.

Throughout the *Aguinda* case, Donziger grudgingly saluted the oil company's willingness to work every angle. "They're evil!" he was prone to exclaim, slamming a large fist on the table before him. At such moments, his broad, tall frame seemed to collapse, elbows dropping to his knees, chin to his chest. Fighting a giant corporation at times seemed futile. "You have to ask yourself," he would eventually admit, "is it a fool's errand?"

Then, without warning, he would become reanimated, rising to his full six-foot-four height, energy pulsing within him: a rumpled Don Quixote, recommitted to his quest, flailing his long arms. Self-pity set aside, he acknowledged the cleverness of his foes' strategy: "I get it. In their place, I would do the same thing." A multinational company like Texaco under attack will use every legal device at its disposal. A single defeat in such circumstances could encourage a barrage of lawsuits from all directions. There would be no end to it. "I get it," Donziger repeated. "It's a battle to the death."

The key, in his view, was not to do combat with Texaco on its own terms. *Aguinda* was about more than civil statutes and procedures. It was a morality play in which the oppressed rise up to challenge their oppressors. "The playbook for this type of case was not taught in law school, because such a case had never existed," Donziger wrote in a proposal for a book he never completed. "My professors—and I had some at the very top of their fields, with names like Dershowitz and Tribe—generally did not encourage students to tackle new frontiers in quite this manner," he explained. "There are obviously personal reasons why this kind of work has become my passion, but the bottom line is that I enjoy the fight." He sought existential validation in his battle with Texaco. Defying conventional odds, he was determined to shape the Ecuadorian narrative. He called it "scripting a legal case."

In a press release inviting reporters to attend the February 1, 1999, hearing before Judge Rakoff in New York, Donziger advertised a no-holds-barred courtroom brawl:

**BILLION-DOLLAR LAWSUIT
BETWEEN RAINFOREST INDIANS AND TEXACO HEADING
FOR TRIAL**

A Real-Life "David v. Goliath" Story

The hearing, the release added, "comes on the heels of a major shift in strategy by Texaco, which recently conceded that the case must go to trial in either Ecuador or the United States." As in the past, he advertised the availability of "Amazon tribal leaders in traditional dress."

Texaco, of course, had not conceded that the case was going to trial in any jurisdiction. The company had demanded that it be dismissed in New York. If it restarted in Ecuador, Texaco would submit to that country's authority only for the purpose of again seeking dismissal.

"The plaintiffs have claimed for years," Donziger's release continued, "that they cannot receive justice in Ecuador, whose civil code sets up many barriers to environmental litigation, including a prohibition on class action lawsuits." In no small measure because of Donziger's "scripting" talent, the influential *New York Times* embraced the plaintiffs' cause. A year earlier, the paper had sent a correspondent to the Oriente and published her dispatch about how "Texaco pumped nearly all the oil this small Andean country produced until 1990, maximizing profits, ecologists here say, by using inexpensive and environmentally unsound methods." The *Times* neglected to inform its readers that the overwhelming majority of the oil money remained in Ecuador or that Ecuador had agreed to release Texaco from liability. Not insignificant details, these facts were also absent from Donziger's rendition of the case.

Texaco submitted a raft of affidavits from Ecuadorian legal scholars and former jurists, who assured Rakoff that their country's judiciary was willing and able to grapple with environmental litigation. One company expert addressed the overthrow of President Jamil Mahuad in January 2000. Not to worry, the paid consultant said, "Ecuador's military has reaffirmed its support for constitutional rule." Apparently reassured, Rakoff again dismissed *Aguinda*. Ecuador, he ruled in May 2001, offered a judicial forum that, while not perfect, was good enough. He rejected the plaintiffs' broad reading of the Alien Tort Statute. The United States "has no special interest," he wrote, "in providing a forum for plaintiffs pursuing an international law action against a United States entity that plaintiffs can adequately pursue in the place where the violation actually occurred." *Aguinda,* the judge concluded, had "everything to do with Ecuador and nothing to do with the United States."

Texaco's lawyers celebrated their jurisdictional victory. They "were confident that the Second Circuit would affirm the dismissal, now that we had said we'd go to Ecuador if the plaintiffs came after us there," recalled the former company executive. "What we were less sure about was the public relations damage that Donziger was doing with the endless press releases and advertisements."

A proud and storied company, Texaco still saw itself in the commercial glow of its glory years. Since the 1940s, it had promoted its retail gas stations with the slogan "You can trust your car to the man who wears the star." The jingle had become part of American popular culture. At the production and refining stages of its business, however, Texaco was struggling. It had access to choice oil reserves, but its increasingly bureaucratic management failed to fully exploit them. In the late 1980s, the company was forced to reorganize in bankruptcy-court proceedings after a disputed attempt to merge with Getty Oil led to a $10.3 billion jury verdict against Texaco. Although it settled the case and survived that debacle, Texaco remained one of the smaller multinational "majors" during a period when hunger for capital for offshore exploration drove the industry toward greater and greater consolidation.

In addition to the intense competitive pressures affecting all oil companies, Texaco had a habit of escalating legal conflicts into disasters. A 1994 job-discrimination lawsuit against the company blew up into a national scandal two years later, when a laid-off white supervisor leaked to plaintiffs' lawyers an audio recording in which he and colleagues spoke disparagingly about black employees and discussed destroying documents. Not long after the tapes became public, Texaco agreed to settle the case for $175 million, the biggest job-bias payout ever.

Donziger capitalized on Texaco's self-inflicted liability woes by suggesting a connection between the frustration of African-American workers and the complaints of indigenous Ecuadorian tribesmen. "Plaintiffs' Attorneys, National Ad Campaign Charges Texaco With Race Discrimination—This Time in the Amazon Rainforest," one Donziger press release declared in the fall of 1999. Paid for by the Kohn Swift firm, the promised advertising campaign featured newspaper spots headlined RACIAL DISCRIMINATION AND TEXACO, CHAPTER 2. Glib as this attempt to link two disparate situations might have been, Donziger rankled his adversary. In a public statement, the company declared its commitment to "equality, tolerance and protection of the environment and the communities in which we operate. To allege that race was a factor in our operations is wrong and it is disgraceful."

"We were just getting the leaked audiotapes and the discrimination settlement behind us," the former Texaco executive said. Then "Donziger starts recycling the whole thing in the context of Ecuador. It drove people crazy, especially when management was trying to work out the Chevron thing."

The "Chevron thing" was a takeover bid in 1999 from the larger company. Mergers and acquisitions in the oil industry were creating a new breed of "super majors": Exxon Mobil, BP Amoco, and Royal Dutch/Shell Group. Texaco lacked the capital to compete against the behemoths, prompting investors to sour on the company's stock. In June 1999, Texaco's board rebuffed Chevron's $37.5 billion offer as inadequate. But Texaco was now "in play." Donziger once again was on the case, purchasing an ad in the *New*

York Times linking *Aguinda* to the proposed takeover. "A Word of Warning to Chevron Shareholders," the ad said. "Texaco Comes With a Lot of Assets. And One Huge Liability."

The heckling from the Oriente plaintiffs' legal team didn't deter a takeover-hungry Chevron. In the context of a proposed acquisition of this size, the theoretical Ecuador liability amounted to pocket change. Still, the nagging presence of *Aguinda* prompted Texaco executives to discuss settling the suit, as they had settled the Getty Oil and job-bias cases. "There were meetings where we looked at possible amounts," said the Texaco executive. "What would it take to make this thing go away?" In late 1999, a Texaco attorney put out a feeler to Bonifaz: Would he consider a settlement?

Bonifaz said he would. He had been involved in the case for more than six years. He lacked the resources for an arduous trial. Like a lot of plaintiffs' attorneys, he filed suits to settle them. Bonifaz was pleased when he was invited to meet in person with Texaco's general counsel, Deval Patrick. An African-American who had headed the Civil Rights Division of the Justice Department during the Clinton administration, Patrick had been hired to mop up Texaco's racial-discrimination mess. He was a political liberal who lacked professional roots at Texaco or in its industry. By predisposition, he had no desire to play the corporate heavy opposing impoverished rain forest victims. At the same time, he had agreed to serve Texaco in exchange for pay exceeding a million dollars a year. He felt pressure to prove to his new colleagues that he wasn't a patsy for plaintiffs' lawyers. And his top priority—what he'd be graded on by the Texaco board of directors, the national media, and Wall Street—was his success in repairing the company's reputation as a racist employer. The *Aguinda* case was an annoying sideshow for Texaco's top lawyer.

Before Texaco's negotiations with Bonifaz got very far along, Chevron returned in mid-2000 with a renewed bid for Texaco. The revised offer, at $36 billion, was less attractive than the earlier one, reflecting the continued deterioration of Texaco's competitive position. This time, though, Texaco's board acceded. Patrick focused on closing the complicated deal; settling with the *Aguinda* plaintiffs slipped lower on his to-do list. The new ChevronTexaco, eventually renamed simply Chevron, would become the world's fourth-largest non-state-owned oil company as measured by its combined $66.5 billion in revenue, 11 billion barrels of reserves, and production of 2.7 million barrels a day. Ecuador faded to an afterthought.

A corporate successor to the old Standard Oil Company of California, Chevron had more streamlined leadership than Texaco. Wall Street applauded the marriage. "Texaco has good assets," said Scott Smith, an oil analyst with Dresdner Kleinwort Benson, "and Chevron has the management to turn them around." With oil prices relatively high, in the mid-$30s, there was talk about new Chevron projects in Kazakhstan and off the coasts of West Africa and Brazil. The danger of litigation in Ecuador received minimal attention within Chevron. "It wasn't on the radar at all," a corporate consultant who advised the company told me. "Years later, the lawyers looked back, or some of them did, and wondered whether maybe the case should have been on the radar."

More out of curiosity than anything else, Texaco lawyers asked Bonifaz to propose settlement terms. He suggested $140 million, or less than 15 percent of the original "billion-dollar" *Aguinda* demand. Assuming that the plaintiffs actually would accept less than they asked for, the final settlement would have been a pittance in the context of the final $45 billion acquisition value announced when the merger formally closed in October 2001.

Still, the newly combined company summarily rejected Bonifaz's request. Chevron did not even bother to make a counteroffer. Patrick, the Texaco general counsel, had already moved to a new post at Coca-Cola (years later, he was elected governor of Massachusetts). The thinking within the merging companies was that the legal proceedings in New York were headed in the right direction. Bonifaz did not exude the confidence or competence needed to export his case to Ecuador. "There were two things that we didn't pay enough attention to," said the former Texaco executive. "One was the Environmental Management Act, and the other was Steven Donziger."

Chapter Eight

JUSTICIA!

For what figured to be a final go-round, the *Aguinda* plaintiffs' legal team revived the ritual journey to New York of wide-eyed Ecuadorian Indians. "Three short, wiry men walked barefoot and lightly clothed in 40-degree weather down Broadway and gazed up at the skyscrapers," the *Times* reported. Donziger took his clients to the East Village for "nouvelle Southwestern cuisine." The Ecuadorians, two Huaorani and a Secoya, told the newspaper that, given a choice, they would have preferred roast monkey. The next morning, Donziger, in a dark trench coat and carrying a briefcase, accompanied the traditionally adorned trio, now wearing shoes, to oral arguments before the Second Circuit. Bonifaz summarized their position in stark terms. "If we can't do this case here," he said, "we're done."

As expected, the appeals court upheld Judge Rakoff and sent the plaintiffs packing. By 2002, it had been nine years since the case had been filed. But the *Aguinda* plaintiffs were far from "done." While jockeying in federal court in New York, Bonifaz and Donziger had been planting seeds in Ecuador. In 1999, their efforts in Quito bore fruit when Ecuador's legislature approved the Environmental Management Act. The statute authorized a group of citizens to seek environmental reparations on behalf of the society. It allowed Ecuadorian judges for the first time to entertain social-reform suits—and without the complication of class representatives demonstrating that they were "similarly situated" to members of a larger group. Private parties in Ecuador could now go to court to vindicate Mother Nature herself.

Passage of the environmental act during the pendency of *Aguinda* in New York was not a coincidence. The Bonifaz-Donziger team helped draft the Ecuadorian law. The Spanish-speaking American lawyers consulted with Quito environmentalists and sympathetic Ecuadorian legislators about how to craft a statute roughly resembling the Superfund law in the United States, which required polluters to pay for cleanups even if they had sold a contaminated site or the industrial activity had long since ceased. In case the federal courts in New York rejected the U.S. class action, as ultimately they did, the *Aguinda* lawyers wanted an Ecuadorian insurance policy.

There was nothing necessarily improper about Americans giving advice to Ecuadorian legislators. It is striking, though, that the *Aguinda* team didn't notify the U.S. courts about the Ecuadorian law, to which Rakoff and the Second Circuit appeared oblivious. Doing so would have undercut the plaintiffs' contention that Ecuador barred mass litigation. In the end, the plaintiffs' silence didn't matter, as the American courts ruled against them anyway.

The oil company's Quito-based lawyers knew about the new environmental law, but they assumed it would not apply retroactively to conduct in the 1970s and 1980s. The Ecuadorian Civil Code forbade the retroactive application of newly created rights. The Quito attorneys, the former Texaco executive noted, overestimated their court system's fidelity to convention, including the rule on non-retroactivity. "It came back to bite us."

* * *

Chevron would deeply regret ever suggesting a move to Ecuador, as became apparent on October 21, 2003, the first day of trial in what might be called *Aguinda II*. The plaintiffs' legal team filed the Spanish-language sequel in the Superior Court in Lago Agrio, seat of Sucumbíos Province, an oblong stretch of intermittently industrialized jungle running along Ecuador's northeastern border with Colombia. Lago had changed over the years. With daily passenger flights from the capital into its tiny airport, it had become a jumping-off point for ecotourists heading to parts of the rain forest not yet overrun by the oil industry and homesteaders. Now a small city of thirty-five thousand, it nevertheless remained grungy and dangerous. Oil workers, most of whom lived in Quito and put in two- or three-week shifts in Lago, filled the run-down saloons. Truck exhaust hung over the main thoroughfares, except in the hour immediately after the daily rainstorm. The cocaine trade bred violence. Guerrillas with the narco-gangster Colombian FARC used Lago for rest and relaxation. Ecuadorian soldiers patrolled the streets in jeeps.

To mark the opening of the trial, several hundred chanting people marched to the provincial court, which was housed, along with law offices and a sundries shop, in a four-story walk-up building. Emergildo Criollo led a Cofán delegation and joined other protesters who carried a road-spanning banner demanding, JUS-TICIA! Donziger helped oversee the raucous street proceedings. At one point, he paused to speak with a group of diminutive bare-chested Huaorani women. A photograph picked up by media outlets around the world showed the tall American lawyer leaning over the Huaorani to reduce the vast difference in height. In one hand, Donziger held a delicate white-feather headdress. Elsewhere, peasant homesteaders and *urbanos* from Lago Agrio and other towns carried signs that said NO MAS MUERTE ("No More Death") and TEXACO, BASTA! ("Texaco, Enough!").

Ecuadorian troops with semiautomatic pistols strapped to

their thighs formed a human barricade in front of the court building. Upstairs, Judge Alberto Guerra Bastides stood in front of about seventy-five plaintiffs' representatives, lawyers, and journalists. Guerra, a man of about forty, wore gray trousers, a pressed white shirt, and a mustard tie. A mural behind him depicted a buxom, dark-haired woman in a short brown skirt, standing knee-high in a rain forest stream. The Amazonian Lady Justice lacked the traditional blindfold but did hold a legal balance, on which perched a yellow-billed toucan.

In the days leading up to the trial's start, Guerra, an experienced civil attorney appointed to the bench in 1998, had doubts about the plaintiffs' claims, he said years later. No Ecuadorian court had ever attempted to sort out such a complicated dispute involving money, politics, and science. As a judge, he had little in the way of support staff. Fearing that he would be overwhelmed, he considered dismissing the case with a ruling that shifted responsibility to the government in Quito. But if he'd done that, he later claimed, he'd have made himself a target of possibly violent political retribution. "Due to public pressure brought to bear by the representatives of the plaintiffs during the first hearing of the case," he recalled, "I allowed the case to continue because I felt that if I didn't, my personal safety would be at risk." No hero, and well aware of his vulnerability on the streets of Lago Agrio, Guerra chose to play for time.

A local radio station broadcast the proceedings live. The judge explained that each side would deliver an opening statement, and then he would receive documentary evidence and interrogate witnesses for six days. There would be no jury. After the courtroom phase, Guerra would preside over a series of in-person visits to well sites and separation stations. Attorneys and their technical advisers would accompany him to make observations and collect soil and water samples. At the conclusion of the "judicial inspections"—122 in all—a team of court-appointed experts would assess the reports compiled by the parties. Based on all of these data and analyses, the judge would issue a ruling.

No one knew how long all of this would take. Ecuadorian trial judges routinely rotate on and off cases, meaning that the man presiding over a suit at the outset might well have passed it to a colleague by the conclusion. Guerra figured he probably wouldn't be the one to issue a verdict. That would become someone else's problem.

Sitting at the plaintiffs' counsel table next to Steven Donziger was Alberto Wray, a former justice of the Ecuadorian Supreme Court. His mere presence spoke volumes. Wray's willingness to join the plaintiffs' team, a favor to Bonifaz, whose family name still carried weight in Quito, gave *Aguinda II* credibility. Trying to signal his own significance, Donziger whispered urgently to his older colleague.

Ecuador's latest president, Lucio Gutiérrez, had declined to take a formal position on the case. Acute observers noted, though, that the former army officer had received critical support from indigenous activists when he led a coup in 2000. Before the trial began, a Gutiérrez spokesman declared, "It is very clear that the people in the region have health problems and suffered for more than ten years. More work is needed to repair the area." Since the Gutiérrez administration showed no intention of paying for that work, one could only assume that the president expected Chevron to foot the bill. The Ecuadorian government deflected responsibility to the gringo corporation.

To display its corporate flag in Lago Agrio, Chevron sent Ricardo Reis Veiga, a Brazilian-born company vice president and general counsel for Latin America. A Texaco holdover, Reis Veiga had supervised the successful push to get the case dismissed in New York. He had correctly predicted that the plaintiffs would stumble in the United States, but he failed to anticipate the *Aguinda* sequel in Ecuador. Like many of his colleagues, he underestimated the willingness of the Kohn Swift firm to continue to lay out hundreds of thousands of dollars a year to finance the suit. The oil executives also failed to appreciate a change in Donziger's priorities. The young American lawyer had left his think-tank job to devote himself fully to the transplanted *Aguinda* lawsuit. Still single, and frugal, Donziger could afford to do this because Kohn Swift put him on a modest monthly stipend. He delighted in spending weeks at a time in Ecuador. "This is about being alive, about exercising the human will against all odds for something you believe in," he wrote in his notes. When meeting with Ecuadorian lawyers, he added, he felt like he was "part of a revolutionary cell."

Donziger viewed the case as a righteous cause deserving widespread attention. He formed an alliance with Amazon Watch, a likeminded anticorporate group based in San Francisco that could mobilize movie stars and rock musicians on behalf of its agenda. Amazon Watch helped arrange for Bianca Jagger, the Nicaraguan-born former model and ex-wife of Rolling Stones front man Mick Jagger, to travel to Ecuador to inject glitz into the *Aguinda* relaunch. A few weeks before the start of the trial in Lago Agrio, Donziger accompanied Jagger, an honorary member of the Amazon Watch board of directors, on a tour of oil pits and spill sites. Dressed in black silk pajamas—an ensemble of "mourning," she said—Jagger told Ecuadorian reporters that the oil company's "practices in Ecuador constitute an environmental crime." Her comments drew international headlines.

"Through his legal and media strategy, Steven made the Ecuador case the center of one of the leading campaigns worldwide against corporate recklessness," recalled Michael Brune, then the executive director of the Rainforest Action Network, another activist group in San Francisco. Like Amazon Watch, Rainforest Action enjoyed a symbiotic relationship with Donziger. The nonprofits promoted his work, and he, in turn, helped them raise money based on their collective crusade against the oil industry. "Steven understood that to win, he had to have not only a solid lawsuit, with all the necessary evidence, but also a way to draw attention and financial backing," Brune said. "That's where the celebrities help a lot." Some environmentalists with bigger, more mainstream groups like the Sierra Club and the Natural Resources Defense Council saw Donziger as a grandstander, interested more in his own fame than the rain forest. Brune, a former Greenpeace activist, thought that was unfair. Donziger's hunger for renown helped sustain him. "It's not like he tries to hide it," Brune said years later, laughing. "While he might rub some people the wrong way, he's just got a big, loud personality."

Chevron's Reis Veiga, a forceful advocate himself, could not compete with Donziger, let alone Bianca Jagger. Deeply loyal to his longtime employer, Reis Veiga stuck to a strategy of expressing contempt for ambulance chasers. The oil company, he believed, had done business with Ecuador in an open manner, fulfilling its part of every contract. Texaco had cleaned up what it agreed to clean up. What remained was the Ecuadorians' responsibility. The deforestation had resulted mostly from agricultural homesteading, he contended, not oil operations (a point supported by scholarly studies). The crop failure had stemmed not from pollution, he said, but from poor soil quality and lack of farming ability on the part of unprepared colonists. This was the message Reis Veiga delivered to Ecuador's attorney general when he paid a call on the official shortly before *Aguinda II* began. Reis Veiga set up the meeting in Quito to ensure that Chevron would receive proper treatment in Ecuador's courts. The oil company felt abused, Reis Veiga complained. In response, the attorney general guaranteed an impartial trial but nothing more.

In the hallway outside the Lago courtroom, Reis Veiga told Ecuadorian and American journalists that, as a wealthy American-based multinational, Chevron provided the plaintiffs with a convenient target. Oil hadn't left rain forest residents worse off, he said. The industry had provided jobs, and according to the company, local health statistics for infant mortality and deaths from childbirth were in line with those throughout Ecuador. "The plaintiffs have failed to present any credible, substantiated evidence," Reis Veiga insisted. What, he asked the reporters, had Petroecuador or the Quito government done to help the poor? Nothing. As he fenced with the media reps, the executive pressed his outstretched hands together in a gesture of emphasis which gave him the appearance of a supplicant praying for absolution.

Inside the courtroom, Reis Veiga deferred to one of the company's native Ecuadorian attorneys. Chevron's argument stuck mostly to procedural points: In naming Chevron as the defendant, the plaintiffs had sued the wrong party. The organization that produced oil in Ecuador had been a "fourth-tier subsidiary" called Texaco Petroleum. The plaintiffs should have sued TexPet. But even that wasn't proper, because statutes of limitation had expired, and the laws in place at the time TexPet was operating its sites had not been violated.

Responding for the plaintiffs in a booming voice, former Supreme Court justice Alberto Wray condemned Chevron as arrogant and disrespectful. Its attempt to evade culpability, he said, insulted all patriotic Ecuadorians.

Judge Guerra did not deliberate for long. Whatever his personal misgivings about the plaintiffs' arguments, he refused to stop the trial based on the company's jurisdictional defense. TexPet may have been a distant subsidiary, but it was still an extension of Texaco, which, in turn, had become part of Chevron. Nor was the company going to escape by means of the 1998 liability release signed by the government of Ecuador. The judge assumed that, as the plaintiffs maintained, the release applied only to potential claims by the republic and by Petroecuador, not by individuals suing under the Environmental Management Act.

On the question of the applicability of that law, which went into effect seven years after Texaco left the country, Guerra again stood aside. With protesters in the street outside every day, he declined to abort the proceedings to uphold an arid abstraction like "non-retroactivity."

Before Judge Rakoff dismissed the original New York version of the suit, the plaintiffs had used the discovery process to gather thousands of pages of Texaco documents. They now filed the documents with the court in Lago Agrio, including the memo from 1972 ordering the destruction of corporate records and the 1980 internal Texaco communication blocking the lining of waste pits to save a mere $4.2 million.

As proof of the human damage done, the plaintiffs submitted a pair of studies claiming to show that petroleum pollution caused cancer. One paper, published in 2001 in the journal *Occupational and Environmental Medicine,* looked at the incidence of cancer from 1989 to 1998 in San Carlos, an Oriente town surrounded by oil wells. The researchers found that because of the contamination of streams used for drinking and bathing, residents had "severe exposure to TPHs." Total petroleum hydrocarbon levels ranged "from 10 to 288 times higher than the limit permitted by the European Community regulations." Of the town's estimated one thousand residents, ten people had been diagnosed with cancer. Eight of the victims were men, 2.26 times higher than the expected number of 3.5 cases. (No excess was found for women.) From these limited findings, the researchers concluded that the elevated cancer rate among men "might be associated with" oil pollution. A follow-up study published in 2002 in the *International Journal of Epidemiology* compared cancer rates in Oriente counties with oil operations to several without oil. The risk of cancer in the exposed populations "was significantly elevated in both men and women," the authors said. The second paper suggested there might be a "relationship" between cancer and proximity to oil, but did not permit an inference linking cause and effect.

Beyond receiving this less-than-overwhelming statistical evidence, Judge Guerra questioned several witnesses. Segundo Ojeda, a former employee of a Texaco subcontractor who witnessed the company's drilling, described how during rainy seasons, waste-oil pits, brimming with crude and drilling muds, overflowed "and emptied toward the marshes." Rene Vargas Pazzos, a senior executive with Petroecuador in the mid-1970s, told the court at the plaintiffs' behest that, while the Ecuadorian government supervised sales and production rates, "all of the technical decisions [that] were made for the development of the petroleum operations in Ecuador were made from the U.S." Ecuadorian oil officials "assumed that the technology employed by Texaco for the exploration and extraction . . . was first-rate technology." Vargas, a former army general, insisted that he and fellow technocrats blindly trusted the Americans.

For this to make sense, the ex-general had to be understood as saying that Ecuadorian officials failed to notice that, over the course of twenty years, millions of gallons of rogue oil spewed from the Trans-Ecuadorian Pipeline. One had to accept that these officials were also oblivious to hundreds of swimming pool–sized pits oozing cast-off petroleum and industrial fluids. The implausibility of the witness's hear-no-evil, see-no-evil account was underscored by the 1976 Texaco letter noting the Ecuadorian government request that the company drain and cover its oil pits. Texaco refused to comply. But in order for the issue to have been raised, at least some officials in Quito had to have been aware of the contamination.

Awareness of the problem was illustrated again in 1979, when the chief of the country's Hydrocarbons Bureau sent an official letter to Texaco listing seven sites around Lago Agrio where poor maintenance caused contamination. The letter bore the government's motto, "Ecuador has been, is, and always will be an Amazonian country." To remind the company of its responsibilities to the rain forest, the hydrocarbons bureaucrat imposed a fine of $3,650, an amount so paltry that it doubtless reassured Texaco that officials in Quito did not, in fact, take their credo seriously. All concerned treated the Oriente as a waste-oil dumping ground and its residents as nonentities.

Donziger made sure that the start of *Aguinda II* received media coverage not only in Ecuador, where it led news broadcasts and dominated front pages, but also in newspapers with international reach. It was no small feat. Generating this kind of coverage revealed Donziger's brilliance for dramatizing obscure events in a simple, easy-to-understand form appealing to harried reporters. "These are not just random spills," he told the *Washington Post*. "This is the result of a decision made by Texaco to install a type of drilling process that would lead to a systematic dumping of toxins." In an article entitled "Ecuador Suit Could Cost Oil Giant," the *Wall Street Journal* noted that Ecuadorians were electrified by "the globalization trial of the century." Dave Russell, an American engineer Donziger hired to provide technical advice, told the *Journal*, "To put this thing in perspective, you're looking at something, sizewise, larger than the Chernobyl disaster." At the beginning of the trial, Donziger released a report he'd commissioned from Russell that estimated it would cost $6.14 billion to dispose of the millions of tons of contaminated soil.

What had begun as a "billion-dollar lawsuit" in New York had suddenly grown sixfold in Lago Agrio. Should the plaintiffs win that sum, it was not clear who would ultimately receive the cash or administer the cleanup. The suit named forty-eight individuals who were suing on behalf of "the community." But the legal papers didn't specify which community. No one knew what a victory over Chevron would look like. Donziger and the other plaintiffs' lawyers, though, knew what they stood to gain: a cool $1.5 billion in legal fees.

Chapter Nine

INSPECTION

Donziger adopted Dave Russell's evocative comparison of the Oriente oil fields to Ukraine's nuclear wasteland. He entitled an article he wrote in 2004 for an academic journal "Rainforest Chernobyl: Litigating Indigenous Rights and the Environment in Latin America." He began to use the term frequently in press releases and interviews and made sure others did, too. Donziger wasn't shy about instructing Amazon Watch how to frame the case. "I was shocked by what I saw in Ecuador," the group's honorary director, Bianca Jagger, told reporters gathered for Chevron's annual shareholders meeting in April 2004. "It was second only to Chernobyl."

Donziger had hired Russell a year earlier by means of a consulting service that put lawyers in touch with paid courtroom experts. Donziger told Russell to calculate "a big number" for the cost of cleaning up the Oriente. With only a month before preliminary court papers were due in Lago Agrio, the Atlanta-based consultant hurriedly toured the rain forest and did back-of-the-envelope calculations in his Lago hotel room to come up with the $6.14 billion estimate. A rotund man with a healthy sense of humor, Russell referred to this kind of analysis as SWAG, or scientifically wild-assed guessing. Unconcerned by this lack of precision, Donziger asked Russell to continue to provide analysis to the plaintiffs' team.

Much about the assignment struck Russell and his sidekick, industrial hygienist Charles Calmbacher, as surprising. On one flight through Miami to Quito, Russell noticed Bianca Jagger sitting a few rows away. She, too, was on her way to help promote the suit. When they met later in Quito, Russell remarked to Jagger that he would not have expected to see her in economy class. Jagger laughed. It had been many years, she said, since she had enjoyed the Rolling Stones lifestyle and traveled by private jet.

A more substantive revelation to Calmbacher was that the judge in Lago Agrio held the courtroom portion of the trial before the litigants headed out to the field to gather the bulk of the evidence. "In the United States, it would have been the other way around," Calmbacher said years later: "discovery first, then the trial." The judicial inspections that began in the summer of 2004 were like nothing either expert-for-hire had ever seen. Calmbacher compared the inspections to "a circus."

At each well site or separation station, judicial employees constructed a makeshift courtroom from plastic chairs, folding tables, and nylon collapsible tents. The Amazon sun pushed temperatures close to one hundred degrees, with humidity to match. Soldiers with automatic rifles provided security. Swatting away insects, opposing lawyers delivered loud, repetitive disquisitions. If television cameras were present, the speeches could last for hours. Technicians hired by Chevron and the plaintiffs dispersed to extract soil and water samples. Calmbacher and the other plaintiffs' experts at first wore white-hooded hazmat suits and gas masks, a flourish Donziger encouraged. Chevron's experts never bothered with the suffocating outfits, and the plaintiffs' team swiftly abandoned them, too.

At many of the inspections, area residents volunteered their woeful histories to the mobile court. As a result of contaminated water, "all the family suffers from headaches and stomach aches," a man named Miguel Zumba testified at a well site called Sacha 13. Instructed to travel to a clinic in Quito, he recounted, the family arrived in the capital only to be told doctors weren't available, so they returned without treatment. At the inspection of the Sacha Sur separation station, José Segundo Córdova Encalada described his understanding of the effects of waste oil spread on roads: "Why did my family get sick? Because we used to walk, since we are not rich. Around noontime, local nature and climate made smoke go up in the highway, which caused many men in these communities to suffer from the lower half of their body, and it gave women cancer in their genitals." Córdova said he knew enough not to drink the oil-stained water from streams and wells. But his uncle "wouldn't stop drinking it, and after more or less one year, he became sick with heartburn. He was taken to Quito, then came back home [for] several months, and finally died. He was diagnosed with cancer." What the personal testimony lacked in terms of medical records or other hard evidence of causation, it made up in heartfelt emotion.

The plaintiffs contended that, rather than releasing tainted produced water, Texaco should have spent millions of additional dollars to "reinject" the fluid into the underground reservoirs from which it had drained crude oil. As early as 1962, two years before Texaco began drilling in the Oriente, the American Petroleum Institute, an industry-funded trade group, had published a monograph entitled *Principles of Oil and Gas Production,* which warned: "The management and disposal of produced water requires extreme caution, not only due to the possible damage to agriculture, but also to the possibility of polluting lakes and rivers that provide water for human consumption as well as for irrigation." By the 1970s, Texaco and its competitors used reinjection widely, if not uniformly, in such places as Louisiana, Texas, and California. In June 1974, Texaco obtained a U.S. patent for an improved reinjection method designed to avoid the "considerable contamination problems" associated with surface disposal of production water.

Chevron's lawyers countered that in the 1970s and 1980s, reinjection was not an iron-clad standard in the United States, especially in thinly populated regions. With certain restrictions, American environmental authorities allowed surface discharge of production water, once residual crude had been removed and the water had been treated to neutralize heavy metals and salts. Chevron, based in San Ramon, east of San Francisco, was allowed by the state of California to discharge produced water at drilling sites in the San Joaquin Valley, not far from large agricultural operations. During the period when Texaco was active in the Oriente, Ecuador did not ban the practice, although by the time of the judicial inspections, Petroecuador was reinjecting produced water at most of its well sites. Other oil-producing nations that permitted surface discharge, depending on local conditions, included Angola, Brazil, Colombia, Indonesia, Kuwait, Mexico, and Nigeria. These places were not famous for environmental rigor, of course, but the point is that Ecuador's lax standards were hardly unique. In a similar vein, Chevron pointed out that while Ecuadorian officials occasionally expressed displeasure over Texaco's management of its unlined waste-oil pits, the Quito government never outright prohibited them.

By 2004, the judge hearing these conflicting entreaties had changed. Judge Guerra had presided over the case for less than a year before it rotated to Judge Efraín Novillo. The customary shuffling of cases heightened the extemporaneous atmosphere of the oil site inspections. Novillo, fifty-six, hurriedly had to get up to speed on the legal arguments and past filings. He admitted that he felt inundated by the attorney diatribes and thousands of pages of esoteric documents cluttering the court in Lago Agrio. "This is the first time," he said, "that I've worked on such a transcendental case."

As the peripatetic inspections unfolded, Donziger was gaining greater influence over the plaintiffs' team. Bonifaz lacked the stomach for tramping around the damp jungle; he mostly remained in western Massachusetts. The patrician Alberto Wray stayed in his comfortable office in Quito. "This was not a case for gentleman lawyers or academics," Donziger boasted in his private notes. "In a highly charged macho culture, this has become a flat-out street brawl."

Chevron often singled out Donziger by name. The company's Ricardo Reis Veiga publicly called him "despicable" and prone to "blatant lies and distortions" when discussing scientific evidence with journalists. Donziger wore the accusations as a badge of honor. At the same time, he did not want a gringo to be the public face of the plaintiffs' team in Ecuador. For that job, he groomed Pablo Fajardo.

An activist with the Lago-based Frente de Defensa de la Amazonia (Front for the Defense of the Amazon), Fajardo had a lowly extension-school law degree. He did not own a suit or tie, and he spoke little English. Donziger saw the wiry Fajardo as the perfect front man for the jungle lawsuit. "Pablo never seemed daunted by the obstacles that stymied the Quito lawyers, who often complained about the heat and whether we had enough Gatorade in the cooler," Donziger noted. Fajardo "not only relished the hot weather, he seemed to come even more alive as the temperature rose." By mid-2005, Donziger had persuaded Wray to make him the plaintiffs' lead local lawyer. Wray seemed relieved to distance himself from the rancorous, exhausting case.

At the Sacha Sur inspection, Fajardo wore a Panama hat over his bushy black hair when he faced off against Adolfo Callejas, an upper-class Quito attorney who spoke for Chevron. "Here we will see something that is common in every oil operation, yet has been demonized by the plaintiffs," Callejas told the judge. Rail-thin, the patrician lawyer had a haughty, condescending tone. Nearby, a network of black-painted tanks and pipes still separated petroleum from salt-laden formation water. "The production stations," Callejas continued, "are necessary, and are the technology that has been used, and is still used, in all crude oil production activities around the world."

Fajardo answered with typical fervor: "They try to deceive public opinion, the court and everyone at this inspection by making us believe that such practices were the way people operated in the entire world," he said. "That's a complete lie, Your Honor." Donziger listened intently from the edge of a crowd of about seventy-five people. "More than a billion gallons of poisonous toxic water were dumped into marshes and rivers in this area," Fajardo added. "What the people demand is the complete remediation of the area Texaco contaminated."

"What these people seek, Your Honor, is not environmental remediation," Callejas responded. "It is not cleanup. It is not a better quality of life. It is two checks." He held up two fingers. "One for the Frente de Defensa de la Amazonia, and the other for the trial expenses, which means for the lawyers."

This accusation, especially from a member of the Quito elite, outraged Fajardo. When it came to the Oriente, he told an interviewer, "I know the problems as they really are, because I live here." He had hesitated about accepting the assignment as the plaintiffs' lead Ecuadorian attorney, worried whether he possessed sufficient professional credentials. He agreed only when it occurred to him that if he took the case, all he would have to think about "is how to tell the truth."

*　*　*

Fajardo was one of thirteen children in a poor family that moved to Shushufindi in 1989 when he was fourteen years old. A drought had driven his parents to the oil-field town fifty miles southeast of Lago Agrio. Though foul and violent, Shushufindi had jobs for desperate people. Fajardo's family was crammed into a tiny shack next to a ruined stream. They had no electricity. Texaco employees in the town lived inside a gated compound with air-conditioning, catered food, and a lighted tennis court. As a teenager, Fajardo worked on a palm oil farm for $50 a month. Because of his serious mien, others asked him to bring complaints to the managers about the lack of drinking water for laborers and the pesticides that made them sick. His activism eventually got him fired. He found a new job cleaning oil-storage tanks, all the while studying for his high-school degree in the evening. In 1993, he joined the Frente de Defensa de la Amazonia, which was formed in connection with the original *Aguinda* case in New York. The Frente, as everyone called it, connected Oriente residents to their American lawyers. Gradually, the group, which was led by mestizo transplants to the region, expanded to become a force in regional politics. The Kohn Swift law firm in Philadelphia provided the Frente with much of its meager budget. It was not lost on the Frente's leaders that if the plaintiffs defeated Chevron in court, the threadbare organization stood to become a far richer and more powerful entity.

In 1997, several left-leaning Spanish-born Catholic missionaries offered Fajardo a scholarship to get a law degree and advance his career. He signed up for a six-year program that allowed him to do most of his course work remotely from Shushufindi. Even before graduating, in 2004, Fajardo began working part-time for the Frente as a paralegal. It was in this capacity that he caught Donziger's eye, and the two became friends. The pollution suit was Fajardo's first significant case, as it had been Donziger's. Even after Fajardo became the nominal lead lawyer in Ecuador, he called Donziger *el Comandante*, "the Commander."

"Things feel like they are falling into place," Donziger wrote in his private notes in the fall of 2005. He was traveling to Ecuador for a week or two each month. The rest of the time, he worked on the case from his apartment in New York. In addition to Fajardo, his team on the ground included Luís Yanza, a taciturn *urbano* organizer who served as executive director of the Frente, and several young leftist Ecuadorian lawyers based in Quito who played supporting roles. From San Francisco, Amazon Watch maintained an active website that promoted *Aguinda II* as part of its "Clean Up! Pay Up!" campaign against Chevron, an initiative Donziger helped to fund with money from Kohn Swift.

As a mechanism for raising money and ecological consciousness, *Aguinda II* steadily gained momentum. As a formal legal proceeding in Lago Agrio, it produced an ever-expanding stream of irreconcilable results.

The plaintiffs claimed to discover contamination everywhere. The San Carlos cancer study, they alleged, demonstrated the damage to human health. Chevron, in contrast, found little pollution that could be traced clearly to Texaco and dismissed the health risks as unproven. The San Carlos study, the company argued, was fatally flawed because it underestimated the population of the town; with the accurate overall head count, the apparent cancer cluster disappeared. In cold scientific terms, Chevron maintained, the study proved nothing at all. The rotating roster of judges from the Lago court made no obvious attempt to evaluate the competing claims.

But beyond the blur of soil and water samples, Donziger was shaping a story about poor peasants confronting a colossal corporate villain. And now he had placed the well-cast Pablo Fajardo at center stage. While Chevron's lawyers harangued the judge about the inevitable environmental costs that came with industry and advancement, Fajardo gave authentic voice to suffering visited from afar. The oil company protested that the plaintiffs couldn't prove a causal connection between Texaco and individual bad fortune. But did that really matter? Donziger sought to demonstrate the essential nature of an uncaring multinational. The legal skirmishing revealed corporate indifference, entirely apart from how many parts per million of total petroleum hydrocarbons remained on the rain forest floor and who had left them there. With Fajardo as front man, he wrote, the plaintiffs were "clearly adopting a more aggressive strategy, with a delicious tray of options to nail" their opponents.

The inclination "to nail" the opposition grew on both sides of the conflict, a tendency favoring Donziger, the more nimble combatant. Ricardo Reis Veiga's boss at Chevron headquarters in San Ramon, Charles James, possessed ample competitive spirit, but James's disdain for the plaintiffs and zealousness on behalf of the company led him to underestimate his competition. This created opportunities for Donziger to counterpunch.

Named Chevron's vice president and general counsel in December 2002, James came to the job from the Bush Justice Department, where he served as assistant attorney general in charge of the Antitrust Division. His main legacy in Washington was settling a monopoly case against Microsoft initially filed by the Clinton administration. James agreed to let the software giant escape any severe penalties, including a possible breakup. A "bedrock conservative," in his own words, James came under heavy criticism from Microsoft rivals, consumer advocates, and state attorneys general for dropping the antitrust case on terms favorable to Bill Gates and his company.

James had spent his career shuttling between government jobs during Republican administrations and a lucrative perch in the

Washington office of the corporate law firm Jones, Day, Reavis & Pogue. He had proven his acumen as a defender of corporate interests, noting during his Senate confirmation hearing for the Justice Department antitrust post that on seven occasions he represented targets of criminal grand jury investigations, "none of which resulted in indictment of my client." He brought the same fervor to defending Chevron, but in Ecuador, he did not enjoy the same kind of success.

In October 2005, the Ecuadorian trial schedule called for the inspection of a processing station called Guanta. The facility was situated near Lago Agrio, on ancestral Cofán land. It had processed huge volumes of crude and discharged oceans of produced water, the drilling by-product that contains naturally occurring salts and other chemicals. Donziger arranged to deliver a busload of traditionally dressed Cofán tribe members to witness the proceedings, and he invited journalists from Quito and abroad.

The evening before the inspection, an unusual document materialized at the Lago courthouse: a report from a nearby military base, saying that an officer had received intelligence that the Cofán were planning an ambush or kidnapping at Guanta. This should have seemed strange because, of all the tribes in the region, the Cofán were generally known for avoiding violence. Nevertheless, Chevron lawyers immediately filed a formal request that the judge stop the inspection, which he did. The next morning, *El Universo* and *El Comercio,* the two largest-circulation Ecuadorian newspapers, as well as several of their leading rivals, carried full-page Chevron advertisements attacking *Aguinda II* as fraudulent. (The timing of the ads was a coincidence, the company later claimed.)

Chevron's foray caught Donziger and Fajardo by surprise. The American watched as Fajardo hurriedly tracked down the judge by cell phone and pleaded for the inspection to proceed. In his notes, Donziger described "seeing [Fajardo's] thin body collapse as he told me, 'No way.'" The company, Donziger wrote, is "more evil and corrupt than we could admit to ourselves." He speculated about "an unholy alliance between the army, Texaco, and PE [Petroecuador] to make sure we do not win the case."

Years earlier in New York, Texaco had promised Judge Rakoff that if he sent the suit to Ecuador, the courts would provide "impartial and independent justice, without corruption or interference from the military." Now, though, Donziger believed Chevron had somehow arranged for a bogus security alert as a pretext for the army's intervention. Rather than concede that he had been outfoxed, however, he began plotting how he could turn the situation to his clients' advantage.

In defiance of the court, Donziger herded the journalists and costumed Indians onto the reserved buses and transported them to the Guanta station. The entire troupe marched through a muddy field and stepped over barbed-wire barriers to reach an oily marsh grown over with grass, where security guards confronted the visitors. At Donziger's direction, Fajardo made a furious speech about military-corporate conspiracies against justice. TV cameras rolled.

Next, Donziger put the crowd back on the buses and took them to the Rayo IV military base, where a Lieutenant Colonel Francisco Narvaez met them at the gate. The commander professed ignorance about any intelligence alert. He knew of no Cofán threat. The report could not have come from Rayo IV. Only he, the colonel, had authority to declare such an emergency. Then the officer made some startling concessions. He admitted that he was a friend of one of Chevron's top lawyers. And, he acknowledged, members of the company's legal team were living at the Rayo IV base, under the protection of his troops.

The television cameras caught it all. Donziger triumphantly claimed that his theory about Chevron's ties to the military had been proven correct. The Guanta episode set off intense controversy in Ecuador. Chevron representatives vehemently denied any impropriety, but Colonel Narvaez promised an investigation. In

November, the Ministry of Defense released a contract between Chevron and the Fourth Army Division. The agreement confirmed that the oil company had built a large residence at Rayo IV for Chevron's legal defense team, with the understanding that, after the trial, the lodging would be donated for the use of army officers. The ministry further admitted that the supposed intelligence about a Cofán threat had been traced back to two sources: an unnamed Chevron employee and a former Ecuadorian army captain who now did security work for the oil company.

The Ecuadorian media had a field day. For good measure, Donziger filed a petition with the Inter-American Commission on Human Rights, seeking protection for the plaintiffs' team in case of military reprisals. In his notes, Donziger celebrated an Associated Press article about the episode that led to other coverage. "We sent a *boletín* to Ecuadorian press, and the response was good—four newspapers covering. . . . Bianca mad [she] could not sign petition . . . AW [Amazon Watch] put it on PR wire and posted on their website. Tomorrow, write another *boletín* to advance story, put pressure on Chevron over its ties to the military."

The oil company continued to deny that it collaborated with current or former soldiers to thwart the Guanta inspection, which, Chevron pointed out, it had requested in the first place. It called Donziger's allegations "completely false and irresponsible." Pointing to U.S. State Department records showing that, since 1998, at least ten Americans had been kidnapped in the area, Chevron said it cooperated with the army only to keep its employees safe. The company's dedication to staff security notwithstanding, the incident fit neatly into Donziger's script about an overbearing company going to extraordinary lengths to prevail, including hiring the Ecuadorian military as its protector and hotelier. He, too, could play rough. Now he felt all the more justified in doing so.

*   *   *

Still, revealing what he portrayed as Chevron's illegitimate modus operandi did not solve Donziger's main legal challenge: The judicial inspections that did occur were producing a morass of incompatible science. Confronted with the opposing parties' contradictory technical information, the latest judge on the case, Germán Yáñez Ricardo Ruíz, decided in 2005 to initiate a new stage of the convoluted proceeding, even as the inspections continued. Yáñez ordered a panel of five neutral experts to review all of the evidence at one disputed well site and deliver an impartial assessment. The expert panel, made up of Ecuadorian engineers, would be paid jointly by the parties and responsible only to the court. Bringing in neutral experts had been an element of the trial plan from the beginning, but it had not been clear when the neutrals would surface. In February 2006, the first panel delivered its verdict on a well site called Sacha 53.

Beginning in 1973, Sacha 53 had produced some three million barrels of oil over eighteen years. Two homes remained in the vicinity of the well head, one owned by Anibal Baños, a farmer whose house was 900 meters away, close to the main road, and the other by a woman named Rosa Ramos, who lived 250 meters to the west. During the initial adversarial inspection of the site in September 2004, the plaintiffs' expert had interviewed Baños about his small farm. "In order to plant the hearts-of-palm plant," the farmer said, "I had to break a piece of land, remove the crude oil, and bring soil from somewhere else and put it around the plant, which is planted only with a bag of soil, and in this way is producing."

In 1996, Texaco sent in workers to clean up two waste pits at Sacha 53. According to the company, the laborers trucked away degraded petroleum, treated the empty pits with industrial detergent, filled the holes with dirt taken from elsewhere, and planted new vegetation. Texaco's mandate under the remediation plan—approved by the Ecuadorian government—was to reduce total petroleum hydrocarbon (TPH) levels to lower than 5,000 parts per million. Eight years after the cleanup, soil samples from the pits showed a maximum TPH level of 520, five times the most stringent standards applied in cleanups in the United States but well within the accepted goal in Ecuador. "These pits are not causing any environmental impacts," Chevron's expert concluded.

The plaintiffs' expert countered that Texaco should never have used unlined pits in the first place, because in the years before the remediation, hydrocarbons probably spread via surface runoff water into the nearby Jivino Negro River. What's more, the plaintiffs said, the detergent, or surfactant, used in the cleanup may have left behind dangerous residue.

In their February 2006 report, the neutral experts more or less sided with the company. They described Texaco's "soil washing" method as standard in the industry. The pits were dug in heavy, impermeable clay-like soil, making it less likely that contaminants escaped in the years before the remediation, the experts added. "In the case of runoff water flowing into the Jivino Negro River and used by people," they said, "the absence of physical-chemical analyses of the water and sediments does not allow for certainty of the existence or non-existence of contamination."

West of the Sacha 53 pits, there was an area where everyone agreed there had been an oil spill that was never addressed. It was in this area that Baños had planted his palm grove. He also grazed cattle there. Soil samples from the spill zone showed TPH levels as high as 20,000—four times the relevant limit. Chevron's expert cavalierly concluded that this was nothing to worry about: "Cows used for meat production," he said, "can ingest over 44,000 [TPH] of crude oil before possibly being affected."

The neutral experts acknowledged that the spill area remained contaminated by chromium VI, copper, and benzopyrene. Any informed outsider would avoid food raised on this poisoned land. But as to who was to blame for the spill and the lack of a cleanup, the experts were unsure. For undetermined reasons, the spill area

had not been covered by Texaco's remediation plan with the Ecuadorian government. "The origin of the contaminants in this zone
has not been accurately defined," the experts said. They could not
tell whether Texaco caused the spill. Perhaps Petroecuador, which
took over Sacha 53 in 1990, was responsible. They threw up their
hands. Making matters even more ambiguous, neither Baños nor
the plaintiffs' legal team had shown that any of his cattle or hearts-
of-palm trees had actually suffered. No human ailment had been
conclusively connected to the pollution. "Thus," the experts concluded, "it is impossible at this time to define the [spill's] impact to
the surrounding areas with the evidence that has been submitted."

In a final twist, tests of the only drinking water well in the area,
owned by Baños, revealed no hydrocarbon contamination. The
well did have dangerous levels of fecal and total coliform bacteria,
the experts reported, indicating the presence of untreated sewage.
But the bacteria could not be blamed on oil activity.

After the PR coup at Guanta, Donziger interpreted the Sacha 53
neutral experts' report as ominous: What if it foreshadowed more
unhelpful assessments by court-appointed neutrals? And what if
the experts weren't really neutral? Although he lacked any hard
proof, Donziger later said that he feared the experts "were very biased in favor of Chevron."

Back when Alberto Wray was nominally in charge of the case
in 2003 and 2004, he had requested a long list of judicial inspections on the theory that the plaintiffs needed as much evidence of
contamination as possible. Now Donziger saw this as a "disastrous
decision," both because the inspections were taking so long and
because Judge Yáñez had indicated that, sooner rather than later,
he wanted to bring in additional batteries of neutral experts. It had
been thirteen years since *Aguinda I* began in New York and three
years since the sequel started in Lago Agrio. Donziger figured that
to finish the remaining adversarial inspections, as well as potential
neutral-expert reviews, might take another six years. Even if other

expert panels issued findings more sympathetic to the plaintiffs, he didn't think his team could hold together that long. Joe Kohn's law firm in Philadelphia was laying out hundreds of thousands of dollars a year. Donziger's personal stipend had grown to between $10,000 and $20,000 a month, plus expenses, and there were other salaries, public relations bills, and international travel and laboratory fees. As time had passed, Kohn had begun complaining about Donziger's loose record-keeping and preference for fine restaurants. At some point, Donziger feared, Kohn would shut the spigot.

Then there was Bonifaz, who had evolved from a boss on the case to a rival. In late 2005, Donziger learned from Callejas, the Chevron attorney, Bonifaz had secretly extended a bizarre olive branch to the oil company. Callejas, according to Donziger's contemporaneous notes, told the plaintiffs' team that Bonifaz had sent a letter "to Chevron asking for settlement, and it had been rejected, and that [Bonifaz] threatened 'violent' reprisals." Donziger didn't know what "violent reprisals" meant—that was the truly bizarre part—but, regardless, the overture had undermined the plaintiffs in Ecuador. "Callejas mocked us," Donziger wrote. "If we were saying we were winning the case, why were we seeking a settlement?" Donziger called Bonifaz's move "the ultimate betrayal of the clients and fellow lawyers. I am convinced this man is truly nutso, totally ego-driven, and desperate." Donziger also fretted about his own image. "Callejas appears to think I am his [Bonifaz's] little tool down here, carrying out his wishes, when the opposite is the truth."

In May 2006, Donziger, Fajardo, and several colleagues held a five-hour strategy session, debating whether to take the emergency step of petitioning the judge to truncate the inspection process and appoint a sole "global expert," who would compile a conclusive assessment of the evidence. Donziger worried about putting their fate in the hands of one person, even a court-appointed neutral.

Fajardo, who had a better grasp of the subtleties of Ecuadorian justice, was more sanguine. "Pablo and our legal team keep insisting that the solution is for the judge to appoint someone who is favorable to us," Donziger wrote. "I don't trust this approach, given our experience so far." How could they arrange for the selection of an independent arbiter who would be "favorable" to the plaintiffs? Fajardo insisted that in Lago Agrio, what sounded like a contradiction made perfect sense.

Chapter Ten

LOBBYING

One evening in April 2006, Donziger met in a guest room in the Crowne Plaza Hotel in Houston with Emergildo Criollo and two staff members from Amazon Watch. The beds were unmade, and cardboard coffee cups littered the crowded space, giving it the feel of a college dorm. Adding to the unusual atmosphere, the documentary film crew that had been trailing Donziger with increasing frequency also jammed into the guest room, camera rolling.

"Let me explain what's going to happen tomorrow," Donziger told Criollo. "They will be sitting up there in their suits and ties," he explained, referring to Chevron's top management. "Don't be afraid. You stand up, walk to the microphone, and talk. If they try and cut you off at the beginning, it could be bad. You have to insist: 'Please, show some respect. You spent twenty-eight years in my territory. I can spend three minutes in your territory.'"

The next morning, the Cofán leader would appear at the Chevron annual shareholders meeting. Amazon Watch had chaperoned Criollo to Houston and acquired the share of Chevron stock that provided access to the event. By enlisting the support of like-minded investors, the activists hoped to reform the company's conduct. "The shareholders speak the one language leaders of

Chevron understand," as Donziger put it, "and that is the language of money."

"Let's practice," Donziger told Criollo in the Houston hotel room. "Pretend you are at the microphone." Chevron, though based outside of San Francisco, was holding its annual meeting in the south Texas city where the American oil industry had grown up. In the hotel prep session, Criollo did not wear the red face markings he favored for public appearances. He put on reading glasses and began speaking tentatively in Spanish: "Okay, my name is Emergildo Criollo, and I am from the Cofán nation. I have come from Ecuador to talk to you." He paused to flip through a small notebook. Donziger, wearing shorts, reclined on a disheveled hotel bed. "The rivers are where the people bathed and drank," Criollo continued. "The forest was wonderful, and the people enjoyed nature."

After a few more meandering sentences, Donziger interrupted. "That was good," he said in Spanish. But he did not actually think it was good. Switching to English, which Criollo did not understand, Donziger said to the bilingual Amazon Watchers, "I want to lay out how I think he should structure his statement." Donziger relished the art of persuasion. He began dictating: "Point number one—you have traveled from Ecuador, from the Amazon, by foot, by canoe, by bus, by airplane . . .'"

When he was done, Donziger told an Amazon Watch staffer named Kevin to coach Criollo until the Cofán leader knew his lines. "What I just prepared is how a lawyer would prepare a witness," Donziger explained to Kevin. "You've got to have that mindset tonight. You've got to control this guy and get him up to speed." Even rain forest authenticity, in Donziger's view, benefitted from polish.

Days earlier, Chevron had issued its annual social responsibility report. It said the company and its leadership "respect the law, support universal human rights, protect the environment, and benefit the communities where we work." Management, however, had squelched an Amazon Watch shareholder resolution calling on the company to adopt a human-rights policy. The measure received support from only 25 percent of shareholders. Chevron similarly deflected a formal complaint Amazon Watch filed with the Securities and Exchange Commission, asking the agency to investigate whether the company had failed to disclose the full liability it faced in Ecuador. (The SEC made inquiries and then dropped the matter.)

When he addressed Chevron CEO David O'Reilly and other senior executives the morning after his hotel-room tutorial, Criollo wore his face paint and beads. He recited Donziger's script flawlessly. "I have traveled a great distance to be here," he said. "I have come by foot, canoe, bus, and airplane. The company was in my territory for twenty-eight years. I ask you to listen to me for just three minutes."

Outside, Amazon Watch protesters chanted, "Chevron, Chevron, you can't hide!"

Inside, Criollo said to O'Reilly, "If you don't fulfill the ethical and moral responsibility that you yourselves say that you have, the Cofán people, my family, my wife, my children, may disappear." Two of his children had, in fact, died of mysterious ailments in the 1970s. Recalling his speech to the shareholders some years later, Criollo said, "I was very, very angry. They gave me three minutes to speak and then turned off the microphone."

The CEO of the second-largest energy company in the United States hastened to correct the Ecuadorian visitor: Chevron had no ethical or moral duty in Ecuador. This was someone else's problem. "Your complaints," O'Reilly said, "have to be taken to your government and national oil company, who are operating in a reprehensible manner."

Did Chevron care about these attempts at public shaming?

To some degree, yes. "Donziger created a drumbeat of criticism," a company public relations person explained. "You can't ignore that. You want to make it go away. But management does not want to be seen as being extorted, especially by this guy. You give in to a Donziger, and God knows who comes out of the woodwork to make claims."

At each step, over the past thirteen years, the oil company had underrated the threat posed by the Ecuador pollution lawsuit. Top executives and their subordinates regarded it as background noise, at worst an annoying distraction from the complicated business of operating a global energy company. Early on, Donziger had been a wet-behind-the-ears attorney, handy with hyperbolic press releases but unproven in the courtroom. Chevron, like Texaco before it, had the best law firms money could buy, both in the United States and in Ecuador. Those firms convinced American judges to reject the suit on procedural grounds. Even when it resurfaced in Ecuador, Chevron assumed that the Andean nation's weak judiciary wouldn't have the gumption to deliver a verdict against an American multinational. That seemed plausible: Texaco had received a formal liability release from the Ecuadorian government. Chevron assumed the release would protect it, as well. The plaintiffs could shout about injustice until the cows came home; the oil company would outlast them.

Charles James, Chevron's top in-house lawyer, was particularly prone to take Donziger too lightly. Over a twenty-five-year legal career, James had developed a fervent belief that if large corporations did not stand up to avaricious plaintiffs' attorneys and thoughtless government overseers, they risked being victimized. The solution, in his view, was to give no quarter and grind down any opposition.

James took these matters personally. He sometimes told an anecdote about how, as a young lawyer working on the staff of the Federal Trade Commission, he and his "bureaucratic friends" pondered how to respond to a congressional mandate to divide up the seven dominant oil producers into smaller companies with less economic and political power. "The fact that none of us knew anything about the oil companies or the industry or anything else, or had no stake or investment in it, didn't bother us at all," he recalled with self-deprecating scorn. The project never got off the ground, but the experience, he said, "helped shape my very strong fear about what happens when people start interfering in the economic realm."

The only scoundrels more deplorable than regulators, in James's view, were plaintiffs' attorneys. "I read an editorial yesterday on the beneficial social role of plaintiffs' lawyers," he said once in an interview. "I laughed and then I threw up. The fact of the matter is litigation is never a way to get appropriate societal results."

James saw *Aguinda* as a transparent shakedown. Compromising in the face of extortion, he believed, invited more extortion. James, who shaved his head shiny-bald and lifted weights as a hobby, had a macho streak not unlike Donziger's. Blustery and profane, he stood out in the hushed, carpeted hallways of the fourth floor of Chevron's Building A in San Ramon, where the most powerful executives had their offices. The Chevron campus, with its gracious courtyards and outdoor walkways, resembled a liberal arts college more than a corporate headquarters. James, however, reminded his colleagues with his in-your-face attitude that they did business in a hostile world of liberal trial lawyers and consumer advocates.

"The way to defuse these controversies," James said, referring to Ecuador, "is to win these cases. We think our record as a company is a superb one." While he had deemed it entirely appropriate for the Justice Department to settle with Microsoft (in a case, to be fair, that James never would have initiated), he wouldn't hear of settling with the *Aguinda* plaintiffs. To him, Texaco had already resolved its legal liability in the mid-1990s with the government of Ecuador. In exchange for its partial cleanup of the waste pits, Texaco had received the release from Quito. Years later, according to James, Chevron had "a responsibility to its shareholders not to pay for frivolous lawsuits."

If blame rested anywhere, James argued, it was on the shoulders of Petroecuador. The state oil company had barely begun to remediate the two-thirds of the sites it was contractually obliged to address. In addition, Petroecuador had drilled more than 700 new wells since Texaco's ouster, compared with the 322 the old consortium operated in the 1970s and 1980s. The Ecuadorian company ran its production, separation, and pipeline sites in a manner that could charitably be described as inattentive. Petroecuador's own records noted more than 1,900 spills in the Amazon from 1995 to 2011, or about one every three days, totaling almost 130,000 barrels of oil. The state-owned company conceded that, beginning in 1990, it had adopted Texaco's practice of releasing millions of gallons of tainted produced water into the environment; only more than fourteen years later did Petroecuador shift completely over to underground reinjection. Ecuadorians who paid attention to such matters compared their country's government-run oil bureaucracy unfavorably to its former American partner. "Since Texaco left here, Petroecuador has inflicted more damage and many more disasters than Texaco itself," Pablo Fajardo had said publicly in 2003 before he assumed a leading role in the *Aguinda II* case and concentrated his ire on Chevron. "There's one spill after another. There's broken pipes. There's contamination of wetlands, of rivers, of streams in great magnitude."

Yet in court, the plaintiffs gave Petroecuador a complete pass. Seeking Quito's backing, Cristóbal Bonifaz had assured the Ecuadorian government as early as 1996 that it would not become a legal target. Donziger upheld that guarantee. All this struck James as the height of hypocrisy. Why should Chevron bear the blame when it was now nearly impossible to say which company had left behind any given oily bog? How did Quito escape responsibility for the deplorable performance of its wholly owned industry?

Donziger, however, refused to divert his focus. He knew his key audiences: Ecuadorian judges, the government in Quito, American environmentalists, and journalists looking for a David-versus-Goliath story. None of these onlookers were overly concerned about apportioning culpability logically among the various companies and institutions responsible for pumping oil in—and contaminating—the Oriente. Demonizing Chevron was much easier to explain to environmentalists and the media.

By studying the legal and political environment in Ecuador, Donziger gained acute insight into a process of boundless malleability. He understood that by shifting all accountability to the American corporate behemoth, the lawsuit shielded Quito from pressure it otherwise might have felt to address the Lago Agrio mess. He also appreciated that the overarching rule in the court in Lago Agrio was that rules changed continually. Sometimes, rules and evidence mattered far less than emotions and personal relationships. In Ecuador, judges mingled privately with lawyers appearing before them to a degree unheard of in the federal courts of the United States. "We can have the best proof in the world, and if we don't have a political plan, we will surely lose," Donziger said, lecturing his Ecuadorian colleagues. "On the other hand, we can have mediocre proof and a good political plan and stand a good chance of winning."

James, a denizen of plush corporate office suites, had no feel for Quito or Lago Agrio. Yet he called the shots for Chevron. The company's representatives on the ground, Ricardo Reis Veiga, the holdover Texaco lawyer, and Adolfo Callejas, the patrician corporate litigator, observed the proceedings in Ecuador firsthand, but even they did not fully comprehend what was taking place. Reis Veiga had fought the *Aguinda* case for so long, and had seen it so close to expiring on so many occasions, he almost could not conceive of a conclusion other than its final collapse. Callejas had trouble accepting that his status and reputation could be overcome by the undistinguished duo of Pablo Fajardo, who rode to court on a bicycle, and Donziger, the loudmouthed American gatecrasher.

The military's involvement in the Guanta episode showed that the company wasn't above unconventional legal warfare. Its lawyers didn't appreciate, though, that when it came to freestyle maneuvering, they were no match for Donziger. If he thought it would yield an advantage, he was willing to try almost anything. And in Ecuador, his go-for-it philosophy was paying off.

Donziger, ever resourceful, developed a three-prong plan: First, convince the Lago court to end the judicial inspections and appoint a sole expert sympathetic to the plaintiffs' case. Second, bring Ecuadorian political pressure to bear on the judge. And third, amp up American media attention, both to increase Chevron's public relations pain and to prime the fund-raising pump so that the plaintiffs' ragged legal team had the money to enable it to survive and see victory.

That Donziger thought he could pull this off can be explained only by imagination and egotism on an Olympian scale. "Steven has the ability to envision what he wants to happen, however unlikely, and then make it happen," observed Karen Hinton, a public relations consultant in Washington whom Donziger hired to help promote the case in the American media. She meant the observation as a compliment. A former congressional aide and official in the Clinton administration, Hinton did her job energetically, as well, but even she sometimes worried about Donziger's obsessiveness. "It's his greatest strength. He never gives up," she said. It could also make him infuriating to work with, since he assumed that with enough persistence he would win every argument.

Donziger decided to lobby Judge Germán Yáñez personally. He asked Yáñez to lunch, and the judge said yes. So Donziger asked the judge out again. They met at hotels and restaurants and at the judge's home, chatting about corruption in the Ecuadorian system and the perils of serving on the bench in a society that often seemed out of control. In the United States, this kind of ex parte contact is strictly forbidden and, if revealed, would torpedo a case. But that was not true in Ecuador. Chevron lawyers, too, met from time to time with the judge. Donziger, however, forged a real relationship with Yáñez.

The judge told him how once, in the middle of a drug-trafficking case, he had been targeted for assassination. Hit men, he claimed, sprayed twenty-two rounds into his car. A woman passenger was killed, but Yáñez somehow emerged without serious injury. In other conversations with Donziger, the judge brought up Marx, Lenin, Heidegger, Montesquieu, and Rousseau. A Catholic, he was studying the tenets of Islam. Donziger described him as "a real humanist."

At the same time, the American plaintiffs' lawyer professed to have mixed feelings about these clandestine contacts. "I love it, this lobbying. I am good at it," he wrote. "But I hate it, hate that it is necessary, hate that it is part of the [Ecuadorian] legal culture." Donziger's affinity for clandestine wheeling and dealing won out over whatever hesitation he might have felt.

Yáñez displayed no anxiety about their meetings. On one occasion, Donziger noted, the middle-aged jurist "brought a young chick in her mid-20s and thought nothing of it." For Yáñez and his comrades on the Lago court, Donziger wrote, "there is little or no intellectual component to the law." They responded, he believed, to favors and threats. An Ecuadorian friend told Donziger that "the only way we will win this case is if the judge thinks he will be doused with gasoline and burned if he rules against us." Given the "immorality of Ecuador's justice system," Donziger wrote, "that type of comment did not even shock me. It is part of the rules of the game here," rules he felt he had to follow.

Sometimes, Yáñez played coy. During a cell phone conversation with Donziger in late spring 2006, the judge "lapsed into canards about 'my office is always open, I want to be fair,' etc.," Donziger noted. "The call was useless and reminded me how weak the judge was." He lacked "self-confidence," in Donziger's estimation. The American lawyer's plan to halt the inspection process and bring the proceedings to a head required "a determined judge willing to make decisions," he worried. "The judge needs to fear us for this to move how it needs to move, and right now there is no fear, no price to pay for not making these key decisions." Donziger's acute reading of the judge showed how attuned he was to the psychology of the Lago Agrio courtroom.

Donziger urged Luís Yanza, the executive director of the Frente, to organize protests at the courthouse. Yanza hesitated. "What are we going to protest about?" he asked. "Oh, maybe the fact we are going to lose the case unless it ends soon?" Donziger answered sarcastically. The American didn't hesitate to browbeat his more submissive Ecuadorian colleagues, a habit some of them came to resent. The Ecuadorians had not had the benefit of Donziger's exposure at Harvard Law School to Critical Legal Studies, which taught that powerful institutions enjoy inherent advantages in the courts. Opponents of power, he believed, had to use irregular tactics if they expected to prevail.

Donziger's creativity in working the case took many forms. He met with the Frente's young female interns, Ecuadorian university students and aspiring lawyers from Quito who sympathized with the poor in the Oriente. They "might want to establish a personal relationship with the judge and lobby him," he suggested to them. "This could help the case." It was an idea that did not go over well. The Ecuadorian interns "took offense at" his advice. In retrospect, he acknowledged, it "was probably a little too much for them to handle." Unapologetic, he looked for other means to influence the court.

The notion of dispatching female interns to flirt with Judge Yáñez did not come out of the blue. On one occasion when he invited Donziger and Fajardo to his home, Yáñez "asked that we bring over some whiskey or some wine," Donziger noted. "We didn't. When we got there, he was clearly drunk and had a young woman." At the Lago courthouse, Yáñez allegedly doled out staff jobs to women based on their availability for off-hours socializing. If Donziger couldn't convince his female interns to seduce the judge, he and Fajardo decided with consummate chutzpah to use the sex-harassment accusations against Yáñez as leverage. They drafted a complaint against Yáñez, playing on his vulnerability because of the harassment allegations. Then they communicated to the judge that they would hold off on filing the complaint, but only if he agreed to truncate the inspection process and appoint as a global expert someone of the plaintiffs' choosing. It was, to put it plainly, pure blackmail.

And it worked. At first, Donziger hadn't been able to wrap his mind around Fajardo's suggestion that they attempt to select the supposedly neutral sole expert. But sure enough, once Yáñez realized how vulnerable to the abuse charges he was, virtually anything became possible. "Pablo met with the judge today," Donziger wrote in an e-mail he sent on July 26, 2006, to Joe Kohn in Philadelphia. "The judge, who is on his heels from the charges of trading jobs for sex in the court, said he is going to accept our request to withdraw the rest of the inspections." Desperate to keep his civil service job, Judge Yáñez, Donziger claimed, "wants to forestall the filing of a complaint against him by us, which we have prepared but not yet filed." In his notes, Donziger wrote that if Yáñez changed his mind, "then we are in all-out war with the judge to get him removed."

While Donziger waged his covert judicial intimidation campaign, Chevron made oblivious public pronouncements and filings, much as the company might have done if it were litigating in federal court in New York or San Francisco. "Plaintiffs have been unable to prove their claims," a company spokesman in Quito said in July 2006, "and it appears that they now realize the continuation of the judicial inspection process will only further weaken their position." Two months later, Yáñez issued an order canceling sixty-four scheduled inspections. The plaintiffs followed with a motion asking him to appoint a sole arbiter "to act as an expert witness to conduct the entire examination."

Donziger was ebullient. In January 2007, he celebrated this extraordinary change in the course of the trial. "Met with the judge last night in [his] house," he wrote in his notes. "Humble house, humble furniture. Made tea. I really like the guy. Remember last August I wanted to ride the wave and get him off the case?" By not publicizing the sex-for-jobs allegations, he wrote, "we saved him, and now we are reaping the benefits."

From time to time, Donziger acknowledged his ambivalence about his tactics. He both "loved" lobbying Judge Yáñez, and he "hated" it. He knew he was on morally suspect ground by urging female subordinates to seduce the judge. It was entirely over the line, he knew, to employ blackmail. But Donziger convinced himself he had no choice. To vindicate his clients, he had made a Faustian bargain. It seemed to him the only way to win against a deep-pocketed global conglomerate determined to bury the case. Only occasionally and in private did he worry explicitly about the price the Devil would ultimately extract. In his personal notes, he wrote, "I feel like I have gone over to the dark side."

Chapter Eleven

PUBLICITY

While he pondered whom to nominate as the global expert, Donziger kept one eye on Ecuador's combustible presidential politics. If the right person prevailed in elections scheduled for late 2006, he thought, the new head of state might lean on the Lago court to rule against Chevron. It was a grandiose idea, but for Donziger, not unusual.

Ecuador, once again, was in political disarray. The country had had seven presidents during the previous decade. Oil continued to dominate the economy, but without bringing economic or political stability. Even during a period of rising petroleum prices, Ecuador's crude production was falling, in part because of a government decision to seize key fields from Occidental Petroleum, at the time the country's largest foreign investor. Also stunting economic growth was Ecuador's failure to develop domestic refining capacity, which meant that, despite its crude reserves, it had to import expensive gasoline from abroad. OPEC offered no help, as cash-strapped Ecuador had left the cartel in the 1990s, unable to pay its dues.

Thirteen candidates competed in the 2006 presidential elections. One, Alvaro Noboa, a banana magnate and the richest man

in a poor country, enjoyed wide name recognition. He wanted
closer ties to Washington and more foreign investment. Donziger
was devastated when Noboa came in first in an initial round of
voting. "Everybody I know is demoralized," he wrote. "People are
focusing on the second round, and everybody thinks it is inevitable
that Noboa will win. Why do [I] feel the hand of the CIA behind
this?"

Donziger preferred a spirited young candidate named Rafael
Correa, previously an obscure leftist academic. He had met Correa
by chance on an Ecuadorian commercial plane flight. The brash
American lawyer introduced himself and explained that he was
"representing the Ecuadorian communities" against Chevron. The
candidate offered friendly encouragement. They knew some people
in common in Quito. Although he had a Ph.D. in economics from
the University of Illinois, Correa bore a grudge against the United
States. As a young boy, he had seen his father arrested for smug-
gling cocaine into the country. The elder Correa was convicted and
spent three years in American prison. When he later turned to politics, the economist chose as his model Venezuelan President Hugo
Chávez, a fiery authoritarian who whipped up his followers with
diatribes against Yankee imperialism. Donziger admired both
Correa and Chávez and applauded their hostility toward American
corporations. During his campaign, Correa described President
George W. Bush as "a tremendously dim-witted president," an assessment Donziger shared.

In a runoff against Noboa, Correa surprised many observers
with his charisma as a campaigner. His promise of a "citizens' rev-
olution," which would concentrate power in the presidency at the
expense of the legislature, ultimately carried him past Noboa in a
second round of voting in late November. In a Correa administration, Donziger expected there would be "sympathetic people and
those we know personally in several key posts directly related to

what we are doing." He anticipated new backing from Quito: "We are getting meetings with people who never used to take our phone calls."

In mid-December, Donziger conferred personally with two incoming Correa cabinet ministers: Rene Vargas Pazzos, the retired general and former senior Petroecuador executive who had testified on the plaintiffs' behalf at the start of the Lago trial, and Alberto Acosta, an eminent left-wing economist. Correa planned to appoint Vargas as minister of defense and Acosta as minister of energy. "Explained case to Acosta," Donziger wrote. "I was struck by his level of honesty, his stature, his intelligence—this is an entirely new thing." Acosta told Donziger that in the new Ecuador, the "economy will exist in the service of humanity, not humanity in service of the economy." During a separate breakfast, Vargas introduced Donziger to a friend as "a good gringo." Donziger mentioned at the breakfast that he had gone to law school and remained in touch with one of the most promising young Democratic politicians in the United States, Barack Obama. Obama, having been elected in 2004 to the U.S. Senate from Illinois, was getting ready to make a precocious run for the White House. "We had a lot of laughs," Donziger wrote, "talking about how I could be the U.S. Ambassador [to Ecuador] under an Obama administration."

Given his impolitic nature, an ambassadorship was the stuff of fantasy. But Donziger's continuing relationship with Obama was real. Earlier in 2006, he had visited his Harvard Law basketball buddy several times on Capitol Hill. The attorney told Obama that Chevron was using political influence in Washington and Quito to deny the rain forest residents justice. Showing the senator photos of the Oriente oil zone, he asked for help in opposing a company attempt to persuade the Bush administration to deny Ecuador certain trade preferences in retaliation for permitting *Aguinda II* to continue. Obama did as Donziger asked, cosigning a letter with

Vermont senator Patrick Leahy, urging Bush trade officials to allow the Ecuadorian peasants "their day in court." Donziger later returned the favor by helping to raise money for Obama's presidential campaign.

In January 2007, Donziger used his fast-improving connections in Quito to obtain credentials for Correa's inauguration ceremony at the Palacio de Carondelet. Politics in Ecuador, and throughout the region, had swung to the left. Sandinista leader Daniel Ortega was an honored guest at Correa's swearing-in. The crowd roared when Venezuela's Chávez stepped out of his limousine: "Socialism, yes! Imperialism, no!"

Caught up in the moment, Donziger observed, "Today is a very, very big day for Ecuador, and the case, really." Correa, he added, "is a progressive, and there is no way under an administration led by this man that Texaco could ever get away with what it usually does here, which is bribes, backdoor meetings, and manipulation of government power."

The new president, forty-four years old, waved from a balcony. He wore a tricolor ceremonial sash over a gray business suit and a high-collared traditional Andean shirt. The crowd shouted its approval. "People are just goddamned fed up with corruption," Donziger said. "They're fed up with U.S. influence. They're fed up with the Bush administration. They're fed up with foreign oil companies making money off of their oil and their natural resources, and they have just had it."

A few days later, Donziger, Luís Yanza of the Frente, and several colleagues got an audience with Correa's interim attorney general. "The door is always open," Ecuador's top legal official told the delegation. "Think of what has happened in ten years," Donziger wrote in his notes. "How we have gone from fighting on the outside of power to being on the inside."

* * *

Buoyed by his hope that the new president would endorse the *Aguinda II* plaintiffs, Donziger turned his attention to selecting a *peritaje global*, a global expert, who would steer the judge in Lago toward a multibillion-dollar verdict against Chevron. Impudent, daring, overconfident—all of these adjectives fairly describe Donziger's assumption that after bullying the judge into aborting the judicial inspection process, he could choose the court adviser who would shape the resolution of the case. Chevron was filing motions objecting to the very idea of a *peritaje global*. Donziger, unbeknownst to the oil company, was already conducting auditions for the job.

In December 2006, the plaintiffs' attorney met for an hour with a petroleum engineer named Fernando Reyes. The purpose of the interview, in Donziger's words, was "to do a hard vet." Reyes disclosed that he had previously published the view that the Ecuadorian government "shares some responsibility" for the contamination of the Oriente. He had also worked as an environmental auditor in Ecuador for an American oil company called Maxus. Donziger didn't see this background as disqualifying, as long as Reyes understood his duty to the plaintiffs going forward. "I told him point blank," Donziger wrote in his notes, that if Reyes accepted the assignment as global expert, "he likely would never work for the oil industry again in Ecuador, at least for an American company." On the other hand, by vindicating the plaintiffs, "he could be a national hero." If patriotic glory weren't sufficient incentive, Donziger assured Reyes he "would have a job for the rest of his life being involved in the cleanup." With all that in mind, Donziger asked Reyes whether he would be "comfortable slamming them with a $10 billion judgment."

That figure made Reyes uncomfortable. Years later, he called it "completely ludicrous." But Donziger came away from their conversation thinking Reyes had said yes. "He was always very persistent and impulsive, the kind of person who never takes no for an answer," Reyes recalled.

In the end, Donziger worried that Reyes lacked "the internal timber to pull it off." To Reyes's relief, Donziger asked him to recommend someone else for the assignment. Reyes suggested a mining engineer he had known since college named Richard Stalin Cabrera Vega. Cabrera didn't know much about oil contamination, but Reyes made the introduction anyway. "For Mr. Cabrera," Reyes said later, "issues such as independence and professional standards were not that important." Reyes, in short, viewed his old friend as a hack: "He would have no problem doing what the plaintiffs were proposing." On a Saturday afternoon in early 2007, Reyes had drinks with Donziger and Cabrera at the bar of the Hotel Quito, where Donziger stayed. Cabrera, it turned out, had once worked for Cristóbal Bonifaz as a paid expert in another case. Unsurprisingly, given that previous association and Cabrera's reputation for malleability, the engineer indicated sympathy for the *Aguinda II* plaintiffs.

"He was a humble man," Donziger wrote of Cabrera, a salt-of-the-earth type. The American lawyer also thought Cabrera would serve as "the perfect foil for Chevron." A couple of weeks later, Donziger met Reyes and Cabrera for breakfast at a Quito restaurant called Mister Bagel. Cabrera responded positively to Donziger's emotional appeal about "the importance of the case, what it means for history, how we can do something that we will always be remembered for." Donziger made his choice: "I have a lot of confidence in Richard—more than before." The American dispatched Pablo Fajardo to lobby the judge to appoint Cabrera, which Fajardo did by means of in-person conversation and e-mail.

In late February, the judge called Cabrera to ask him to recommend an expert. This struck Donziger as "odd," since "we had set it up that Richard would be appointed." Fajardo explained that the phone call to Cabrera was for show: "It is likely part of the judge's complicated plan to protect himself." The judge, according to Fajardo, wanted it to appear that his mind was open and that he was canvassing for candidates, when, in fact, Cabrera was himself going to be selected.

Assuming that Fajardo was correct—that Cabrera's appointment was essentially a done deal—the plaintiffs' team invited the engineer to an all-day planning meeting on March 3, 2007. At least a dozen people attended, including Donziger, Fajardo, and several members of the expanding group of American technical consultants Donziger had hired to advise the plaintiffs. Donziger and Fajardo briefed the presumptive global expert on the evidence. "Great spirit and energy in the room," Donziger noted. "I spent the whole day making comments and mostly directing them to Richard. We laid out our entire case and legal theory—what a benefit! We need to do the same with the judge. Richard seems low-key and cooler than I thought."

Donziger told the attendees that he and the other Americans would form a "work committee" to present a "draft plan" for Cabrera. Looking at Cabrera, Donziger said, "Richard, of course you really have to be comfortable with all that, and we'll define the support the expert needs."

Fajardo gave a PowerPoint presentation the title of which translated as "Plan for the Global Expert Assessment." "Here is where we do want the support of our entire technical team," Fajardo said, "experts, scientists, attorneys, political scientists, so that all will contribute to that report." Cabrera's report to the court, an ostensibly disinterested analysis of the evidence, would in fact be a collective product of the plaintiffs' team, Fajardo explained. "The work isn't going to be the expert's," he told the attendees. "All of us must bear the burden."

One participant objected. Wasn't Cabrera supposed to be independent? Shouldn't his report reflect only his work?

No, Fajardo said. Cabrera would "sign the report and review it. But all of us . . . have to contribute to that report."

"Together?" asked Ann Maest, one of the American consultants paid by the plaintiffs.

Yes, Fajardo said.

"But not Chevron," Maest added. Her joke was met by laughter around the room.

From $1 billion in New York, the target verdict had inflated to $6.14 billion in Lago. The judicial site inspections produced ambiguous evidence, soon to be overcome by the appointment of a supportive global expert. Donziger joyfully told his colleagues, "We could jack this thing up to $30 billion in one day."

Three months later, on June 13, 2007, Cabrera took an oath at the Lago courthouse to serve as the neutral global expert in *Aguinda II*. He swore he would carry out his duties "faithfully and in accordance with science, technology and the law, and with complete impartiality and independence vis-à-vis the parties."

Chevron seemed flummoxed by Cabrera's appointment. "We are dismayed that the court has yet again succumbed to plaintiffs' pressure tactics and violated the spirit and letter of the law by appointing a lone expert, unfamiliar with the proceedings," Ricardo Reis Veiga griped. He called the development "another vivid example of the unacceptable potential for bias." Reis Veiga didn't know the half of it. He had no idea that the plaintiffs were already prepping Cabrera and telling him they would do his work.

In an e-mail to Joseph Berlinger, a New York–based filmmaker, Donziger wrote of the Cabrera appointment: "This is a huge victory!!!!!!!!"

Making the March 3 briefing for Cabrera all the more remarkable was the presence, once again, of a cameraman and audio specialist recording the event. The crew worked for Berlinger, whom Donziger had recruited to make a movie about the Ecuador case. Berlinger had directed a number of acclaimed documentaries, including *Brother's Keeper,* about a murder in upstate New York; *Paradise Lost,* the story of a controversial murder trial in Arkansas; and *Metallica: Some Kind of Monster,* a portrait of the heavy-metal rock band. The Berlinger crew began shadowing Donziger in early 2006; they captured such memorable vignettes as his thunderous condemnation of "the corrupt Texaco lawyer" before the elderly judge in Quito and Donziger's attendance at the Correa inauguration.

Berlinger, a rumpled romantic with a thick, black beard, considered himself an advocate for underdogs. He saw Donziger as a promising main character for a serious film. Donziger convinced the filmmaker that, in Berlinger's words, "a shocking ecological disaster" had occurred in Ecuador. After his first trip to the Oriente, Berlinger left "feeling sick—literally, from noxious fumes I ingested—and figuratively, from the things I saw and stories I heard." He returned "to my comfortable home in Westchester and tucked my kids into bed, and I guess I felt guilty. Here I was, someone who had had some success in life, and it seemed like the universe was tapping me on the shoulder and saying I should do something about this situation."

That an award-winning documentarian would agree to take on a project about Donziger's case signaled an important elevation in the profile of *Aguinda II.* Over the years, dozens of American and European journalists had visited the Oriente to report on the lawsuit for various newspapers, magazines, and TV news shows. Berlinger's presence meant something more. His documentaries were treated as events unto themselves. They debuted at Sundance and were reviewed reverentially by the *New York Times.* A cause embraced by a filmmaker of Berlinger's heft would likely attract a new wave of financial support in the United States, allowing the plaintiffs to survive Chevron's objections and foot-dragging.

Donziger displayed a virtuoso's touch in weaving together promotional and financial support for his lawsuit. To close the deal with Berlinger, the lawyer introduced the filmmaker to Russell DeLeon, one of Donziger's more colorful classmates from Harvard Law School. DeLeon and Donziger shared an interest in poker, which they agreed was too often derided as mere gamblers' fare when it deserved the respect afforded chess. DeLeon had turned his passion into a multibillion-dollar fortune in the controversy-ridden online gambling industry. One of his businesses was called PartyGaming, which had its headquarters in the tax haven of Gibraltar. DeLeon generally stayed out of the United States, which banned operators of digital gambling parlors, and where he feared he might risk arrest. Donziger persuaded his wealthy buddy to provide $750,000 for Berlinger's film, financial records show. The Netflix online movie service chipped in another $300,000, and Donziger himself contributed more than $30,000. Eventually DeLeon invested a total of some $900,000 in the movie, or more than 70 percent of its budget. In return, Berlinger gave DeLeon a lead producer credit. "Russ at that time wanted to get into the movie business," Berlinger recalled, "so that was part of his motivation for investing."

Donziger reveled in his dual roles of film coordinator and on-screen lead. Only occasionally did it occur to him that Berlinger's crew was memorializing exchanges that normally would remain cloaked by lawyer-client confidentiality. On the day after the March 3 conclave with Cabrera, the camera was recording when Donziger reiterated to his American technical consultants at a Quito restaurant that all of the arrangements the plaintiffs were making with Cabrera were to be concealed from Chevron, the "goal [being] that they don't know shit." During the meal, the American advisers questioned skeptically whether the plaintiffs had sufficient evidence that contamination from the waste pits had spread to surrounding groundwater.

With characteristic bravado, Donziger responded that the

scientific details didn't matter. "You can say whatever you want, and at the end of the day, there's a thousand people around the courthouse, you're going to get what you want" from the judge, he declared. "If we take our existing evidence on groundwater contamination, which admittedly is right below the source . . . and wanted to extrapolate based on nothing other than our . . . theory," then, "we can do it, and we can get money for it."

He seemed oblivious to the camera. "This is all for the court just a bunch of smoke and mirrors and bullshit," he announced.

Unused to Donziger's cavalier attitude, one consultant persisted about the groundwater data.

Donziger suddenly remembered the presence of the filmmakers. He abruptly broke off the discussion, saying to the documentary crew, "There's another point I got to make to these guys, but I can't get this on camera." The recording stopped. Berlinger's team did not capture whatever Donziger had to add that was even more problematic than his already dubious seminar on stage-managing Ecuadorian justice.

The voluble lawyer intensely enjoyed the company of Berlinger and his crew. They talked about sports and women. Donziger regaled the filmmakers with stories of his fencing with Chevron. He struck Berlinger as perhaps fanatical—an Ahab chasing his Moby Dick in the form of a vast corporation—but the filmmaker couldn't help liking his mercurial subject. For his part, Donziger seemed to feel liberated by the camera's gaze, akin to an actor who discovers new depths to his emotions while onstage. Once he even mused aloud that he could have performed in feature movies if he hadn't chosen law as a profession. Only occasionally did Donziger have a twinge of concern. "Sometimes," he wrote in his notes, "I feel I am letting Berlinger in too much."

* * *

Within months of taking office, Ecuador's new president ful-filled Donziger's grandest hopes. *Aguinda II* provided Correa with an ideal vehicle for stirring populist sentiment against Ameri-can corporate power. In March 2007, he agreed to meet in Quito with Pablo Fajardo and several other plaintiffs' representatives. The presidential press secretary then issued a release offering the Frente "all the support of the national government." In nationwide radio addresses, Correa labeled the Ecuadorian lawyers represent-ing Chevron as traitors to their people. He described as heroes the "representatives of the Amazon Defense Coalition, who have been fighting with ChevronTexaco for years, even decades."

Correa elevated the Lago lawsuit to an emblem of national pride and resistance. In April 2007, he ordered up an entourage of politi-cal aides, bodyguards, and Ecuadorian journalists for an expedi-tion to the Oriente. Correa decided to make the trip so suddenly that Donziger, in the United States at the time, could not get down to Ecuador in time to participate. Pablo Fajardo and Luís Yanza ac-companied the president on his pea-green military helicopter, in-stead. Ecuadorian TV cameras (and Berlinger's film crew) recorded Correa as he descended on the homestead of a man named Manuel Salinas. Fajardo served as the president's guide. "The owner of this farm," Fajardo told Correa, "lives in extreme poverty, possibly has cancer, and the water he drinks is totally contaminated." Dressed in casual jeans and, for dramatic effect, a neon-orange hard hat, the president expressed outrage. "This pit was never operated by Petroecuador," he said, "and now Texaco doesn't deny the envi-ronmental damage, but they blame Petroecuador. Please!" Well briefed for the event, Correa asked: "How many times bigger [is this] than the *Exxon Valdez*?" Then he answered himself: "Thirty times more damage, but the *Exxon Valdez* was in the United States, so this doesn't matter."

"This is the water he drinks," Fajardo said to Correa, as they peered into Salinas's well. A cup of liquid was presented to the president. "Just look at the color," Fajardo said. "It smells like . . ."

"Gasoline," Correa interrupted, his timing perfect.

Donziger could not have scripted a more memorable media moment. Without pointing to any specific evidence of causation, Ecuador's newly elected young president had endorsed the idea that the American oil company bore responsibility for an innocent farmer's poverty, his bad water, and his "possible" case of cancer. No judge sitting in the courthouse in Lago Agrio could have missed the signal that Correa wanted Chevron to pay a steep penalty for all of these ills.

Fajardo's extraordinary oil-field tour with the president played out for the benefit of the public, with large audiences watching on television, listening on radio, and reading about it in the next day's headlines. One telling exchange, though, involved no words and was witnessed by only a few people. During the flight on the presidential helicopter, someone handed Correa a copy of *Vanity Fair*, the glossy American monthly best known for chronicling the rich, famous, and beautiful. The May 2007 edition was entitled "The Green Issue," and its centerpiece was an admiring profile of Pablo Fajardo. Correa turned the pages, nodding his approval. He looked up and smiled warmly at Fajardo.

In an epic 13,300-word article, William Langewiesche, *Vanity Fair*'s foreign correspondent, described Fajardo with a tone approaching awe. "It is an observable fact," Langewiesche wrote, "that Fajardo never sweats, and furthermore that when he moves through the jungle in his tidy-lawyer clothes, he does not get dirty or wet." Even in translation from the Spanish, Fajardo sounded like a philosopher of uncommon fluency: "One of the problems with modern society," he told Langewiesche, "is that it places more importance on things that have a price than on things that have a value." Chevron and its minions, by contrast, did not appear in a favorable light. Langewiesche reported that in August 2004, Fajardo's beloved brother Wilson, an evangelical minister and radio reporter, had been murdered in Shushufindi. "Do you suspect he was killed because of you?" the journalist asked Pablo. The lawyer answered that he had been led to believe that it was he who had been targeted, because of his battle against Chevron, "and that the killers had made a mistake." *Vanity Fair* did nothing to cast doubt on Fajardo's unsubstantiated accusation (which Chevron vehemently denied).

The *Vanity Fair* piece, illustrated with lavish photographs, represented another Donziger promotional feat. The lawyer had encouraged Langewiesche to shape the article as a profile of Fajardo. The award-winning journalist agreed that the imperturbable jungle lawyer perfectly embodied the struggle against the powerful American oil company. In Donziger's opinion: "This is the kind of paradigm-shifting, breakthrough article that I think is going to change the entire case from here until it ends, in a way that is favorable to us."

Not long after the Fajardo profile hit the newsstands, subscribers' mailboxes, and the Internet, Trudie Styler, the wife of the British rock star Sting, was asked by an Ecuadorian interviewer why she decided to visit the country and lend her celebrity glow to the *Aguinda II* case. One reason was that Donziger had traveled to London to plead personally with Styler to accompany him on a tour of the Oriente oil fields. Donziger arranged to meet Styler because she and Sting, who first gained global fame in the late 1970s as the front man of the Police, were longtime advocates of preserving the Amazonian rain forest. "This is a story that we've been aware of for a while, and then obviously [we got] to know the story better through the *Vanity Fair* article that came out in America a few weeks ago," Styler told the interviewer. She said she had been "reading a lot about Pablo Fajardo, who is the David in this David and Goliath story." Inspired by a man "who is speaking on behalf of his people," she and Sting decided "we also would like to get involved in perhaps identifying a project in which we can support the indigenous communities."

Styler accepted Donziger's invitation, and her Oriente passage in the spring of 2007 received abundant international media coverage. Draped in a translucent white veil, she traveled with Donziger by canoe to the Cofán village at Dureno and paid her respects to families with grievous health problems they blamed on Chevron. A statuesque model and actress by profession, Styler did not shy from attention. "Trudie's method of dealing with me is generally very seductive," Donziger wrote. "She has a need to know that each man around her is attracted to her, and she is good at turning it on so each man is."

At one dinner with Donziger and several Ecuadorian notables, Styler admonished her tablemates to look each other in the eyes as they toasted, or risk not having sex for seven years. "Such a cultural disconnect," Donziger observed. Styler made large groups wait in the tropical heat while she shopped for native trinkets. "None of these people had heard of Sting and could have given a damn," Donziger noted. Still, he thought, "Trudie's presence was generally uplifting."

In July, Styler and Sting repaid Donziger for his hospitality. The jet-setting couple invited the lawyer and his comrades Fajardo and Yanza to the United States for a Police reunion performance at the environmentally themed Live Earth concert at Meadowlands Stadium near New York. After the band played "Roxanne," "Every Breath You Take," and other hits, Donziger and Fajardo went backstage and chatted with the spike-haired Sting. Former vice president Al Gore ambled by and shook Fajardo's hand. NBC's *Today Show* sent cohost Ann Curry to interview Sting and Styler. During the interview, Styler accused Chevron of committing atrocities in Ecuador. *Today* ran tape of her Donziger-arranged tour of the Oriente.

After the TV appearance, Sting respectfully introduced Fajardo and Yanza at a Live Earth press conference, resulting in yet another round of international coverage. Styler accompanied Fajardo to an interview on the Bravo cable TV channel, which separately hosted the actress Daryl Hannah, who spoke about her own trip to the Oriente oil pits. Best known for her portrayal of a winsome mermaid in the movie *Splash*, Hannah had posed for photos in Ecuador with her outstretched hand covered in black petroleum; these images zinged digitally around the world. "I don't think Donziger could have planned and coordinated every piece of the promotion," said Berlinger, who recorded much of the activity for his documentary. Donziger retained some of the country's best-known spin artists—among them former Clinton White House aides Chris Lehane and Mark Fabiani—to help plot media strategy. "The whole thing took on a momentum of its own," Berlinger said. "It was pretty amazing to watch."

The publicity barrage continued. Styler published a long article in London's *Daily Mail* newspaper condemning the Oriente oil pollution. Chevron answered with a pleading "Open Letter to Trudie Styler," which, if anything, ratified her gravity as a spokeswoman for the plaintiffs. (Why correspond publicly with a rock star's wife if she did not deserve to be taken seriously?) Chevron acknowledged that rivers and groundwater in the rain forest were polluted. Petroleum, however, wasn't the cause of the problem. Echoing the court-appointed experts who assessed Sacha 53, the company noted that there was "compelling evidence showing a connection to other, non-oil-related issues, including dangerous levels of human and animal waste in the water supplies."

The oil company couldn't slow, let alone stop, the PR juggernaut. In December 2007, CNN broadcast its annual *Heroes* awards show from the cavernous main hall of the American Museum of Natural History in New York. "They're men and women who save lives and do what is right in this world, which, frankly, often does not reward doing the right thing," cohost Anderson Cooper told viewers. The winners, he said, were chosen by a panel whose members included Nobel Peace Prize recipient Muhammad Yunus, a pioneer of third-world "micro-finance," and Lance Armstrong, the (since disgraced) cycling champion. Actor Jimmy Smits took the stage to introduce the Fighting for Justice Hero: none other than Pablo Fajardo. The Ecuadorian lawyer, Smits said, "believes it is his responsibility to get up every day, ride his bike to court, and fight for his dream—a world where every family can enjoy access to pure water and air."

In a celebratory video that followed, Fajardo explained, "I am on trial against Chevron Corporation." Strangely, he added that the plaintiffs "don't want any money." Instead, he said, "we just want them to let people live with dignity. That's all we want." He did not mention Donziger's ambition to "jack this thing up to $30 billion."

Chapter Twelve

RELATIONSHIPS

Even before he watched his protégé Fajardo take a star turn on CNN, Donziger sensed a shift in momentum in Ecuador. "I feel us in control of the case in [a] way I have not felt before," he wrote in his notes during a plane ride home to New York in late 2007. Referring to his success in engineering the appointment of Richard Cabrera as *peritaje global,* or global expert, he wrote, "The design of the PG is brilliant."

The self-congratulation seemed warranted. The plaintiffs had put in place a court-sanctioned figure poised to issue a definitive report calling for the judge to impose a monumental penalty on Chevron. "We control the frame of the debate," Donziger observed. Chevron "just cannot get around the visuals, the fact that they did this, and the fact that their only defenses are technical. They are a big oil company."

In most modern courts, of course, technical defenses are legitimate (and often effective). Law is a realm of procedure and technicality. And merely being "a big oil company" ordinarily is not a legal wrong meriting punishment. Still, on a practical level, Donziger had a point: An American oil company came to the jungle and left a noxious mess. Poor people suffered through no fault of their own, or, at least, they suffered more than they otherwise might have, because of drilling residue in their water and oil on their roads. They were not in good health, whatever it was that had made them ill. Ideally, some organization or institution would have paid to clean up the pollution and improve the lot of the destitute Indians. Donziger was correct that when he told the story in this manner, many people would agree that the profitable American oil company was the likeliest candidate to write the check.

Roughly calibrated redistribution doesn't sound unfair under these circumstances: Robin Hood and his merry men, reincarnated as lawyers, relieve the rich of some of their wealth for the benefit of the poor. Move the action from Sherwood Forest to the Amazonian rain forest. One difference, though, was that according to legend, Robin Hood lived as an outlaw, beyond the bounds of respectable society. Donziger sought to accomplish his version of redistribution via the courts—a more complicated, real-world endeavor.

Like the hooded archer of yore, Donziger paid a price for pursuing his unconventional mission. Far-flung legal swashbuckling taxed his ability to maintain a normal personal life. Donziger's girlfriend, Laura Miller, kept to a more ordinary routine, if one that was glamorous in its own way. She worked as a corporate publicist in New York, promoting the wares and reputations of Cartier, Anne Klein, and magazine publisher Condé Nast. Stylish and sophisticated, she organized sumptuous receptions for her clients and solicited sympathetic press coverage. While their professional orbits seemed distant, Miller and Donziger actually shared an interest in using celebrities to draw attention to a business or a cause. Miller admired Donziger's single-minded dedication, even though he tended to rail broadly against corporate perfidy and American greed, while she spent her days cultivating New York's corporate elite and celebrating conspicuous consumption. People learn to tolerate contradiction, especially for the sake of love. They compartmentalize. Miller overlooked Donziger's stridency and accepted him as he was. In her company, he toned down his self-righteousness, at least some of the time.

In January 2006, Miller and Donziger learned that she was pregnant. On his next visit to Ecuador, he mused in his notes about becoming a father: "It feels completely different to come here knowing that." The couple decided to marry. Donziger had a history of passionate relationships that ended with emotionally explosive breakups. His marriage would be different, he told friends. He would settle down, romantically speaking. He would help raise a child. On the other hand, he did not see why fatherhood required him to ease up in his pursuit of Chevron. Donziger developed a theory of marriage that conveniently accommodated his needs. For a domestic union to work, he believed, the spouses could not compete; one would naturally dominate. In his marriage, he explained to friends, he played the dominant role. He knew he had a big ego, and he appreciated Laura's willingness to subordinate herself.

Miller deeply loved her husband, despite his flaws, and she admired his intense involvement with *Aguinda II*. She assumed he'd adhere to some new limits. Before giving birth to a son they named Mateo, or Matthew, she had gone along on several trips to Ecuador. Her pleasant personality made her popular with the Ecuadorian plaintiffs' team. Her patience with Donziger was not infinite, however. When he chose to extend one trip so he could attend a political reception in Quito, he and Laura had what he described as "a series of very negative conversations where she accused me of choosing work over family." With young Mateo in diapers, she had a point. Still, Donziger didn't relent. "It was really unpleasant," he said of the disagreement with his wife, "but I have made the right decision." Several months later, he recorded another "intense argument with Laura last night. The travel and being away is taking its toll; we are not taking care of our relationship. I am very worried about this." But his worry did not slow his travel schedule.

*   *   *

While not a materialistic person driven by financial reward, Donziger sometimes groused about the cost of his career choices. His low-six-figure annual stipend from the Ecuador case, combined with Laura's larger corporate PR salary, allowed them to live comfortably even in high-cost-of-living Manhattan. Donziger's family in Jacksonville was well-to-do, and there was trust-fund money waiting for him. But he paid jealous attention to law school peers who were becoming far wealthier or more famous. "Obama has become a U.S. Senator and a likely presidential contender, gracing the cover of *Time* and now a best friend of Oprah," he wrote. "Another Harvard Law classmate, Hill Harper, is an accomplished actor and a star on *CSI New York*." Donziger noted that he had "lost a tremendous amount of income and future income potential by focusing my professional life so narrowly in the last few years. . . . I own no car, and almost all of my equity has gone to keeping this single case alive. My guess is that last year I probably made less money than 95% of my law school classmates who are employed." Nor was he immune to vanity. "I glance at myself in the mirror as I pound away at my computer," he wrote, "and I look so much older than I remember, so much less handsome."

If he won the case, he acknowledged, he stood "to collect an exorbitant amount in fees—probably enough to set up my family for life, with plenty left over to fund other cases and possibly start a foundation." On the other hand, if he lost, "I can imagine roaming barefoot with my clients through the rain forest to hunt the last dying monkeys." Empathy and exaggeration colored Donziger's daydreams. "My personal struggle," he averred, "has taken on an odd parallel to the survival game in which the clients are engaged." Except that while his Indian clients lived in shacks without indoor plumbing, he drank wine with dinner and shared a two-bedroom Upper West Side apartment filled with high-end appliances.

*   *   *

For all his tactical progress against Chevron, Donziger's ability to vindicate his monkey-hunting clients and get his hands on those mammoth fees depended on the case staying alive long enough for the plaintiffs to grasp victory. And that was far from assured.

The Philadelphia plaintiffs' attorney, Joe Kohn, a wealthy man from a wealthy family, was crying poor. Having fronted the anti-Chevron legal campaign more than $5 million over the years, his firm now had a cash-flow problem, Kohn claimed. Payment of several large contingency fees related to other cases had been delayed. Kohn told Donziger he was lending personal money to the firm to meet payroll. "I knew we were testing his limits," Donziger wrote, "but I never knew how close we were coming."

Periodically, Donziger paid visits to Kohn's wood-paneled seventeenth-floor offices in Philadelphia to plead for more time and additional funds. While the law firm his father founded enjoyed a venerable reputation in the Kohns' native Philadelphia, the son struggled to live up to the family name. Gangly in appearance and lacking Donziger's forceful physical presence, he had run twice for Pennsylvania attorney general, in 1992 and 1996, losing both times. He contributed to Democratic political candidates, but had not achieved the rank of first-tier power broker. On the largest professional challenges, he tended to come up short, and now he was beginning to worry that the Ecuador case might fit the pattern.

During one of Donziger's visits, Kohn flipped distractedly through computer printouts showing the perilous state of the *Aguinda II* case finances. "Okay," he said, "so we have been sort of living on a shoestring for the last couple of months."

Yes, Donziger confirmed. The plaintiffs' legal operation needed an emergency infusion of cash. It was $100,000 in debt in Ecuador and still faced daunting expenditures for salaries and technical fieldwork. "We also have to recognize," Donziger said, "that part of [Chevron's] strategy is to bankrupt us."

Kohn understood the plaintiffs' predicament. Corporate defendants targeted in litigation by customers, employees, or pollution victims commonly use their greater resources to try to grind down opponents. But Kohn had always made it clear that he expected a healthy return on his investment. Donziger worried that the Philadelphia lawyer would resolve this tension by pressing for a settlement with Chevron and walking away from the class-action marathon.

This wasn't an idle fear. While Donziger was jabbing and feinting in Lago Agrio in 2007, Kohn opened negotiations in the United States with Tim Cullen, one of Chevron's main outside attorneys. Cullen headed the litigation department at Jones, Day, Reavis & Pogue, where the oil company's general counsel, Charles James, had once been a partner. At James's behest, Jones Day was coordinating the Ecuador case for Chevron. Cullen told Kohn that the oil company would contemplate settling, but only if it cost Chevron shareholders less than $100 million. Forget about the $6 billion dream, Cullen said. It was never happening.

Donziger worried that Kohn might snap at this bait, taking less than $100 million. After all, the lawyers would still divvy up 25 percent of that amount, allowing Kohn to enjoy a fat return on his investment.

One morning in February 2007, Cullen, a by-the-book corporate defender, agreed to sit down with Kohn and Donziger at the Jones Day offices in New York. Kohn displayed the requisite bluster for such an occasion, warning Cullen that the plaintiffs expected to win a multibillion-dollar verdict in Ecuador. It was not clear to Donziger whether Kohn believed his own harangue.

Cullen, in any event, seemed entirely unruffled. The case, he said, had dragged on for far too long. If Ecuadorian lives had been harmed, nothing was being done to ease the suffering. The legal bickering needed to end; they didn't want their children and grand-children to inherit the dispute.

Donziger felt relaxed enough with Cullen to indulge in some friendly joshing. He warned the Chevron lawyer that the new Ecuadorian government favored the plaintiffs, but then insisted, with the guileless dishonesty of a five-year-old, that he had not personally met with anyone from the Correa administration. Cullen "laughed his ass off," Donziger noted. "As I tell my kids," the Chevron lawyer said, teasing Donziger, "if you're going to lie, lie big." Donziger, strangely, appeared to take the comment as a compliment.

The meeting wrapped up quickly. Cullen didn't take a lot of notes. He received his visitors in a cramped conference room. The Jones Day partner had not arranged for the standard morning-meeting spread of coffee, orange juice, pastries, and fresh fruit. Donziger knew this was not how big-firm lawyers treated plaintiffs' attorneys whom they took seriously.

As he showed his guests the door, Cullen said that he would confer with Charles James at Chevron, but the promise seemed halfhearted. Cullen, in fact, did report in dutifully to his client, but James was not in a settling mood. As long as he called the shots, Chevron would keep fighting.

With compromise unlikely, Donziger knew he would have to string Kohn along until the court in Lago reached a verdict. Despite this financial dependence, Donziger consoled himself that at least he had sole command of the proceedings in Ecuador. In 2006, he had persuaded Pablo Fajardo and Luís Yanza, once and for all, to cut ties to the eccentric Cristóbal Bonifaz. The two Ecuadorians cited Bonifaz's failure to consult with them and his reluctance to visit the rain forest.

Bonifaz was not taken by surprise by Donziger's maneuver; he had seen the split coming. He was not, however, prepared to walk away from the case. He had initiated the legal war against Texaco in New York more than a dozen years earlier. To Bonifaz, this was his crusade, on his native turf. It was his legacy. Donziger and Fajardo, in his view, were mere upstarts. Bonifaz had a plan, and he didn't care what it might cost his former underlings.

Chapter Thirteen

FIASCO

To execute his plan, Bonifaz wrote to an acquaintance in Ecuador, what he needed was "three or four people who have resided close to the lakes of petroleum left by Texaco and who have discovered in the last four years that they have some form of cancer." He also requested a letter from "any medic who has examined these persons that says that in his opinion there is at least a 51% probability the cancer was caused by the fact that these people have been exposed to the petroleum contamination in the Amazon." Finally, he ordered up "some sort of simple document by which these persons give you authorization to seek a remedy in court to compensate them."

Armed with these rudimentary materials and some client names, Bonifaz believed he could launch a parallel Oriente pollution lawsuit in the United States, one that would put him back in the game against Chevron. He intended to be at the table if there were settlement talks. "It is possible that with this last action in court that I am planning," Bonifaz wrote to his friend in Ecuador, "we will give Chevron *'la copa de gracia.'*"

Bonifaz's Spanish version of the French term *coup de grâce* ("blow of mercy") would literally translate as "cup of mercy" in English. What he meant to express was something more along the lines of "we will really stick it to Chevron." His confidence, however, exceeded both his linguistic and legal capabilities.

Before filing suit in the federal court in San Francisco, the oil company's home jurisdiction, Bonifaz did not take the trouble to meet the seven Ecuadorian clients who had been rounded up at his request. He did not verify the medical records he had solicited or the paperwork authorizing him to take legal action on the Ecuadorians' behalf. Calling this quick-and-dirty lawsuit unpromising would be charitable. Nevertheless, Bonifaz got two other activist attorneys from the United States to sign the federal-court complaint. The suit sought class-action status on behalf of thousands of oil-field victims.

Donziger quickly learned about the rival legal action but was helpless to do anything about Bonifaz's escapade. Publicly discrediting Bonifaz would risk undermining the Lago case and raising doubts about the larger campaign to hold Chevron culpable.

This was not the first rival lawsuit to threaten the legitimacy of *Aguinda II*. Judith Kimerling, the environmental lawyer whose research provided the foundation for the entire endeavor, remained intensely interested in the Amazon after she was marginalized by Bonifaz and then Donziger. Her involvement with the rain forest and its inhabitants had only deepened over the years. She visited the Oriente frequently, forming close personal bonds with members of the Huaorani and Kichwa. At the City University of New York, she built an academic career on law review articles about the litigation against Texaco and later Chevron. And at scholarly conferences, she became a spokeswoman for indigenous people who believed that their interests weren't represented by the American lawyers and their homesteader allies in the Frente. With her guidance, a dissident group of Huaorani and Kichwa filed their own legal action in a provincial court in the Ecuadorian town of Tena.

Kimerling had distrusted Bonifaz and Donziger from the outset. She resented their usurping her role as advocate for the Indians. She was convinced they just wanted to get rich and didn't care, as she did, about reviving the jungle environment and its indigenous cultures. She also thought the amount of money the *Aguinda II* lawyers sought was fanciful. No one had a real plan for spending $6 billion, she wrote in one journal article, and "the basis for the estimate is murky." Whenever her Huaorani and Kichwa friends inquired about the management of the case in Lago Agrio, they were rudely rebuffed by Donziger and his allies, she added. That's why she encouraged them to file their own suit.

To Donziger's great relief, Kimerling's competing litigation foundered. The judge in Tena wanted no part of an international controversy, citing as one basis for his dismissal of Kimerling's complaint the picky technical flaw that Chevron had not been served with a certified English translation of the original Spanish documents. Kimerling encountered only frustration when she tried to appeal in the Ecuadorian court system. Defeated, she returned to New York, where she continued to write profusely footnoted essays about Indians who had been betrayed not only by the American oil industry and the government in Quito, but also by their ostensible legal representatives.

The Bonifaz suit in San Francisco flamed out in far more spectacular fashion. Chevron sent lawyers to the Oriente to question Bonifaz's supposed clients. In sworn depositions, the plaintiffs confessed that they had not suffered the various ailments Bonifaz attributed to them. A woman named Gloria Chamba, for example, supposedly had experienced emotional distress over her son's contracting leukemia as a result of exposure to petroleum. Under oath, she was asked about a sentence in the complaint stating that she "provides care to her son as he slowly deteriorates from his cancer." That, a Chevron attorney inquired, "is false, isn't it?"

"Yes," Chamba said.

"Did you ever authorize your lawyers to sue [Chevron], claiming that your son has leukemia?"

"No."

Chamba's son "does not have and has never had leukemia," concluded U.S. District Judge William Alsup. Similarly, plaintiff Luisa Gonzales "alleged that she had breast cancer when she knew that she did not," the judge said. Dismissal of injury claims before a trial was a "severe sanction," Alsup acknowledged in an August 2007 ruling, but one that was justified in this case because the plaintiffs had "engaged deliberately in deceptive practices that undermine the integrity of judicial proceedings." Moreover, the judge added, "This is not the first evidence of possible misconduct by plaintiffs' counsel in this case. It is clear to the court that this case was manufactured by plaintiffs' counsel for reasons other than to seek a recovery on these plaintiffs' behalf. This litigation is likely a smaller piece of some larger scheme against [Chevron]." Three months later, in another harsh opinion, Alsup shut down the entire fiasco, reiterating that Bonifaz and his co-counsel had brought suit in California "for reasons that have more to do with internecine quarrels among [Chevron's] antagonists than the interests of their plaintiffs."

Chevron wasted no time in trying to use the Bonifaz debacle to undermine *Aguinda II* itself. The San Francisco suit, the company said in a court filing, was part of "a long-standing and ongoing unlawful effort by Bonifaz and other lawyers and entities to extort money from Chevron by blaming it for harms that are as nonexistent as the false cancer claims" disowned by Chamba and Gonzales. Whatever pollution existed in Ecuador, the company added, was "the sole responsibility of the Ecuadorian government and its state-owned oil company, Petroecuador."

Donziger's clients scrambled to distance themselves from Bonifaz. They issued a scathing press release asserting that Bonifaz had been fired from the case in Ecuador for "ethically questionable" conduct. "Bonifaz purports to fight for human rights," they said, "but as one can see from the federal court's decision, he regularly forgets to respect the human rights of his own clients in the Amazon rain forest." The release criticized Chevron "for trying to use the sanctions against Bonifaz in the San Francisco case as a vehicle to discredit" the case in Ecuador.

The self-immolation of Bonifaz was a cause for celebration at Chevron. In speeches and interviews, Charles James vowed that the company would redouble its effort to crush the Lago Agrio case, as well. "I've got a docket of lots of people who have brought lots of lawsuits against Chevron who all believe, 'You've got a lot of money. Why don't you just give me some?'" he told an industry trade publication in October 2007. "We owe it to our shareholders not to do that."

The Donziger case, James added, was nothing more than "a farce."

Chevron's attempt to link the two cases was not surprising, but the suits were actually quite different. U.S. court rules required the Bonifaz plaintiffs to submit to pretrial questioning by Chevron's lawyers. Neither Ecuador's Environmental Management Act nor Ecuadorian court procedure obliged Donziger's clients in the Oriente to do the same—and they never had. Not that the *Aguinda II* plaintiffs would have admitted to faking illness. They had a long list of real maladies and family fatalities, not least Emergildo Criollo's sad account of his children dying.

During one of my own visits to the Oriente, a campesino named Servio Curipoma told me how his family moved from Loja to the town of San Carlos in 1981. He was ten years old at the time. They settled near an operating Texaco oil well. The only roads were built by Texaco, to and from drilling platforms, well heads, and separating stations. Curipoma's family intended to farm cacao and coffee; they had to be able to get crops to market. "We didn't understand how [proximity to the oil] would affect our health," he explained.

His mother, Rosana, bore ten children. The family discovered sometime after it arrived, he said, that the house Curipoma's father had built was located between two open, unlined Texaco waste pits. Chickens and rabbits the family raised would sometimes fall in. The children or their parents would pull the animals out and try to clean them, but they usually died anyway. Eventually, contractors sent by Texaco covered over the pits with dirt. As far as Curipoma knew, the waste oil and drilling muds were never removed; they were merely buried. During rainstorms, greasy black fluid would run from the former pits into nearby streams, he said, the same streams from which the family drew their water for drinking and cooking. They bathed there, too. "We had no choice," he said. "That was the only water. It was shiny with oil."

In 1988, his mother was diagnosed with uterine cancer. A few years later, his father was diagnosed with stomach cancer, which killed him in 2000 at the age of sixty-four. His mother received radiation treatment at a hospital and later had a hysterectomy. She lived longer but suffered terribly from stomachaches and diarrhea, her son said. Emaciated and in constant pain, she succumbed to the cancer in 2006. He was not sure of her age.

"It is my duty as a son to fight Chevron and achieve justice," Curipoma said. "The oil company killed my parents, and it killed my sister-in-law, who also got cancer." While he could not prove the causal link between petroleum and illness, that fact did not diminish his anger.

About eight years earlier, Curipoma had decided to build a new home for his wife and three children. He began to lay a concrete foundation on family land a short distance down the road. He discovered, he said, that directly beneath the new structure was another waste-oil pit that had been covered by just a foot or so of soil, enough to allow foliage to grow back. He asked me to have a look. We walked a hundred yards along a dusty single-lane road and reached a clearing with a partially built house.

"It looks green here," he said, "but you have to look closely." A squat man in his forties, he began hacking at the ground with a machete. Small pieces of asphalt, the hardened remains of abandoned crude, became visible as he cleared the grass. It was as if a parking lot had once existed just below the dirt and grass and trees.

We walked to an adjacent area near one of his cacao groves. The ground grew spongy, and the smell of petroleum became evident. "Stop here," Curipoma said. "Otherwise you will sink in." Apparently in honor of my visit, he was wearing polyester slacks instead of his usual farming clothes. He reached for a stick several feet long and plunged it into the moist soil. When he pulled the stick back out, it was covered with stinking black goo.

"This is what Texaco left us," he said with disgust. "When there is rain, this petroleum still washes into the San Carlos River, which is where this community gets water. I do not want my three children to suffer the way my parents did. I do not want to die of cancer."

What did he want?

"We don't want money to get rich," he said. "We just want someone to clean up the oil. Chevron has plenty of profits. Why don't they give us justice?" He stared at me for a while, as if waiting for an answer.

The town of San Carlos has special significance in the legal battle because it was the site of one of the two studies that the *Aguinda II* plaintiffs put forward as their strongest evidence that cancer rates were elevated in the oil-producing areas of the Oriente. But Chevron had insisted that the San Carlos study underestimated the population of San Carlos—and, as a result, proved nothing at all.

Chevron did more than critique the plaintiffs' research. The company sponsored its own peer-reviewed study, published in 2008 in the *International Archives of Occupational and Environmental Health,* which compared mortality data from oil-producing provinces in the northern Amazon to that of the non-oil-producing province of Pichincha, which included Quito. The company-funded study found "no evidence of increased rates of death" from all causes or from cancer in the oil-extraction zone. In fact, mortality rates from all causes and from cancer in the Amazon provinces, the study concluded, "were significantly lower" than those in the Quito area. In other words, a resident of the capital city was statistically more likely to be diagnosed with cancer and die than a farmer living in San Carlos or a storekeeper in Lago Agrio.

Servio Curipoma, however, was uninterested in company-financed findings that contradicted the earlier studies suggesting increased cancer risks due to oil. A farmer with limited formal education, he was not that impressed by any of the research. As a boy, he swam in polluted streams. He had watched his parents waste away and die. There was no doubt in his mind what caused them to perish. He saw his own children come home from playing in the fields and surrounding forest, their limbs smudged with petroleum. "You cannot tell me," he said, "that the oil has not made us sick. The question is: Who will do something about it?"

Chapter Fourteen

AUTHORSHIP

By mid-2007, Richard Cabrera, the court-appointed global expert secretly selected by Donziger, had become the unlikely central figure in *Aguinda II.* The process of identifying Cabrera and ensuring his appointment had consumed a long five months, as Donziger noted during an informal moment captured by Joe Berlinger's film crew. The judge, he added, "never would have done it had we not really pushed him." Donziger drew a lesson from the experience: "All this bullshit about law and facts" was secondary. "In the end of the day, it is about brute force."

At times, Donziger sounded less like an attorney than a movie-screen mob boss. On June 6, 2007, he met in Ecuador with Atossa Soltani, the head of Amazon Watch, and Luís Yanza, director of the Frente. The plaintiffs, Donziger told his friends, needed to "do more politically, to control the court, to pressure the court" because Ecuadorian courts "make decisions based on who they fear most, not based on what the laws should dictate." He worried that, to win, the plaintiffs had to make the judiciary fear them. Donziger suggested taking over the Lago court with a massive protest to send a message to the judge: "Don't fuck with us anymore—not now and not later." He proposed raising "our own army . . ."

"A specialized group ... for immediate action," Yanza inter-jected.

A woman who had organized her fair share of protests, Soltani seemed alarmed by the militant turn the conversation had taken, and equally worried that it was being filmed. She interrupted to ask whether anyone could subpoena the video of their exchange.

Not in Ecuador, Donziger said.

"What about the U.S.?" Soltani asked.

Donziger unwisely ignored her.

Soltani persisted: "I just want you to know that it's ... illegal to conspire to break the law."

"No law has been conspired to be broken," Donziger said.

Chevron petitioned the court repeatedly not to appoint Cabrera and instead to continue the laborious judicial inspections. The company argued that without as many samples as possible, gathered from throughout the former concession area, any finding of liability would amount to a denial of due process. Chevron executives "suspected that Cabrera, this mining engineer, who didn't have any relevant experience, was going to be friendly with Donziger," one member of the company's senior management told me. When court filings did not work, Chevron bought newspaper advertisements in July 2007, impugning Cabrera's "complete lack of integrity" in the pages of *El Universo, El Comercio,* and *La Hora El Pais.* Chevron mounted the ad hominem attack without knowing just how closely Cabrera was working with the plaintiffs. To a degree difficult to believe, given the company's enormous financial advantage, Donziger seemed to be outflanking his opponent.

Over a period of six months, Cabrera attended four dozen site visits, making a big show of his imperviousness to partisan influence. In fact, it was the plaintiffs who had recommended to Cabrera which sites he ought to inspect, steering him to those with the most egregious contamination. One of these episodes was captured on film by the Berlinger crew. "I have been named the expert for the global assessment report," Cabrera told the public gathering, as soldiers and police officers monitored the crowd. He had shed some of the modesty Donziger noted when they first met. "At this juncture," the engineer said, "I am the highest authority at this examination."

Diego Larrea, an Ecuadorian lawyer for Chevron, asked Cabrera whether the parties could make suggestions on soil sampling.

"Wait, wait, wait," Fajardo objected, raising his hands. "What we agreed on was that the expert has the authority to say what is and what isn't going to be. We can't say, 'Take samples here and there.' Excuse me, but that is something he [Cabrera] has to decide."

"You can make a suggestion," Cabrera told Larrea, "but I can't work under your criteria. I decide where to take samples, and that's it, Counselor." In reality, Cabrera had already met extensively with Donziger and other members of the plaintiffs' team and agreed to work under *their* criteria.

While in the United States, Donziger wrote an e-mail to Fajardo in July 2007, with the subject heading *Ideas para reunion con Richard* (Ideas for meeting with Richard): "When I get there," Donziger instructed, "we'll re-analyze the work and the budget with Richard. And we'll adjust with a much smaller team. My tendency is to stop Richard from working much more in the field . . . or, if he continues doing it, he should continue under the most strict control and with an extremely limited number of samples. And we'll change the focus of the data at our offices." Unknown to Chevron, Fajardo remained in regular contact with Cabrera, keeping tabs on the expert's activities.

Chevron was equally oblivious to another development that motivated Donziger to monitor and steer Cabrera: The plaintiffs' earlier in-house estimate of potential cleanup costs had fallen apart.

As the Donziger legal team and Amazon Watch routinely asserted in press conferences and releases, the $6.14 billion figure to clean up the rain forest came from Dave Russell, the Atlanta-based environmental consultant hired by Donziger. After offering what he conceded was a "wild-assed guess," however, Russell had second thoughts. In February 2005, he e-mailed Donziger to say, "From the data I have seen so far, we are not finding any of the highly carcinogenic compounds one would hope to find when investigating the oil pits."

These doubts did nothing to endear Russell to Donziger. Their relationship deteriorated, and Donziger refused to pay the consultant's invoices. Then Donziger fired him.

In February 2006, Russell sent Donziger a letter with the heading "Cease and Desist." Russell said that after being let go, he continued to follow the case and eventually realized that his 2003 cleanup cost estimate "is too high by a substantial margin, perhaps by a factor of ten or more." He wasn't saying that the Oriente was pristine, but he now believed that a decent remediation could be done for $600 million. Russell asked Donziger to stop publicizing the $6 billion estimate and quit citing Russell as his expert authority. He wanted nothing more to do with *Aguinda II*. He had prepared the $6.14 billion estimate, he added, "with only a week of review time in the jungle, heavily influenced by you in the writing." Russell called the figure "a ticking time bomb which will come back to bite you and very badly if any one attempts due diligence on it."

Enraged by Russell's defection, Donziger understood how damaging it could be. "I don't care what the fuck that guy says," the lawyer told a colleague with Amazon Watch. "The $6 billion thing is out there. The reality is, based on what this guy is telling me [it] would cost less than that, significantly less than that." In a separate e-mail to members of the plaintiffs' team, he acknowledged that Russell's cease-and-desist letter "has a certain amt [amount] of danger for us."

In Donziger's eyes, the Cabrera global expert report would be the antidote to Russell's attempt to poison the $6 billion cost estimate. If Cabrera, with behind-the-scenes assistance from the plain-tiffs' team, arrived at his own multibillion-dollar damages figure, Russell's change of heart would become irrelevant.

Donziger's experience with Russell did not diminish the law-yer's ambition for a truly stupendous judgment. In conversation with Ann Maest, another of the plaintiffs' paid scientific consul-tants, he explained, "If we have a legitimate $50 billion damages claim," that would give the judge cover to say, "Well, I can't give them [the plaintiffs] less than $5 billion." Under those circum-stances, Donziger reasoned, the judge could tell Chevron he had done the company a favor by knocking out "90 percent of the dam-ages claim."

Relying on Kohn Swift's bank account, Donziger retained a Boulder, Colorado, firm called Stratus to generate the guts of the report Cabrera would give the Lago Agrio court. A respected litiga-tion adviser to federal and state agencies, Stratus brought an aura of technical credibility to Donziger's enterprise. Ann Maest worked for Stratus. She had attended the March 2007 Cabrera prep session in Ecuador and was the participant who joked about keeping the proceedings secret from Chevron. David Chapman, a colleague of Maest's, e-mailed Donziger after the meeting suggesting that "the way this would work best is that if Stratus did much of the work, putting the pieces together and writing the report," which Cabrera would then sign and file with the court. Donziger traveled to Boul-der to give the Stratus employees marching orders. *Aguinda II*, he told them, had "a larger meaning." The report Stratus was poised to produce for Cabrera, he told the technical experts, would be-come well known among "academics, people in your field, other lawyers."

Stratus's top executives responded positively. "We loved the whole package," Joshua Lipton, the president, said at the time. Stra-tus also enjoyed the remuneration. Its initial contract with Kohn Swift called for compensation of $125,000. That amount ballooned to $1.7 million, according to court filings. Donziger also suggested that if there were a verdict against Chevron, Stratus stood to make a lot more helping to oversee the remediation work in Ecuador.

Drawing on measurements from the judicial inspections, among other sources, Stratus began churning out multiple "annexes" on water, soil, and air pollution. These were intended to undergird the Cabrera report proper. Donziger and Kohn exchanged scores of e-mails with Stratus principals and staff members in late 2007 and early 2008. To make sure that they produced the expansive dollar figure he was hoping for, Donziger suggested to Stratus in September 2007 that it "define the norms of clean-up" and then "propose these norms to the Ministry of Energy, which governs these norms and whose Minister is a good friend of ours, so that the Ministry issues them as an official decree before the trial ends." Donziger sought to influence not just the judicial process in Lago Agrio, but also the Correa administration in Quito.

In January 2008, Douglas Beltman, the executive vice president of Stratus, traveled to Ecuador with his subordinate Maest to meet Richard Cabrera in person. In addition to their Ph.D.s, the American consultants had years of experience evaluating pollution sites. They were unimpressed by Cabrera. As Beltman later put it, the Ecuadorian mining engineer "lacked the skill, qualifications, and experience" to assess environmental damage. It also struck Beltman as odd that Cabrera lacked an "independent team" to assist him. Instead, his aides "were affiliated with or working at the direction of" the plaintiffs. Yet another peculiarity: Donziger told Beltman that Stratus's role had to remain "absolutely secret." At the same time, the American lawyer assured Beltman that Ecuador's informal legal culture tolerated all of these arrangements, raising the question of why secrecy was required.

During his visit, Beltman felt uncertain about the situation. Donziger obviously cared about getting something done in Ecuador. The contaminated sites he showed the Stratus experts needed attention. Beltman, a committed environmentalist, years earlier had helped clean up Superfund disasters in the United States as an employee of the Environmental Protection Agency. He had no affection for big oil companies, and he wanted to improve conditions in the Oriente. In the end, Beltman decided to suspend his skepticism and work with Donziger. The important thing, Beltman felt, was to make sure people had clean water and a safe place to raise their children.

Upon returning to Colorado, Beltman rallied his subordinates. "We have to write, over the next 2 to 3 weeks, probably the single most important technical document for the case," he said in a February 2008 e-mail. "The document will pull together all of the work over the last 15 years or so on the case and make recommendations for the court to consider in making its judgment." This document and Richard Cabrera's report, he suggested, would be one and the same.

Once he had an initial draft, Beltman sent it to Donziger, inquiring whether he was "on track in terms of tone, language level, and content." The three-thousand-page compendium, drafted in English and then translated into Spanish, included an introduction stating, "This report was written by Richard Cabrera." But, of course, Cabrera did not write it. Caught up in Donziger's campaign against Chevron, Beltman didn't question the propriety of putting words in Cabrera's mouth.

Stratus continued to tinker with its magnum opus until the end of March. On April 1, accompanied by armed guards, Cabrera filed the report with the Lago Agrio court. He recommended that Chevron pay damages in excess of $16 billion—not as much as the amounts Donziger had bandied about, but nearly three times the sum calculated—and then retracted—by Russell.

In the months that followed, Donziger and his consultants at Stratus reminded one another by e-mail to keep the true authorship of the report confidential. At one point, Beltman, sounding half-mischievous, half-nervous, joked in an e-mail to colleagues: "Oh what a tangled web . . ." The complete quotation, often wrongly attributed to Shakespeare, is from Sir Walter Scott's epic poem *Marmion* (1808): "Oh, what a tangled web we weave/When first we practice to deceive!" Like Donziger, Beltman seemed to recognize that he had taken a fateful step over to the dark side.

In the months after Cabrera gave the Lago court "his" global expert's report, Chevron objected to just about every statistic and claim filed under Cabrera's name. Surprisingly, Donziger's unit also protested the report, arguing that it was not generous enough. Chevron's lawyers did not realize that the plaintiffs were objecting to their own consultants' numbers. Compounding the charade, Stratus drafted Cabrera's responses to the objections Stratus had written to the "independent" expert's report that Stratus had also composed. Beltman later acknowledged he had never before engaged in such subterfuge. Working closely with Donziger, the scientist absorbed, as if by moral osmosis, the attorney's attitude that extreme corporate misconduct justified extreme countermeasures.

To formalize Stratus's critique of its own analysis, Cabrera issued a revised version of the report in November 2008, declaring an even larger damage estimate of $27.3 billion. By bidding against themselves, the plaintiffs had got the number close to the $30 billion to which Donziger said he'd like to see the verdict "jacked up."

Chevron generated thousands of pages of court filings disagreeing with Cabrera. The company pointed out that his cleanup estimates attributed all oil pollution to Texaco, entirely exonerating Petroecuador, the sole operator for the previous two decades and the culpable party in more than fourteen hundred spills just since 2000. Chevron contended that the Cabrera estimate included millions of dollars for nonexistent pits, which were actually mere shadows in aerial photographs of the rain forest. The Cabrera report used inflated U.S.-based cost figures, rather than Ecuadorian price estimates: $2.2 million to remediate a pit, for example, rather than the actual amount of $85,000 per pit that Petroecuador had spent on its sporadic cleanup effort. The report recommended $8.4 billion in damages for "unjust enrichment," when Texaco enjoyed less than one-eighth of that sum in profits, according to Chevron. The report pushed for another $9.5 billion to compensate for thousands of "excessive cancer deaths" attributed to petroleum exposure, but did not identify a single person with cancer or refer to a single medical record. There was no discussion of scientific proof that oil pollution caused cancer, either. Instead, the excessive deaths were "assessed" on the basis of the epidemiological cancer studies (which Chevron challenged) and self-reporting of cancer cases at public meetings of Oriente residents. The meetings were overseen by Dr. Carlos Beristain, a Spanish physician investigating health problems in the region.

Cabrera's revised figures made Charles James apoplectic. He'd never seen what he considered such a barefaced corruption of a legal proceeding. In a company press release, he lashed out at Cabrera's "undeniable disdain for science, transparency, and Ecuadorian law." James accused the expert of "ongoing collaboration" with the plaintiffs. "An extraordinarily disturbing pattern has emerged," James said. Cabrera's report "and plaintiffs' counsel's demands read like two parts of the same script." James pointed to language in Cabrera's revised report in November that appeared to have been "cut and pasted" from plaintiffs' filings in September (the only differences are marked in bold):

Donziger's team wrote:

Therefore **the cost** analysis to remediate to 1000 ppm of TPH as stated in Attachment N calculates a cost that is lower than the actual one in order to achieve this level of cleanliness (even though it should be taken into account that 1000 ppm of TPH is not adequate level of cleanliness, as previously mentioned). The real cost to remediate the soils to 1000 ppm of TPH is approximately $2,034,000,000.

Cabrera wrote:

> Therefore **my** analysis to remediate to 1000 ppm of TPH as stated in Attachment N calculates a cost that is lower than the actual one in order to achieve this level of cleanliness (even though it should be taken into account that 1000 ppm of TPH is not adequate level of cleanliness, as previously mentioned). **Using my revised calculations** the real cost to remediate the soils to 1000 ppm of TPH is approximately $2,034,000,000.

Coming to Cabrera's defense, the plaintiffs filed a fifteen-page document in December 2008 in which Doug Beltman and Ann Maest of Stratus, while not exactly denying that Cabrera had submitted their work, nevertheless insisted that he operated at arm's length from the plaintiffs. Cabrera, they said, acted as "a neutral 'expert' to the court."

The Lago court had ordered that the parties jointly pay Cabrera for his work. The plaintiffs enthusiastically did so. "We have met with Richard and everything is under control," Luís Yanza, the director of the Frente, wrote to Donziger just weeks after Cabrera's appointment in 2007. "We gave him some money in advance." The plaintiffs' team paid Cabrera about $392,000 in total. Approximately $272,000 of that sum was approved by the Ecuadorian court. The Frente paid Cabrera another $120,000 from what Yanza called the organization's "secret account." In some of their e-mail, Yanza and his colleagues mysteriously referred to the engineer by the code name "Wuao." Chevron assumed Cabrera was working for the plaintiffs, which indeed he was. The company refused to pay him anything. Chevron's boycott only reinforced Cabrera's tilt toward Donziger, who had chosen, bought, and paid for the "neutral" expert.

The company made some thirty court filings objecting to Cabrera's methods and questioning his impartiality—all to no avail. The judge stressed that both sides had been welcome to provide the expert with whatever information they thought relevant. In response to the company's repeated impugning of his work, Cabrera declared in his own filing in October 2008 that he was an "honest man with nothing to hide." His "conduct as an expert in this case," he added, "has been as professional, impartial and objective as possible." He claimed that he did "not take orders from either of the parties to the lawsuit" and that he had not been "subject to the view or whims of either of the parties." Four months later, Cabrera told the court that "the entire expert investigation procedure was completed by me personally." The engineer's misrepresentations and impudence rivaled those of his employer, Donziger, who stood by silently as Cabrera lied to the judge.

Donziger's astonishing good fortune in orchestrating and promoting the case continued in January 2009, with the gala premiere of Joe Berlinger's *Crude* at the Sundance Film Festival in Park City, Utah. Accompanied by Pablo Fajardo, Trudie Styler, and Sting, Donziger joined Berlinger for a question-and-answer session following the screening. Actor Robert Redford, the festival's founder, was among those in the audience at the posh ski-resort theater. The crowd applauded Donziger's self-praise about "taking standards of the developed world regarding oil production and applying them to developing countries." Styler exhorted listeners to open their checkbooks and contribute to the litigation cause. "It's very clear where our sympathies are," Berlinger said when it was his turn. According to the website Indiewire, Fajardo was "the man of the hour, receiving a standing ovation from the audience." With Donziger translating, the Ecuadorian said of *Crude*: "I really think this is a very important documentary." Sting told CBS News: "All the things we've been arguing [for] ... are involved in this film—the right to breathe clean air, to drink fresh water, to feed your children and have a healthy life." The reviews were strong. Manohla Dargis of the *New York Times* praised "a forceful, often infuriating story about Big Oil and little people."

Berlinger's film combined footage of the oil-slicked Oriente and its residents with a narrative of how Donziger turned the case into a media sensation. *Crude* tracked Fajardo's rise to fame, from the *Vanity Fair* profile to his receiving the prestigious Goldman Prize, an award frequently described as the Nobel for environmentalists. With an emotional scene of Fajardo visiting his brother Wilson's grave, the film dramatized Fajardo's allegation that Chevron was somehow responsible for Wilson's violent death. On this point, Berlinger, like the author of the *Vanity Fair* article, apparently allowed his predisposition toward the plaintiffs to dull his journalist's instincts. Years before Fajardo insinuated that the oil company was complicit in Wilson's murder, he had filed a statement with the local prosecutor's office accusing three local men of committing the homicide. Pablo had made no mention to investigators of any suspicions about Texaco or Chevron. At the time of the 2004 killing, Pablo had not yet begun to play a major role in the pollution case, making his claim that he was the intended murder target all the more unlikely. In fact, an editorial published in *El Comercio* implied that Wilson's death resulted from public comments he had made about the Colombian FARC guerrilla movement and drug trafficking. Neither Berlinger's film nor *Vanity Fair* raised these complicating facts.

The filmmaker conveyed how Donziger and Fajardo, with financial backing from Joe Kohn, kept Chevron continually on the run. *Crude* showed Fajardo aboard Correa's helicopter and at the president's elbow as Correa recoiled from the smell of polluted drinking water. On the day after Correa toured the oil fields, the president underscored his loyalties by delivering a speech calling for the criminal prosecution of lawyers who years earlier had helped arrange for Texaco's liability release from the Ecuadorian government. Correa referred to Ecuadorians who worked for Texaco or Chevron as *"vende patrias,"* or people who sell their country. In *Crude,* Donziger is shown celebrating this brazen presidential intervention. The oil company lawyers, Donziger joyfully speculated, "are shitting in their pants right now."

Donziger's campaign to have Ricardo Reis Veiga and one of his colleagues on Chevron's Latin American legal team thrown in prison for their representation of Texaco began even before Correa took office. The stratagem had two goals: distract Chevron's attorneys and undermine the 1998 release, a critical element of the company's defense. Donziger and Fajardo lobbied Ecuadorian officials in Quito to investigate Reis Veiga and provided documents they hoped would lead to prosecution. As early as 2005, an Ecuadorian government lawyer friendly with the plaintiffs' legal team wrote to them in an e-mail that the Attorney General's Office in Quito was "searching for a way to nullify or undermine the value of the remediation contract (between Petroecuador, the Republic of Ecuador, and Texaco Petroleum)."

On a personal level, Donziger saw the potential prosecution and humiliation of Reis Veiga as a form of revenge. The company attorney had belittled the lawsuit ever since Donziger helped file it in New York in 1993. "Some days, I fantasize about putting my strong hands around Reis Veiga's neck and squeezing until he begs for mercy," Donziger wrote in 2006. "I want him to know how it feels to suffer." If Donziger couldn't literally strangle the man, imprisonment would do.

Over the years, various Ecuadorian prosecutors looked into Reis Veiga's actions but dropped the matter after determining he hadn't violated any criminal laws. Donziger's team didn't give up easily, however. In March 2008, Fajardo wrote to Donziger about an imminent appointment with a senior government official. Fajardo promised to "insist" that the government "reopen the criminal investigation against Texaco for the remediation." That same month, on March 31, the day before Richard Cabrera filed his report with the court in Lago Agrio, the Correa administration followed through and announced the revival of the criminal investigation of Reis Veiga and another Chevron attorney, Rodrigo Pérez Pallares, an Ecuadorian national. Combined with Cabrera's breathtaking damages assessment, the revived probe clarified the degree to which the oil company was losing control of the situation in Ecuador. In San Ramon, Charles James fulminated against plaintiffs' lawyers. *Newsweek* magazine quoted an unnamed Chevron lobbyist in Washington as saying, "We can't let little countries screw around with big companies like this—companies that have made big investments around the world." But the lawsuit kept going. A corporation with $200 billion in annual revenue and operations in one hundred countries seemed like a muscle-bound Gulliver, besieged by legal Lilliputians.

"*Chevron* is America's third-largest company, behind ExxonMobil and Wal-Mart," CBS correspondent Scott Pelley said by way of introduction to *60 Minutes* one Sunday evening in May 2009. "One way it got that big was by buying Texaco in 2001. Now that purchase of Texaco has pulled Chevron into a titanic struggle in the Amazon." Soon, Pelley added, "a judge in a tiny Ecuadorian courtroom will decide whether the company must pay as much as $27 billion in damages. That would make this the largest environmental lawsuit in history."

Airing just five months after the Sundance premiere of *Crude*, the thirteen-minute segment on America's most popular television news program reinforced the spreading impression that Chevron faced big trouble in Ecuador. *60 Minutes* showed image after gripping image of seeping crude and blazing gas flares set against the verdant jungle. "It's a disgrace. They treated Ecuador like a trash heap," Doug Beltman told Pelley. CBS identified the Stratus consultant as a former EPA official and "the scientific expert for the people suing Chevron."

60 Minutes cast Donziger as the hero of the piece. In archival footage from the 1990s, he appeared, young and dark-haired, accompanying his indigenous clients into the federal courthouse in New York. A decade and a half later, beefier and gray, he answered Pelley's questions without his usual bombast. They spoke in the rain forest, and Donziger seemed relaxed, several of his top shirt buttons undone in the jungle heat. Like Berlinger, the producers of *60 Minutes* adopted the plaintiffs' point of view. Chevron made this easier by offering as its main spokesperson an executive named Sylvia Garrigo, corporate manager of global issues and policy. On camera, she came off as bureaucratic and stiff. If she conveyed any humanity during her interview, those moments didn't make the cut that aired. Instead, viewers watched her argue that human exposure to hydrocarbons was not necessarily dangerous. "I have makeup on, and there's naturally occurring oil on my face," Garrigo said. "Doesn't mean I'm going to get sick from it."

In opposition to Garrigo, *60 Minutes* introduced Manuel Salinas, the kindly-looking campesino who lived near the well site visited by President Correa during his helicopter tour two years earlier. Salinas obligingly scratched the ground with a stick and produced black petroleum gunk. The water from his drinking well, he said, was polluted. *60 Minutes* did not mention that, while Texaco had drilled and once operated the well, the site had been run for the past two decades by Petroecuador. (Correa, of course, had not noted this fact, either.) While someone undoubtedly should have cleaned up the Salinas property, the site happened not to have been among those Texaco agreed to remediate; the state oil company was obliged to do the cleanup.

In his narration, Pelley mentioned that Petroecuador was emptying some waste-oil pits. What he failed to note—perhaps because he and his colleagues didn't know—was that Donziger for years had actually been trying to impede the national oil company's cleanup. In late 2006, Donziger and Fajardo exchanged e-mails discussing their partially successful campaign to get Petroecuador to leave hundreds of pits as they were. In the spring of 2007, Fernando Reyes, the environmental specialist Donziger had considered as a candidate to be the global expert, ran into Fajardo at Petroecuador's executive offices. Fajardo mentioned that he had been lobbying a Petroecuador vice president "to suspend all remedial activity in the area run by the Petroecuador-Texaco consortium, because the remediation was depriving the plaintiffs of clear evidence on which to base their claims for damages in the case." In an e-mail to Fajardo, Donziger recommended that in pursuing this perverse goal, Fajardo engage in "informal and oral meetings" with Petroecuador officials. They didn't want Chevron "to use some letter to say we are obstructing remediation."

That, however, is exactly what the plaintiffs' team was doing. Three years later, in an e-mail to Donziger with the subject heading "WORRISOME," Fajardo described an Ecuadorian newspaper report that the Correa government had announced an acceleration of pit remediation. Worse, Fajardo added, the Quito regime estimated that its entire cleanup initiative would cost an "extremely low" $96 million, a different order of magnitude from the billions that the plaintiffs were demanding. Fajardo fretted, believing that this could allow Chevron to "say that the State finally assumed its duty and is going to clean up what it ought to."

In a furious e-mail response, Donziger instructed the Ecuadorian legal team: "You have to go to Correa and put an end to this shit once and for all." The "shit" Donziger wanted to end was the mopping up of the waste oil. The lawyer who had raised millions of dollars from environmentalists committed to saving Indians and the rain forest was actively blocking attempts to clean the contamination. Donziger's deal with the Devil was becoming increasingly perverse.

When Pelley made his visit to Lago Agrio, the judge overseeing *Aguinda II* was Juan Nuñez, a balding man in wire-rimmed glasses. "Nuñez struck us as serious and thoughtful," Pelley told viewers. Contradicting this warm endorsement, Chevron's Garrigo stated flatly that the judge and Cabrera were part of a "corrupt and politicized judicial system." Her language echoed Donziger's from years earlier, before the Lago litigation began to go his way. In light of President Correa's endorsement of the Frente and its lawsuit, Garrigo asked Pelley incredulously: "Do you think that this judge is going to feel any independence? Is going to look at the rule of law? Is going to look at the contracts? Is going to look at the evidence and determine what is legitimate and illegitimate?"

Pelley asked Nuñez on camera about the company's charge of misbehavior. The judge looked bewildered. Nuñez compared himself to "a good father of a family," who is duty-bound "to give a child what a child is entitled to." It was an odd metaphor. Since it was unlikely that Nuñez had Chevron in mind when he described the child he planned to protect, perhaps Garrigo was correct that the judge favored the plaintiffs. Pelley asked her, "What do you think your chances are of winning this case?"

"In Ecuador?" she responded. "Very little." Chevron management realized that if something drastic did not change the course of the trial, the company was going to lose to Donziger in Lago Agrio.

* * *

Paul M. Barrett

In October 2009, the Frente sponsored a macabre parade in front of the Lago Agrio courthouse. The procession featured effigies of the indicted Chevron lawyers Reis Veiga and Rodrigo Pérez Pallares. Protesters announced the "crimes" committed by the company figures: destroying the rivers, sickening innocent children, betraying the nation's cultural patrimony. A man dressed as the Grim Reaper carried out the mob-imposed punishment: decapitation by scythe. The headless Chevron corpses were dumped in a group coffin, carried into the jungle, and buried in a shallow grave.

Chapter Fifteen

ENTRAPMENT

Just a couple of months after Chevron's Garrigo announced on *60 Minutes* that the company was resigned to losing in Lago Agrio, another company spokesman, Donald Campbell, declared: "We're going to fight this until hell freezes over, and then we'll fight it on the ice."

One reason for the apparent disconnect was the way some financial people view money. Each year that Chevron did *not* pay out a multibillion-dollar verdict, the company enjoyed the benefit of retaining that money. On paper, Chevron accountants could translate the benefit into a dollar amount equivalent to the bank interest on a potential verdict. On a year-by-year basis, that interest was greater than the tens of millions of dollars that Chevron was spending annually on legal fees. From a certain short-term perspective, therefore, it made sense to pay the legal fees and postpone a judgment. In hindsight, of course, it would have been much less expensive for Texaco to have settled the original case in New York in the 1990s. (If one wanted to go back futher, it would have been smart and morally proper for Texaco to obviate the need for a lawsuit in the first place by spending relatively modest sums in the 1970s to line its waste pits and reinject most of its produced water.)

But decades later, the bellicose Charles James could argue within Chevron that the company ought to continue to pay its outside lawyers as an unfortunate cost of doing business, with the hope that Donziger, at some point, would run out of financing.

This plan for a war of attrition meshed with another line of thinking James favored: that settlement would encourage other plaintiffs to try the Chevron litigation lottery. Better to send the message that Chevron would never play the patsy. The strategy had worked in another long-pending lawsuit over the company's conduct abroad. In December 2008, a federal jury in San Francisco cleared Chevron of claims brought by Nigerian villagers who had occupied an offshore drilling platform ten years earlier. Like the *Aguinda II* plaintiffs, the Nigerians objected to what they said was the American company's indifference to the environment. In response, Chevron summoned government security forces to break up the demonstration, resulting in injuries and two deaths. The protesters said they were unarmed; Chevron's witnesses countered that villagers took hostages. "At the end of the day," James told the *San Francisco Chronicle,* "our position was vindicated, and we were able to prove in the trial that what was alleged to have happened didn't happen that way." The lesson the company wanted to teach plaintiffs' lawyers was that, whatever their clients' complaints, this wealthy American company would not roll over.

In Ecuador, Chevron had never acquired any assets to speak of. If it lost in the Lago court, the company simply planned to refuse to pay. That would force Donziger and his colleagues to take an Ecuadorian judgment to the United States or other countries where the company did have assets and ask judges in those countries to enforce the verdict via seizure proceedings. In third-country enforcement cases, which could take years to unfold, Chevron would argue, as Garrigo did on *60 Minutes,* that it did not get a fair trial in Ecuador.

If the $27 billion Cabrera report was a serious warning that Chevron had deep problems in Lago Agrio, the company was signaling that the marathon confrontation would not conclude in Ecuador. It would not end "until hell freezes over." And in the meantime, Chevron developed new plans for disrupting the Lago trial and proving that Ecuadorian justice did not deserve respect in the rest of the world.

Some of these plans resembled little more than dirty tricks. In early 2009, a young freelance journalist working in Latin America received an intriguing inquiry: Would she take a "research" assignment in the Ecuadorian jungle? Kroll Associates, a New York–based private investigation firm for large corporations, wanted Mary Cuddehe to gather information on the *Aguinda II* plaintiffs under the guise of reporting an article. The pay would be generous. Broke and curious, Cuddehe agreed to hear more.

Kroll invited her for an expenses-paid weekend at a luxury hotel in Bogotá, Colombia, where she would learn more about the mission. Sam Anson, a Kroll managing director, took Cuddehe out to lavish meals and even a night of dancing. A former journalist, Anson said his client Chevron was being unfairly pilloried. Cuddehe found him convincing.

Anson wanted her to travel to Lago Agrio and reveal that the plaintiffs' lawyers and Cabrera were perpetrating a fraud. Specifically, the Kroll operative asked her to investigate Carlos Beristain, the Spanish physician, with an eye toward proving that the health survey he conducted for Cabrera was in some way fixed. Beristain had declined to reveal the names of the villagers he questioned, and Chevron suspected that Donziger's team had conspired in selecting them.

Cuddehe understood that her value lay not in her skill or reputation, but the fact that she was unknown. "No one would suspect that the starry-eyed young American poking around was actually shilling for Chevron," she wrote later. Kroll would pay her $20,000, plus all expenses, for six weeks of faux journalism—five times what she would typically make for a real freelance assignment.

"You know, you're irreplaceable," Anson told her seductively on her last night in Bogotá. They were sitting outside a fancy Peruvian restaurant. Inside, Kroll employees were dining on grilled fish and sipping passion-fruit cocktails. "The smoke from Sam's cigarette," she wrote, "curled in the lamplight, giving the moment a film-noir feel."

Cuddehe felt the tug to say yes. She needed the money. An undercover adventure had a dark Hollywood appeal. "Were the plaintiffs colluding with Beristain?" she wondered. "Was Chevron desperate and paranoid, merely trying to smear its opponents?" In the end, though, she pulled back. "Despite my curiosity, I knew I had to say no," she wrote in a tell-all article for the website of *The Atlantic* magazine. "If I'm ever going to answer those questions, it will have to be in my role as a journalist, not as a corporate spy."

The man from Kroll seemed disappointed. "There is no other Mary Cuddehe," he told her. "If you don't do this job, we'll have to find another way."

Chevron later claimed that it didn't approve of Anson's attempt to recruit Cuddehe. "He was off the reservation," a company spokesman told me. Then again, part of the reason large corporations and their lawyers retain firms like Kroll is so that, if an espionage mission goes bad, it can be disowned as off the reservation. In any event, on August 31, 2009, Chevron announced that it had found, in Anson's words, another way.

The company said it had uncovered a "bribery scheme" implicating Judge Nuñez. Chevron turned over to Ecuadorian and American prosecutors undercover video it said showed Nuñez secretly saying that he would rule against Chevron, even though the trial was continuing. The video, according to the company, included evidence of an agreement to share $3 million in bribes in return for access to environmental-remediation contracts that would follow a victory for the *Aguinda II* plaintiffs. "We think this information absolutely disqualifies the judge and nullifies anything that he has ever done in this case," Charles James told the *New York Times*.

The story defied belief: Two businessmen, an American and an Ecuadorian, met several times with Judge Nuñez to discuss lucrative pollution-cleanup contracts. Using tiny cameras embedded in a spy pen and watch, the businessmen recorded their clandestine conversations. Chevron said it received the videos from one of the James Bond wannabes, Diego Borja, who formerly worked as a logistics contractor for the company and whose wife and uncle also had been on Chevron's payroll. Neither Borja nor his partner, an American named Wayne Hansen, had been paid for their private-eye work, Chevron said. But, because of safety concerns, the company had moved Borja and his family from Ecuador to the United States and was paying their expenses. Chevron portrayed Borja as an opportunist-turned-hero. "I'd like to think he brought [the recordings] to us out of respect for our company and concern for what seemed to be transpiring here," James said. At Chevron's behest, the U.S. government granted Borja political asylum.

The covert video told a foggy story. In one grainy tape, a man identifying himself as a representative of Correa's political party referred to $3 million in bribes, presumably to be paid by Borja and Hansen. The political emissary appeared to indicate that the money would be split three ways: among the judge, the plaintiffs in the lawsuit, and the Correa administration. Nuñez was not present for that exchange. Following Chevron's release of the tapes, Ecuador's prosecutor general opened a criminal investigation of everyone involved, including Nuñez. The judge denied wrongdoing but stepped down from the case, making way for another jurist to take over, the sixth in as many years.

Chevron's explosive revelation made headlines and then, within weeks, began to deteriorate into confusion. It turned out that Borja's partner, Hansen, was a convicted drug dealer who in the 1980s had been sentenced to nearly three years in American prison for conspiring to import 275,000 pounds of marijuana into the United States from Colombia. Then it emerged that, after three get-togethers with Judge Nuñez, Borja, the former Chevron contractor, met in San Francisco with lawyers for the company. Next, Borja returned to Ecuador and held a fourth meeting with the judge. That sequence, the plaintiffs asserted, suggested that Chevron may have been a more active participant in the sting than the company acknowledged. Chevron insisted that its lawyers told Borja not to meet again with the judge.

No one came out of the Borja-Hansen affair looking especially virtuous. Judge Nuñez had no good explanation for meeting repeatedly with obviously corrupt interlopers pressing him about the outcome of the biggest-dollar case in his country's history. On the other hand, this was Ecuador. As illustrated by Donziger's earlier access to Judge Germán Yáñez, one of Nuñez's several predecessors on the case, some Ecuadorian jurists feel comfortable schmoozing with just about anyone. Conflict of interest seems to be an unknown concept there.

A close examination of the muddy tapes revealed the thoroughgoing ambiguity of the entire situation. Whatever his reasons for conversing with Borja and Hansen, Nuñez never said he would accept a bribe for throwing the case. Borja and Hansen pressed him to confirm that he had decided to hold Chevron liable. Finally, on one occasion, the judge responded perfunctorily, "Yes, sir," to the question of whether the company would lose. It was far from obvious, though, whether Nuñez was really answering the query about Chevron's culpability or trying to end the conversation without giving offense.

Even as its gotcha disclosure eroded, Chevron continued to deny any role in the videotaping. Borja, the supposed Good Samaritan, did, however, become a ward of the corporation. Court filings in the United States showed that the company was paying him a generous monthly stipend, covering his lawyers' fees, and providing him with the free use of a luxury home and a sport-utility vehicle. In Lago Agrio, the trial did not go back to square one, as Chevron had hoped it would. Instead, Nuñez's replacement stepped in and pressed on toward a verdict. The Correa administration accused the company of engineering the scandal to delay justice.

Borja repaid Chevron's largesse by getting snared in yet another video sting. (A Hollywood screenwriter wouldn't dare make this up.) In Skype conversations with a childhood friend, Borja boasted that by getting Nuñez dismissed, he had accomplished in a matter of days what Chevron had been unable to do in a year. "There was never a bribe," he acknowledged to his friend. If Chevron ever turned on him, Borja said, he could reveal incriminating information about the company. "I have correspondence that talks about things you can't even imagine," he told his friend. "I can't talk about it here, dude, because I'm afraid, but they're things that can make the Amazons win this, just like *that,*" he added, snapping his fingers. The Skype exchanges ended up in the possession of the plaintiffs, who made them public.

Borja's inscrutable performance continued. At Chevron's behest, he recanted the Skype statements, claiming that for some unspecified reason he had been blowing smoke to mislead his friend. As much con man as whistle-blower, and quite possibly a lunatic, Borja relished tricking people and making himself seem important. He garishly embodied the ethical rot endemic in Lago Agrio. By getting into bed with him, Chevron associated itself with Borja's dishonesty. In Donziger's mind, Chevron's relationship with Borja confirmed his view that in Lago Agrio, no holds were barred. Both sides were doing business of one sort or another with the Devil.

Chapter Sixteen

CLEANSING

Not embarrassed by the Borja episode, Chevron plotted an even more aggressive line of attack. Attorneys from the Jones Day firm had defeated the Nigerian villagers' wrongful-death lawsuit in San Francisco, but they had not solved the company's problems in the wilder, woollier jurisdiction of Sucumbíos Province. So Chevron brought in a Los Angeles–based firm called Gibson, Dunn & Crutcher and gave it the assignment of destroying Donziger.

"We are the firm that clients in distress have turned to when they are facing their worst problems, or when they have in fact faced defeat," Gibson Dunn partner Randy Mastro told *American Lawyer* magazine in late 2009. "We have been the problem-solvers, the game-changers." A hundred years old and a thousand lawyers strong, Gibson Dunn was not known for humility.

Previously the oil company's lawyers had aimed to refute Donziger's message. Mastro would shoot the messenger. Girding for a loss in the Lago Agrio court, he and his firm aimed to undercut the legitimacy of a plaintiffs' verdict and make it difficult for Donziger to enforce a judgment outside of Ecuador.

Mastro, cochairman of Gibson Dunn's national litigation practice, worked in New York, where, before going into private practice, he enjoyed success as a federal prosecutor. He had the mind-set of an organized-crime investigator. He saw Donziger and his clients as conspirators to be exposed and punished.

Gibson Dunn lawyers, assisted by gumshoes from Kroll, began the assignment for Chevron by conducting a frame-by-frame examination of *Crude*. Sam Anson and his colleagues at Kroll remained convinced that the Spanish physician Dr. Carlos Beristain would provide an incriminating link between the plaintiffs' legal team and Richard Cabrera. The Kroll investigators scrutinized the documentary as if it were stakeout surveillance video. In a windowless war room decorated with empty pizza boxes, they studied the film like FBI agents monitoring the comings and goings at a Mafia social club. They even used facial-recognition software to try to identify Beristain in the background of scenes depicting Donziger, Pablo Fajardo, and their comrades. Eventually this painstaking analysis revealed that there were two slightly different versions of *Crude* in circulation. One, available online from Netflix, included footage of Donziger and Fajardo consulting with Beristain as the Spaniard conducted focus-group-style research on self-reported incidents of cancer and other illnesses. That struck Kroll and Gibson Dunn as significant because Cabrera later relied on Beristain's findings to arrive at his recommendation that the Lago Agrio court impose $9.5 billion in damages for statistically "excess" cancer deaths.

While the Netflix version of *Crude* showed Donziger and Fajardo associating with Beristain, Berlinger had edited the physician out of the scene for the other version of the film, which was available for sale as a DVD. Netflix, it turned out, had mistakenly released the wrong cut of the movie, an error that raised tantalizing questions. Why, Mastro wondered, would Berlinger take the trouble to erase evidence of Beristain's connection to the plaintiffs' lawyers? Did this confirm Kroll's suspicion that Beristain worked with the plaintiffs and Cabrera at the same time? Perhaps Donziger had requested the change. What might other "outtakes" from Berlinger's filming reveal? Mastro wanted to see all of the footage from the cutting-room floor.

Within its large litigation department, Gibson Dunn identified a subset of its most experienced courtroom lawyers as the Transnational Litigation Group—a marketing conceit meant to impress corporate general counsel grappling with hostile foreign court systems. "When faced with significant non-U.S. and cross-border litigation," the firm's website promised, "members of the Transnational Litigation Group work with their clients to respond to these often massive and multifaceted assaults with more than a series of defensive tactics, but rather, an affirmative strategy to ultimately end the litigation."

Chevron liked Gibson Dunn's philosophy of offense as the best defense. The company was particularly impressed by Gibson Dunn's success in extricating Dole Food from expensive legal trouble in Nicaragua. In 2007, plaintiffs' attorneys convinced a California jury to hold Dole responsible for illness and sterility suffered by Nicaraguan banana workers allegedly exposed to a potent pesticide in the 1970s and 1980s. The company faced billions of dollars in potential liability and thousands of similar claims in other countries. Dole hired Gibson Dunn based on the firm's advice that the way to defeat the pesticide claims was to show that they were fake. "Take the fight to the other side," Mastro said.

Over the next eighteen months, Gibson Dunn lawyers and investigators proved that, regardless of what environmental harm and worker sickness may have occurred in Nicaragua, the attorneys who had sued Dole were untruthful. Some of the alleged pesticide victims were shown not to suffer from sterility. Others had not even worked for Dole. One purportedly injured person admitted that he had been coached to testify "like a parrot." Gibson Dunn got a California state court judge to dismiss two of the central cases against Dole. A federal judge in Miami refused to enforce another large verdict obtained against the company in Nicaragua. *American Lawyer* honored Gibson Dunn in 2009 for having the Litigation Department of the Year. The magazine noted that in addition to rescuing Dole, Gibson Dunn had extricated Wal-Mart Stores from an employee class-action disaster and won a Supreme Court victory for a notorious West Virginia coal mine operator. "I call them lifeboat lawyers," said Thomas Mars, Wal-Mart's executive vice president.

Someone with a more jaundiced view of corporate conduct might compare Gibson Dunn to the character Winston Wolf in the 1994 Quentin Tarantino movie *Pulp Fiction*. Played by Harvey Keitel, Wolf was a "cleaner," an underworld specialist in the art of tidying up bloody crime scenes. If, after other law firms had taken a few whacks at a problem, the client still had a mess on its hands, Gibson Dunn arrived with the legal equivalent of sponges, mop, and a bucket of Clorox.

A changing of the guard in Chevron's in-house legal ranks smoothed Gibson Dunn's retention. In mid-2009, the oil company began the process of replacing general counsel Charles James. Having served zealously, but without neutralizing the threat in Ecuador, James received a short-term promotion to executive vice president as a step toward a consensual retirement. James recommended as his replacement R. Hewitt Pate, also a politically conservative Republican, who had succeeded James as head of the Justice Department's Antitrust Division. Pate had no hesitation about displacing Jones Day (James's former law firm). With Gibson Dunn, Chevron bought the talents of numerous accomplished attorneys in Los Angeles, Washington, and New York. None would become more of a nemesis to Donziger than Randy Mastro.

In his early fifties, Mastro had wavy white hair and a matching snowy beard. He peered over wire-rim glasses, which perched at the tip of his nose. He typically wore a dark business suit, French-cuffed shirt, and burgundy tie. His Santa Claus–in–Brooks Brothers look was misleading, however. Mastro had learned about brass-knuckled investigation under the supervision of Rudolph

Giuliani. In the 1980s, when Giuliani was the headline-seeking Manhattan U.S. attorney, Mastro prosecuted mob cases as one of his senior assistants. Giuliani moved to city hall as mayor in 1994 and hired Mastro as his chief of staff, later promoting him to deputy mayor for operations. Mastro endured death threats when he tangled with organized crime families over control of New York's private garbage industry and the Fulton Fish Market. Sometimes he semi-jokingly brought a baseball bat to staff meetings. His " 'we-hit-them, they-hit-us' approach," the *Daily News* once reported, "made him the No. 2 player on Team Rudy, the mayor's alter ego, and the only trigger man in town who can make Giuliani look like Mr. Nice Guy."

Against Donziger, Mastro's weapon of choice was Title 28, Section 1782, of the U.S. Code. The obscure legal provision allows a civil litigant to seek a federal court order for testimony or documents that might be useful in a proceeding overseas. Worded broadly, it is ideal for prying into an antagonist's private doings. Attorney-client privilege applies to a Section 1782 inquiry, but the privilege can be overcome if targeted attorneys are accused of committing fraud or discuss their legal strategy publicly—for example, in a documentary film.

Beginning in January 2010, Gibson Dunn blanketed the federal courts with 1782 petitions, seeking practically every communication exchanged among anyone who had worked for or with Donziger. In New York, Mastro demanded that Berlinger turn over hundreds of hours of outtakes from *Crude,* on the theory that the video might be useful to Chevron in defending itself in Lago Agrio. Berlinger hired top-flight lawyers to argue that his First Amendment free-press rights shielded him from such a "fishing expedition." In Colorado, New Mexico, Texas, Georgia, and New Jersey, Gibson Dunn attorneys asked federal judges to force the Stratus firm and other environmental consultants to divulge their dealings with Cabrera, Donziger, and Fajardo. Eventually, Chevron's law firm would file 1782 petitions in more than twenty federal courts, seeking hundreds of thousands of pages of confidential records, e-mails, memos, and even Donziger's diary-style notes to himself about the case.

The Gibson Dunn probe swiftly revealed how Donziger's relationships with former comrades had devolved into rancor. One person the law firm deposed was Charles Calmbacher, the industrial hygienist who had worked alongside Dave Russell as a technical expert for the plaintiffs' team in Ecuador. Like Russell, the author of the "rain forest Chernobyl" catchphrase, Calmbacher was at first an enthusiastic backer of the case. Referring to Chevron, Calmbacher told the *New York Times* in August 2004, "Their defense is a lot like the tobacco industry saying there is no evidence linking smoking and lung cancer." But also like his friend Russell, Calmbacher underwent a radical change of perspective. As they studied the results from oil-field sampling, they became less confident that the pollution could be tied with scientific certainty to cancer or other illnesses. And they resented Donziger's pressure to get them to say otherwise.

"You know what I think of Steven Donziger?" Calmbacher asked me when we met several years later. Silently, he held up his middle finger.

When Gibson Dunn lawyers questioned Calmbacher in Atlanta in March 2010, they asked him about environmental-damage assessments of two key Texaco drilling sites. The written assessments were filed with the Lago court in Calmbacher's name. He said that, at Donziger's request, he had signed several blank signature pages. Then, Calmbacher explained, someone appended the signature pages to versions of his analyses that had been altered.

"To the extent that someone took this signature page," a Gibson Dunn attorney asked Calmbacher, "and attached it to this report and represented to the court in Lago Agrio that you had written this report and reached these conclusions—that would be false, correct?"

"That's correct," Calmbacher answered. "I did not reach these conclusions, and I did not write this report."

"While you were working as a judicial inspection expert for the plaintiffs," the Gibson Dunn lawyer continued, "did you ever conclude that TexPet had failed to adequately remediate one of the sites?"

"I didn't, no." Donziger, he said, "wanted the answer to be that there was contamination and people were injured."

Why?

"Because it makes money. That's what wins the case."

Mastro's firm wasted no time in e-mailing the Calmbacher deposition transcript to Hew Pate at Chevron's San Ramon headquarters. The new general counsel saw the statements of the disgruntled former plaintiffs' expert as the biggest, easiest-to-understand crack the company had found in Donziger's case. This was not a matter of dueling scientific statistics. "Their own expert," Pate said, "has testified that two of the plaintiffs' earliest reports are fraudulent." The trial in Ecuador, he added, had been "tainted from the outset."

In New York, Mastro's Section 1782 petition seeking access to the *Crude* outtakes landed by random assignment in front of U.S. District Judge Lewis Kaplan. A former partner at Paul, Weiss, Rifkind, Wharton & Garrison, one of New York's most prestigious corporate firms, Kaplan was named to the bench by President Clinton in 1994. He had a reputation as highly intelligent, technically adept, and consistently irascible. He wore large aviator-style glasses and a permanent scowl.

Mastro asked Kaplan to focus on three scenes from *Crude*. The first depicted Dr. Beristain conferring with Donziger and Fajardo.

Kaplan quickly agreed that it was fishy that the plaintiffs' attorneys were working with a member of the supposedly neutral global expert's staff. Even more suspect, the judge ruled, was that Berlinger tried to eliminate images of Beristain from the film. In a January 22, 2009, e-mail, Fajardo had begged Berlinger's team to delete Beristain. "This is so serious that we could lose everything, or a great deal, just because of these minuscule shots," Fajardo wrote.

"I liked Pablo," Berlinger told me. "He was pleading with me, teary-eyed, about how important this was, that it would ruin the case. I said okay because it didn't seem significant to the film at all. I didn't appreciate how it would look in retrospect." In a declaration to the court, Berlinger confessed to the Beristain edit, an act of suppression that Kaplan called "suggestive of an awareness of questionable activity."

A second scene that troubled Kaplan was the one in which Donziger ostentatiously told Berlinger's camera in 2006 that he would use "pressure tactics" to intimidate the elderly judge in Quito. Kaplan seemed offended by Donziger's comment that in Ecuador "this is how the game is played. It's dirty." Chevron, Kaplan ruled, deserved to see what other "dirty" tactics Donziger had used. Finally, Kaplan noted the scene in which Donziger speculated that the pair of Chevron attorneys were "shitting in their pants" because they'd been indicted by Correa's chief prosecutor. Kaplan observed that the plaintiffs had provided information to the Ecuadorian government and encouraged the prosecutions. There was even a scene in *Crude* in which Correa physically embraced Donziger and told the American lawyer, "Wonderful, keep it up!"

Kaplan brushed off Berlinger's objection that he had a First Amendment right to keep his raw footage confidential. Such a privilege might protect a legitimate news-gatherer, the judge said, but he adopted Chevron's description of *Crude* as "a piece of theater deliberately designed to win over audiences to the plaintiffs' side and to facilitate the Lago Agrio litigation." Neither the company nor the judge was aware at the time that Donziger had helped get the film financed by his wealthy law school friend DeLeon.

Granting Mastro's demand for six hundred hours of out-takes, Kaplan invoked the wisdom of Supreme Court Justice Louis Brandeis about sunlight being "the best of disinfectants." Review of Berlinger's outtakes, Kaplan said, "will contribute to the goal of seeing not only that justice is done, but that it appears to be done."

Chapter Seventeen

OUTTAKES

Risking the wrath of the gods of irony, Chevron in 2010 brought the battle back to its starting place. In the 1990s, Texaco had argued in federal court in New York that justice demanded the question of pollution liability in Ecuador be adjudicated in Ecuador. Lawyers for the rain forest residents insisted that the Andean country was too corrupt. The oil company won, and the case was exiled from American shores. Donziger and his fellow plaintiffs' lawyers did not surrender, however. They took up the fight in Lago Agrio. Convinced that the oil company would play rough, Donziger preemptively did the same. In the free-form litigation that followed, he gained the upper hand.

So Donziger's corporate opponents now blithely reversed course. They insisted that the New York court where they had once said the case did not belong provided a fine venue to litigate the rights and wrongs of the rain forest. Chevron branded the judicial proceedings in Ecuador—which in the 1990s, Texaco had sworn would be squeaky-clean—a cesspool of vice. Donziger, who had warned against official impropriety in Ecuador, now defended the trial in Lago as perhaps unconventional by American standards, but essentially fair. With billions at stake, no one worried about consistency.

Thirteen years had passed since the start of *Aguinda I*. The protracted clash had yet to improve either the ecology of the jungle or the health of its inhabitants. The spongy black gunk remained everywhere.

Horror and indignation gripped New York's media establishment when word spread about Judge Kaplan's order requiring Berlinger to surrender his *Crude* outtakes. The filmmaker appealed, and Floyd Abrams, longtime First Amendment counsel to the *New York Times*, filed a friend-of-the-court brief on behalf of the *Times*, the *Wall Street Journal*, the *Washington Post*, ABC, CBS, and NBC. Abrams warned that the constitutionally protected work of all newsgatherers would be "seriously jeopardized" if a corporate target of journalistic inquiry could root around in reporters' notebooks and digital files. The media titans argued that Judge Kaplan had "made it far too easy for Chevron to obtain far too much."

In July 2010, the Second Circuit rebuffed Abrams. Ruling for Chevron, the appellate court concluded that Berlinger had not acted as an independent journalist and, as a result, did not enjoy free-press protection. His "making of the film was solicited by the plaintiffs in the Lago Agrio litigation for the purpose of telling their story," the court said. This criticism betrayed a deeply naïve understanding of documentaries and other long-form journalism. Many such projects begin with a participant in a controversy seeking someone to tell their story. The fact of the solicitation alone does not necessarily taint the resulting work. Serious journalists aspire to dispassion and integrity regardless of how they initially learn of a potential topic.

The appeals court was on firmer if still narrow ground when it criticized Berlinger for altering the film at the plaintiffs' request.

The change seemed minor to Berlinger, and he claimed not to understand its significance at the time he made it. But to the judicial panel, the edit proved that Berlinger's larger purpose was not news gathering but propaganda.

Hard cases, the legal saying goes, make bad law. The Berlinger matter produced an unfortunate precedent making journalists and documentarians more vulnerable to corporations seeking to undermine the First Amendment right to probe the economically powerful. For Donziger, the ruling created an immediate crisis of exposure.

It is difficult to overstate the thrill Mastro and his team experienced when they got their hands on Berlinger's raw field tapes. A squad of Gibson Dunn associates and Kroll investigators spent the summer dissecting the haul. Once again, the war room filled with fast-food detritus as young lawyers pored over scores of video clips a day. Mastro then went back to Kaplan with what he considered the greatest (meaning worst) hits from Donziger's oeuvre of cinematic braggadocio. With these excerpts as ammunition, Mastro asked Kaplan to order Donziger to turn over every piece of paper and every computer file he had on the Ecuador case. "If we were on a 'fishing expedition,'" Mastro told the judge, "we caught a whopper."

In his elegant high-ceilinged Manhattan courtroom, Kaplan permitted the Gibson Dunn partner to put on a festival of *Crude* outtakes: Donziger holding forth in Quito cafes, Donziger pressing Joe Kohn for more money, Donziger declaiming on corporate greed. The plaintiffs' lawyer had not merely grown comfortable in front of the camera; he had fallen in love with it. Mastro showed Donziger explaining the imperative to bend reality: "Science," he said in one clip, "has to serve the law practice; the law practice doesn't serve science." In another, he preached a coarse version of Critical Legal Studies: "I once worked for a lawyer who said something that I have never forgotten: 'Facts do not exist. Facts are created.' Ever since that day, I realized how the law works." The witticism might elicit nods in a Harvard seminar on the elusive nature of knowledge; from the mouth of a practicing lawyer, it suggested a willingness to manipulate evidence.

Kaplan watched video of the March 2007 all-day meeting when Donziger & Co. told Cabrera (before he had even been appointed) that they would do his work for him. In another scene, Donziger attended a glass-clinking dinner in Quito during which the conversation turned to what might happen to a Lago judge who vindicated Chevron. Another participant suggested that such a judge would be "killed." Donziger calmly replied that the judge might not be killed, "but he'll think he will be, which is just as good."

Kaplan described the presentation as "disturbing." Donziger's statements, the judge added, "raise substantial questions as to his possible criminal liability and professional discipline." Kaplan granted Mastro's request for complete access to Donziger's files. The plaintiffs' every communication would be laid bare—a profoundly rare development in civil litigation. In addition, Kaplan said, Gibson Dunn could depose Donziger under oath. These extraordinary steps reflected the judge's conclusion that Donziger had waived lawyer-client confidentiality by inviting the filmmakers to follow him and by acting as a political organizer as much as an attorney. They also reflected Kaplan's palpable distaste for Donziger's arrogance.

Kaplan's suggestion that Donziger deserved to be investigated by the New York Bar Association, or even a prosecutor, did not go unnoticed at Gibson Dunn's offices in the MetLife Building above Grand Central Terminal. Mastro instructed his subordinates to begin gathering material for a fresh legal action aimed at Donziger personally.

* * *

As the disclosures of Donziger's collaboration with Cabrera came to light, some of those under him panicked. Julio Prieto, a young attorney in Quito, sent Donziger an e-mail in March 2010 warning that the revelations could be "devastating in Ecuador." Prieto added that "apart from destroying the proceeding, all of us, your attorneys, might go to jail."

In Philadelphia, Joe Kohn decided that he had heard enough. The financial anchor of the lawsuit had laid out more than $7 million for the case, including more than $1 million for Donziger's compensation and expenses. Even as Donziger continually complained that he needed more money, he refused to share control. In November 2009, Kohn had sent a letter to the Frente's Pablo Fajardo and Luís Yanza warning about Donziger's "excessive amounts of travel, stays at hotels, and meals at expensive restaurants." Even more irritating, Donziger "purports to make all decisions on his own, without any contact or input from our firm."

In late 2009, Kohn laid out a plan for settling with Chevron—and ending his collaboration with Donziger. The time was right, he argued. David O'Reilly, the company's CEO, had announced his retirement at the end of the year and wouldn't want to bequeath *Aguinda II* to his successor. Kohn recommended that the plaintiffs demand $1 billion and be prepared to accept $700 million, or less. Chevron, he predicted, would resist for five, ten, fifteen years rather than pay a settlement in excess of $1 billion. "During that time," he noted, "the people in the Oriente will continue to suffer and die from the pollution, drink contaminated water, and lack basic medical care." Even a victory at trial would not produce quick cash. Lacking assets in Ecuador, Chevron would refuse to honor a judgment there.

Donziger didn't buy it. Although he had contemplated settlement in the past, he believed that, with the $27.3 billion Cabrera report in hand, the plaintiffs were within striking distance of an enormous judgment. The time to negotiate was after a verdict, when they'd have more leverage. As for Kohn's complaints about control of the case, Donziger could only shake his head. Kohn had never been more than the treasurer of Aguinda Inc. Since his hostile takeover from Cristóbal Bonifaz, Donziger had reigned as chairman and CEO of the case.

Kohn thought Donziger's stubbornness had ripened into megalomania. Donziger hadn't settled so much as a fender bender. What did he know about big-dollar cases? Kohn happened to be in the midst of resolving his firm's long-pending $2 billion human-rights verdict against the estate of Philippine dictator Ferdinand Marcos. In the end, thousands of plaintiffs in that case settled for a total of only $10 million, or half a penny on the dollar. You took what you could get. With $700 million, Kohn argued, the Ecuadorian plaintiffs could "provide for virtually 100% clean-up of all of the oil pits; $100 million or more towards clean water programs; $100 million or more towards establishing healthcare facilities and treatments, and still leave tens of millions of dollars for other important programs." Such a settlement, he said, "would be one of the most outstanding humanitarian achievements ever obtained in a court of law."

Donziger refused. In July 2010, with his approval, the Frente fired Kohn, his $7 million in financing be damned.

Kohn reacted bitterly, blaming Donziger's greed. "I am also shocked," Kohn wrote in a letter to the Frente, "by recent disclosures concerning potentially improper and unethical, if not illegal, contacts with the court-appointed expert, Mr. Cabrera, which are coming out in the U.S. discovery proceedings being initiated by Chevron." Kohn added: "I have come to realize that my firm and I were deceived, in part apparently driven by a combination of Donziger's conceit and naiveté, a dangerous combination which is leading the case rapidly towards disaster."

* * *

As a result of Gibson Dunn's prolific Section 1782 filings, Donziger gained notoriety throughout the American court system. "The release of many hours of the outtakes has sent shockwaves through the nation's legal communities," one federal judge in New Mexico wrote in an opinion. "The footage shows, with unflattering frankness, inappropriate, unethical and perhaps illegal conduct." A federal judge in North Carolina agreed: "While this court is unfamiliar with the practices of the Ecuadorian judicial system, the court must believe that the concept of fraud is universal, and that what has blatantly occurred in this matter would in fact be considered fraud by any court."

Chevron brought such judicial condemnations to the attention of the court in Lago Agrio, seeking to get *Aguinda II* dismissed on the basis of ethical taint. Even if the Ecuadorian court proceeded to a verdict, the oil company's lawyers figured that the Section 1782 litigation would raise doubts about the validity of that verdict, making it impossible for Donziger to enforce it in the United States or anywhere else Chevron had assets.

Donziger had alienated Kohn, his main source of financing. His original technical experts, Russell and Calmbacher, had turned on him. The *Crude* outtakes revealed the plaintiffs' covert ties to Cabrera. Judge Kaplan in New York publicly suggested Donziger was a candidate for professional discipline or prosecution. Many lawyers at this point would have run up the white flag.

Instead, Donziger plowed ahead. "Chevron is using me as a whipping boy," he complained to an interviewer in late 2010. "They want to make me into a cartoon villain." He was essentially right. The oil company had decided that its best hope for countering the case in Lago Agrio lay in decimating Donziger. But he refused to surrender. His capacity for defiance knew no bounds.

With Kohn's wallet closed, Donziger needed fresh sources of funds. He had already persuaded his Harvard friend DeLeon to double down on the case. After helping to finance *Crude*, DeLeon agreed to sink millions more into *Aguinda II* itself. Multiple written agreements described DeLeon's investment in the litigation. At one point, Donziger promised his friend a 6 percent share of any recovery, according to a "Confidential Investor Document" dated April 14, 2009. Another agreement, dated just a few weeks later, referred to DeLeon having provided funding in the puzzlingly specific amount of $6,536,624.20. Yet another accounting suggested contributions of $5,487,315 from DeLeon and entities affiliated with him.

Despite the disheveled state of Donziger's paperwork—and the possibility of future disagreements over who owed what to whom—the lawyer was pleased with his ability to fund the litigation even after Kohn had been sidelined. Indeed, Donziger decided he could turn the rain forest lawsuit into a vehicle for financial speculation, not only for DeLeon, but other wealthy people as well.

Plaintiffs' attorneys for generations had fronted clients money in exchange for a percentage of verdicts or settlements. In the 2000s, a marketplace for third-party "litigation finance" developed, in which hedge funds bought interests in other people's lawsuits. Speculating on litigation became just one more unconventional investment, an alternative to junk bonds or synthetic credit default swaps. Historically known as "champerty," investing in third-party lawsuits had once been prohibited, for fear that investors' interests would conflict with those of litigants. These restrictions gradually receded, though. The U.S. Supreme Court held in the 1960s that civil-rights organizations have a constitutional right to finance other people's lawsuits. As hedge funds increasingly gambled on big-dollar disputes between companies, Donziger adapted the practice to the mass-tort lawsuit. He had something of value: the prospective judgment in Ecuador. Like an entrepreneur seeking to sell shares in a start-up enterprise, he engaged a financial middleman named Nicolas Economou, who ran a firm called H5. Economou functioned as a broker, shopping assets—in this case, a potential verdict—to investors. One of the men he introduced Donziger to was Christopher Bogart.

A former executive vice president and general counsel of Time Warner, Bogart had moved on from the practice of law to run Burford Capital, the U.S. arm of a British hedge fund. Burford was raising $300 million from pension funds, insurance companies, and other institutional investors with which it proposed to bet on litigation. Given the $27.3 billion Cabrera valuation and the pro-plaintiffs environment in Ecuador, Donziger assured Bogart that the oil company would lose in Lago Agrio and have to pay billions. Bogart wasn't completely convinced, but he did think it likely that Chevron eventually would settle for an amount in the hundreds of millions of dollars. Even a modest slice of such a recovery would allow for a hefty return on Burford's investment. Bogart, born and raised in Canada, had a courtly, almost aristocratic manner. He found Donziger irritatingly grandiose. But the plaintiffs' lawyer displayed an impressive familiarity with the workings of the Ecuadorian legal system. In the hedge-fund business, big rewards necessitated large risks. So Bogart and his partners at Burford decided to roll the dice.

The hedge fund would invest, however, only if a major outside law firm agreed to join the plaintiffs' legal team and devised a strategy for collecting on the verdict anticipated in Ecuador. Donziger, desperate for Burford's infusion of cash, shopped around and settled on Washington, D.C.-based Patton Boggs. The choice reassured Bogart. James Tyrrell, a senior partner at Patton Boggs, already had a close relationship with several principals at Burford and had publicly endorsed the nascent litigation-finance industry. Tyrrell produced an opinionated assessment of the case that greatly encouraged Bogart to move ahead. Rather than dispassionate analysis, the Patton Boggs memo read like a legal brief. It dismissed as "frivolous" Chevron's objections to the Cabrera report. "Cleverly using the lens of U.S. norms to distort what transpired in Ecuador, Chevron has used its findings regarding plaintiffs' involvement with the Cabrera report to create the impression that it is the victim of an injustice in Ecuador," the memo said. Specifically, Patton Boggs endorsed what Donziger had told Bogart: that the plaintiffs' dealings with Cabrera had been limited and permissible under the Ecuadorian system. Patton Boggs clearly wanted to get into what Tyrrell saw as a potentially lucrative fight.

In November 2010, Burford invested $4 million in the case, with an option to put in $11 million more. Donziger now had the money and the legal manpower to keep Chevron on the defensive. For its financing, Burford stood to receive as much as 5.5 percent off the top of any recovery. Patton Boggs agreed to participate for a 25 percent cut of any legal fees. Down the line, Donziger's Ecuadorian clients would have to share whatever prize they won with a widening circle of outsiders.

Donziger boasted about his innovative arrangements. "You cannot sustain this kind of case without money, and a lot of money," he told students during a speech at Duke University Law School in November 2010. "I don't see a model in the nonprofit world where you could actually bring a lawsuit like this and sustain it over time against a big oil company." From the beginning, he said, "we wanted to make this a business, a business model for a human rights case." *Aguinda II*, he argued, would set a precedent not only for achieving transnational justice, but also for righteous financial engineering.

What Donziger did not tell the Duke students and other audiences was that the overlapping agreements he had struck with various funders could leave relatively little for an actual cleanup. The more modest the potential recovery from Chevron, the larger the proportion of the take was now guaranteed to investors. If Chevron ultimately settled for $100 million, for example, DeLeon, Burford, and other financiers would get paid $69 million, according to a forensic analysis done at the oil company's behest by the accounting firm KPMG. Attorneys and other advisers—including Donziger—would share $22 million. Administrative expenses would consume $8 million. That would leave a paltry $1.5 million for repairing damage to the jungle and its inhabitants.

Advocating for Ecuadorian peasants was an unlikely assignment for Patton Boggs and Jim Tyrrell. Tracing its roots to the politically influential Boggs family of Louisiana, the five-hundred-lawyer firm specialized in Washington lobbying and international trade. It routinely represented foreign governments, including the government of Ecuador, but it didn't ordinarily assist poor farmers or Indians. Tyrrell, who joined Patton Boggs after establishing himself as a corporate-defense litigator at another large law practice, represented the chemical manufacturer Monsanto when it was sued over the Vietnam defoliant Agent Orange. After 9/11, he defended New York City and its contractors against injury suits filed on behalf of firemen and cops who became ill following extended exposure to the smoldering remains of the World Trade Center. The *New York Post* called him "the Devil's advocate." A fastidious man in his early sixties, Tyrrell preferred another of his nicknames, "the master of disaster." In *City of Dust,* a book about the trade center case, author Anthony DePalma wrote that Tyrrell's clients "love him and pay mightily for his services," while antagonists "accuse him of being rapacious and underhanded." Tyrrell recommended the book.

Tyrrell sold the *Aguinda II* engagement to his partners at Patton Boggs as a contingency-fee deal that, according to Donziger's most optimistic scenario, could earn the Washington law firm tens of millions of dollars. With Tyrrell in the hunt, Chevron could no longer assume that Donziger would exhaust himself and slink away. Patton Boggs boasted a specialty that was the mirror image of Gibson Dunn's expertise in undermining foreign judgments: Companies that had won verdicts overseas, but were having trouble getting defendants to pay up, hired Patton Boggs to find a jurisdiction where the courts would enforce the verdicts. If the law firm could do this for corporate clients, Tyrrell urged his partners, why not for a group of Ecuadorian villagers?

Once Tyrrell joined the plaintiffs' team, he immediately turned his attention to the Cabrera problem: Assuming the Lago court delivered a judgment against Chevron, would courts elsewhere view the compromised expert's role as such a serious blot that they would reject the verdict? Judge Kaplan's appalled reaction did not bode well. Tyrrell came up with a possible solution: Patton Boggs would procure a fresh set of expert opinions from U.S.-based scientists. In e-mail exchanges with Donziger, Tyrrell's top lieutenant, a Patton Boggs attorney named Eric Westenberger, referred to this project as an "effort to 'cleanse' any perceived impropriety related to the Cabrera Report." If Chevron could bring in Gibson Dunn as its *Pulp Fiction* cleaner, the plaintiffs would do the same with Patton Boggs.

By late 2010, Tyrrell's team had put together a report in which a fresh group of American Ph.D.s-for-hire calculated the Oriente pollution damages at a gargantuan $113 billion, four times as great as Cabrera's estimate. The spirit of the plaintiffs' eleventh-hour cleansing seemed to be: As long as we're asking for a lot, why not go for broke? In December 2010, Fajardo filed the new demand with the court in Lago Agrio.

In its opposing submission, Chevron argued that Patton Boggs's experts, without doing any original research, had spun out theoretical computations designed to generate an even-more-breathtaking total. "At this point, the plaintiffs' lawyers have no legitimate evidence to advance their claims," said the oil company's Hew Pate, "so they've resorted to a shell game."

While Chevron sneered at the proceedings in Ecuador, Tyrrell directed his associates to map the world for places to collect a verdict. He and Donziger knew that because of Gibson Dunn's dissemination of the *Crude* outtakes, most judges in the United States would blanch at enforcing an *Aguinda II* judgment. "But one of Chevron's vulnerabilities is they have assets in over a hundred countries, and you could enforce a judgment out of Ecuador in any of many countries where they have enormous assets," Donziger said in his speech at Duke Law School. Judges in other Latin American countries might look favorably on the Lago proceedings. His high-spirited campus talk followed a celebratory airing of *Crude* as part of a Latin American film festival. Donziger displayed pride in the buccaneering antics Berlinger depicted. He conjured an image of a righteous pirate, plying the high seas: To enforce a Lago judgment, "you could seize assets, seize boats," he told the law students. "You know, there's all sorts of legal theories we're thinking about."

A different Donziger appeared the following month, December 2010, for his court-ordered Section 1782 deposition in New York. With Mastro supervising, a pack of Chevron lawyers interrogated Donziger on what had transpired in and around Lago Agrio. Uncharacteristically reticent, Donziger surrendered as little information as possible. For thirteen days, the Gibson Dunn lawyers had him trapped in a conference room. He hunched over the table before him, shifted in his chair, asked frequently to be excused for bathroom breaks. Hostile attorneys circled like hungry wolves.

As Donziger once enjoyed bullying Chevron's lawyers in Ecuador, imagining that they would soil their trousers, the company's attorneys relished their ambush in New York. They asked Donziger about his goading the Ecuadorian government to prosecute members of the Chevron legal team.

He responded that he had merely done what any law-abiding person would do: "share publicly available information that was being generated in the Lago Agrio trial that we felt proved that the remediation conducted by Texaco was a fraud." This was just the way the game was played, Donziger added. "Both sides try to put pressure on the other side. There is nothing unusual about it. It is the essence of any contested litigation."

In 2007, had he gone so far as to draft a press release for an Ecuadorian legislator, calling for criminal investigation of Chevron lawyers? Hadn't he shared the press release with his wife, Laura, boasting to her in an e-mail, "I write well, don't I? I love this shit."

"I don't remember," Donziger said, "but it is possible I did."

"Are you aware, sir," Donziger was asked, "that there are professional restrictions on using threats of prosecution or efforts to achieve prosecutions in aid of a civil matter of any kind?"

"I am aware, but to me that wasn't what this was."

Launched in 2008 at Correa's direction, the criminal investigation of the Chevron lawyers for allegedly falsifying remediation records had been suspended and then reinstituted in 2010, only to be dropped again the following year. Wasn't the prosecution threat part of an attempt "to help you get more money out of Chevron in the civil case?"

"It wasn't a question of money," Donziger answered. "It was a question of getting the parties to the table to reach some sort of resolution."

What about his *Crude* outtake remark about "jacking up" the verdict to $30 billion?

Donziger claimed he had said that "for dramatic effect."

"It is fair to say," he was asked, "that you have an expectation that you, Steven Donziger, might receive as much as hundreds of millions of dollars?"

"It is possible."

He was asked about his numerous private meetings with the Lago Agrio judge and the statement in his personal notes, "I love it, this lobbying."

"I think a lot of my language, sir, was not exactly accurate," Donziger said. "Contacts with the judge, which are permissible in Ecuador, based on my understanding of the rules, were efforts to explain some legal issue or the like. So . . . the reality is there was lobbying going on of government officials generally, and I think I got the two confused."

Was Donziger really saying his own notes were false?

"I have come to the conclusion," he responded, "that some of the notes were either exaggerated or inaccurate or the like."

Asked about the Cabrera report, Donziger at first tried to duck the question with similarly unconvincing results.

"Sir," a company lawyer said, "do you agree that the *peritaje global* report, ultimately signed by Richard Stalin Cabrera Vega, was in fact drafted by persons at Stratus and edited by you personally?"

"Well, that's a complicated question," Donziger responded. "I can't answer that yes or no."

After lengthy resistance, though, he grudgingly conceded that Stratus prepared the bulk of the Cabrera report and its annexes, altogether four thousand pages. He reviewed and edited parts of it. And that work was "pretty much adopted by Mr. Cabrera."

How much?

"He adopted pretty much verbatim what had been provided to him."

"Now, sir," the questioning continued, "at times after the report was issued by Mr. Cabrera, did you take steps to make sure that it was not known that the plaintiffs had been involved in any way in the preparation of the report?"

"I might have," Donziger said.

When Cabrera himself told the court in July 2007 that it was "an insult" for Chevron to suggest that he had "any relation or agreements with the plaintiffs," that was false, was it not?

"I don't think it was an accurate statement," Donziger admitted.

Mastro believed he had unmasked Donziger as a liar, his case as a fraud. Donziger continued to insist otherwise—that he had sought to achieve legitimate ends by unconventional means.

Tyrrell of Patton Boggs, whose firm had joined the case only a few months earlier, read the Donziger deposition transcripts and concluded he'd been snookered. On January 27, 2011, Tyrrell called Burford's CEO, Bogart. "Tyrrell told me that Donziger had not told Patton Boggs the truth about the extent of his prior contacts with Cabrera," Bogart later recalled. Burford Capital had invested millions in Donziger's cause based on Tyrrell's due diligence. "Donziger was a fool," Tyrrell added, according to notes Bogart made of the conversation. The Patton Boggs partner said that in light of Donziger's admissions, his firm was evaluating its "ethical obligations," suggesting the possibility of withdrawing from the case.

And yet Tyrrell did not want retreat. He was intrigued by the gigantic fee he could earn—and the return Burford could collect—if Patton Boggs somehow extricated Donziger from his troubles. "I feel good about the underlying case," he told Bogart. It was "difficult to believe," the lawyer added, "that no award of significant damages" would result.

A lieutenant in the navy as a younger man, Tyrrell decided to sail ahead, despite the gathering storm.

Chapter Eighteen

RACKETEERING

As Gibson Dunn attempted to rip Donziger apart in New York, the trial process in Ecuador neared its conclusion. The latest judge in Lago Agrio, Nicolás Zambrano Lozada, issued the *autos para sentencia,* a document indicating that he had reviewed all of the evidence—more than two hundred thousand pages of testimony and scientific data—and was prepared to render judgment. Having taken over the case only three months earlier, Zambrano implied that he had digested the dense record at a superhuman rate, nearly seventeen thousand pages a week. Making the the feat even more impressive and possibly flat-out incredible, Zambrano received assistance from a staff of one: an eighteen-year-old woman whom he paid $15 a day to do his typing. In December 2010, the judge invited the parties to submit *alegatos finales,* or final arguments.

The respective positions on pollution liability were well established. Chevron argued that Texaco had cleaned up what it agreed to clean up, the Ecuadorian government had granted it a formal and binding release, and the relevant soil and water samples didn't show a threat years later to human health. The plaintiffs countered that Texaco had behaved barbarously, conducted a sham cleanup, received a phony release from corrupt government officials, and ought to be held responsible for the entirety of the resulting ecological and human wreckage.

Tyrrell of Patton Boggs viewed the nearly two-decade-old case from a different vantage point: How could he help Judge Zambrano tolerate Donziger's avant-garde legal tactics? Since Chevron had made clear that it would not respect an adverse judgment in Ecuador, Tyrrell needed to point the Lago judge toward a pro-plaintiff ruling that judicial systems elsewhere might enforce. Filed with the Lago Agrio court in January 2011 under Pablo Fajardo's name, the Patton Boggs *alegato final* emphasized that with its blunt vows to defy any judgment, Chevron was the party that had shown contempt for Ecuadorian justice. The company brazenly violated its "earlier promises to abide by a judgment in Ecuador—promises it made to the American courts." Chevron sought "to destroy the very idea that indigenous communities can empower themselves to vindicate their legal rights." Confronted by this kind of opponent, Patton Boggs implied, Donziger might be forgiven his irregular methods.

The plaintiffs reminded Zambrano that the oil company had insulted the Lago court in other ways. Over the years, Chevron had bombarded Ecuadorian judges with repetitive motions in an apparent attempt to create a record that the court neglected the company's right to due process. On August 5, 2010, the company's attorneys filed no fewer than twenty motions, eighteen of which related to the same July 30 court order. The following month, Zambrano was brought on as the new presiding judge after his predecessor was removed for having failed to cope with the backlog of Chevron motions. In December, Chevron accompanied one of its demands for dismissal of the case with a threat that Zambrano could face criminal liability if he did not act as the company asked. "Chevron's tack is an obvious one," Patton Boggs argued. "The more absurd motions it files that are not granted, the greater opportunity for the company to cast this court as biased and incompetent in a subsequent enforcement proceeding."

In the kidney-punching, shin-kicking contest that the Ecuadorian litigation had become, Chevron seemed determined to maintain parity. If Donziger threatened one judge facing sexual-harassment allegations, the company menaced a subsequent one with the threat of criminal prosecution. The plaintiffs' lawyer thought he could engineer an Ecuadorian fraud investigation of Chevron's attorneys? Well, the company would accuse Donziger in New York of being a racketeer.

On February 1, 2011, with Judge Zambrano in Lago Agrio expected to issue a ruling imminently, Gibson Dunn lawyers filed suit against Donziger in federal court in Manhattan. The civil action invoked the Racketeer Influenced and Corrupt Organizations Act, known as RICO, a statute enacted in 1970 as a weapon against the Mafia. As Gibson Dunn intended, the clerk of the court assigned the RICO case to Judge Kaplan, because he had handled the Section 1782 proceedings. Kaplan had practically invited Chevron to file the RICO suit when he suggested that Donziger merited professional discipline or indictment.

"Over the course of several years," the Gibson Dunn suit began, "defendant Steven Donziger and his co-defendants and co-conspirators have sought to extort, defraud, and otherwise tortuously injure plaintiff Chevron." Federal prosecutors use the RICO law in criminal cases, but it also has civil provisions available to private litigants. It provides for stiff financial penalties if defendants are shown to have colluded in a racketeering "enterprise." Chevron named as Donziger's co-defendants Pablo Fajardo; the Frente director, Luís Yanza; the Stratus consultants in Boulder; and all of the named *Aguinda II* plaintiffs. For good measure, the RICO suit labeled as "co-conspirators" the Patton Boggs and Kohn Swift firms, Amazon Watch, and financiers Russell DeLeon and Burford Capital.

"The enterprise's ultimate aim," Gibson Dunn asserted, "is to create enough pressure on Chevron in the United States to extort it into paying to stop the campaign against it." By this reasoning, any corporate defendant—the asbestos-products and tobacco industries come to mind—could file a RICO lawsuit against plaintiffs' lawyers on the theory that the attorneys exerted pressure in pursuit of a lucrative settlement. Lawsuits are by their very nature a form of civilized extortion: pay up, or Lord knows what a jury will do to you. Companies use intimidation every time they sue each other over contracts gone bad, ambiguous insurance policies, or disputed patents. Very few defendants, however, hit back with the racketeering law.

The RICO suit cited plaintiffs' expert analyses that had been disowned by their authors, as well as the ghostwritten Cabrera report. Gibson Dunn dismissed the entirety of *Aguinda II* as a "sham." Chevron sought unspecified reimbursement for its legal expenses and an order from Kaplan blocking enforcement of the anticipated Lago judgment outside of Ecuador. Since Chevron had already said it wouldn't pay damages in Ecuador, a sweeping injunction would, in theory, nullify an Ecuadorian judgment everywhere else.

"It is sad to see American citizens organizing a shakedown of a U.S. company while pretending to be helping Ecuadorians and the environment," Chevron's Hew Pate told reporters on the day of the RICO filing. "Equally sad is the pattern of fraud and obstruction in multiple U.S. federal courts in a vain attempt to try to keep the truth from coming out. But now, the truth has been revealed."

Donziger's PR woman, Karen Hinton, called the RICO suit a diversion. There remained, she told the *Times*, "overwhelming evidence of guilt in the intentional contamination of one of the most pristine rain forests in the world." Privately, though, Donziger worried that Judge Kaplan took seriously the evidence Chevron had amassed. Not shy about using his power, Kaplan might agree with the oil company that an American judge possessed the authority to smother the Ecuadorian verdict before it had even been delivered.

On February 8, Mastro stepped up to the lectern in Judge Kaplan's courtroom. The judge, a bear of a man, sat behind a high desk, looking down on the attorneys before him. Mastro had brought a platoon from Gibson Dunn, as well as his client, Chevron's patrician Hew Pate, a former U.S. Supreme Court clerk who spoke with the distinct accent of his native Virginia. Behind the company contingent sat a smaller group representing the Ecuadorian plaintiffs; in their midst was a stooped and disgruntled Donziger.

Why, Kaplan asked Chevron's lawyers, should he block an Ecuadorian judgment that had not yet occurred?

"They will get their judgment in Ecuador and immediately start to use it in ways to disrupt Chevron's operation," Randy Mastro replied. "They intend to use it to cause maximum harm to Chevron, to try to extort a settlement out of Chevron." Mastro did not have a commanding courtroom delivery. His voice was raspy and nasal. But he was dogged, and he showed no embarrassment about portraying his mighty client, the third-largest corporation in America, as Donziger's hapless victim.

Mastro referred to a thirty-page strategy document written by Patton Boggs and obtained when Kaplan ordered all of Donziger's files disclosed to his opponents. The memo, entitled "Invictus," after the Victorian poem favored by Nelson Mandela ("My head is bloody, but unbowed"), laid out a sophisticated plan for securing seizure orders from courts around the world willing to attach Chevron refineries and ships. Patton Boggs had gone so far as to identify partners and affiliates of the law firm who had political connections in Asia and Latin America and could use that influence in going after Chevron vessels. "This is an opportunity to prevent an extortion and fraud from being effectuated," Mastro said.

Kaplan warmed to the argument. "Did I correctly understand your papers to take the position," he asked, "that, given the nature of the Ecuadorian judicial system over the past several years, you would contend that the judgment would not be conclusive or entitled to recognition?"

"That's correct, Your Honor," Mastro happily responded. He pointed to e-mails in which Fajardo and Donziger had communicated in code about wiring the appointment of Cabrera. Fajardo referred to himself as "the messenger," who would meet with "the cook," meaning the judge, who, in turn, would meet with "the waiter," meaning Cabrera. Once he was appointed, Cabrera would coordinate "the menu," or expert assessment, although there might be a challenge from the other "restaurant," meaning Chevron. Mastro called this foolishness the "classic style of people who are engaging in knowing criminal acts, [using] code words in their own internal communications to try to hide it." Mastro peppered his argument with references to "the Pizza Connection case" and "the Sicilian Mafia." He tried everything short of whipping out a violin and playing the theme from *The Godfather*.

"Mr. Donziger," Kaplan finally asked, "do you want to be heard?"

All eyes turned to the plaintiffs' attorney. To the surprise of nearly everyone in the courtroom, Donziger demurred. He told the judge that he had not yet hired a lawyer to represent him against the RICO allegations. "Your Honor," he said, "I don't feel comfortable responding, much as I'd like to, to Mr. Mastro's presentation without counsel."

Kaplan did not mask his disdain. He thought Donziger a coward, as well as a rogue. "Just so the record is clear," the judge said, "Mr. Donziger is an attorney admitted to practice in the State of New York."

This left the proceeding at an awkward pass. If Donziger refused to engage, who would represent the interests of the Ecuadorian claimants? Jim Tyrrell of Patton Boggs refused to appear before Kaplan, because Chevron had named his firm a co-conspirator in the racketeering enterprise. So Patton Boggs retained a New York attorney named Sheldon Elsen to speak on behalf of the Ecuadorians. Elsen had practiced for many decades and knew Kaplan personally. That recommended him for the job. On the other side of the ledger, he was in his eighties and long past his prime.

"Your Honor," Elsen began, "Mr. Donziger seems like a nice-looking gentleman, but I don't represent him."

Kaplan said he understood that.

Elsen noted that Patton Boggs had drafted the papers submitted to the court, which Elsen found lacking. "Your Honor has been in a big firm, and you know the arrogance of large law firms," Elsen said. The odd, gratuitous swipe got everyone's attention. After some more verbal meandering, Elsen got to his point. Chevron, he said, had no business asking a judge in New York to protect it from a prospective judgment in Ecuador: "What you have is a big-bucks corporation who knows their way around the world, who said we will abide by the judgments of the courts in Ecuador, and now they are coming in, crying, 'We don't want a judgment against us because of the courts in Ecuador.'" If Elsen had sat down then, he would have earned his fee. "Now," he continued, "Mr. Donziger may be a knave or a thief; I don't know whether he is or he isn't. Some of the things he said, I am glad I was not representing him."

"They are statements made by your clients' agent in the course of his employment," Kaplan pointed out. It was impossible to tell whether the judge found Elsen entertaining or pathetic.

"I certainly want to disassociate my clients from Mr. Donziger," Elsen persisted. "What he did is not defensible, and I am not trying to defend him."

"Have you read the Patton Boggs memo, 'Invictus'?" Kaplan asked.

Elsen: "In-what?" The old man was at a loss.

Kaplan: " 'Invictus.' "

Elsen: " 'Invictus.' "

Kaplan: "I commend it to your attention."

Elsen: "What do you mean by 'Invictus'?"

Kaplan: "That's the code word for the memo analyzing how to use enforcement proceedings simultaneously in multiple jurisdictions and prejudgment attachment 'largely as a means of attaining a favorable settlement at an early stage'—essentially by causing as much trouble and disruption as is humanly possible."

Elsen: "I am not associating either my clients or myself with such a strategy."

Kaplan appeared to lose interest.

Elsen: "You can appreciate, Your Honor, my clients and I are not on a steady telephone exchange."

Kaplan: "I do appreciate that. Thank you. Nice to see you again." Elsen would not be seen again in the Ecuadorian litigation.

A jurist who speaks extemporaneously in complete paragraphs, Kaplan immediately began his verbal ruling: "Among the obvious facts here are that the Ecuadorian plaintiffs are in this for money. They may be in it for other things, but they are in it for money. Someone engaged a Washington law firm on their behalf to develop a strategy for getting money, assuming for the sake of discussion that they prevail in Ecuador."

He reviewed the "Invictus" memo and Patton Boggs's plans to use political connections overseas to exert leverage against Chevron. While clever, "this worldwide, full-court press" struck Kaplan as having "very little legitimate basis to it, apart from the harassment it will cause." Kaplan said that he had not reached any final conclusions, but he reiterated his suspicions about Donziger and his tactics. "There is evidence," he said. "It is troublesome. It is sufficiently troublesome that Mr. Elsen has walked away from Mr. Donziger as to some of it."

The idea of crippling Chevron offended Kaplan. "We are dealing here with a company of considerable importance to our economy, that employs thousands all over the world, that supplies a group of commodities—gasoline, heating oil, other fuels, and lubricants—on which every one of us depends every single day. I don't think there is anybody in this courtroom who wants to pull his car into a gas station to fill up and find that there isn't any gas there because these folks have attached it in Singapore or wherever else."

Following this logic, Kaplan might have ruled against any plaintiff, no matter how righteous, posing a substantial financial threat to Chevron—a one-sided perspective for a supposedly disinterested judge. Kaplan, in fact, sounded very much like the corporate-defense lawyer he had been in private practice before being named to the federal bench. He granted Chevron a "temporary restraining order" and said he would consider turning it into a longer-lasting injunction. He forbade Donziger and his clients from seeking to enforce any victory they might win in Lago Agrio. His hostility to the plaintiffs undisguised, Kaplan did not explain the source of his authority to prevent enforcement of an Ecuadorian judgment in Singapore or Brazil or Canada. What was clear: Chevron had a powerful ally on the federal bench in New York, and Donziger had yet another enemy.

Chapter Nineteen

DECISION

On February 14, 2011, six days after Judge Kaplan prohibited enforcement of any Ecuadorian judgment, Judge Zambrano in Lago Agrio published a 188-page, single-spaced ruling. As expected, Chevron lost. The initial price tag was set at more than $9 billion. Unless the company promptly apologized, the ruling stated, the damages would double, a say-you're-sorry penalty not found in American jurisprudence. Chevron, unsurprisingly, refused to apologize, pushing the verdict to $18.2 billion. Various incidental enhancements soon inflated the amount to $19 billion. At the time, the company had $17.1 billion in cash on hand.

Zambrano, a fifty-four-year-old former Ecuadorian air force officer, had produced the lengthy judgment in a mere six weeks from the time the parties submitted their final written arguments. He later said that in a marathon of legal composition, he dictated the entire judgment to his secretary, a recent high school graduate from Lago Agrio whose mother asked him to hire her. In an interview just before he issued the ruling, Zambrano displayed a jaunty personality. He kept his head shaved, he said, "to stay cool, so I can think better." He didn't answer unidentified callers on his cell phone to avoid distractions and threats. At night, he left the court building alone, without a bodyguard. "It's our supreme creator who protects me," he said. "I don't have anything to be afraid of."

The trial judge's confidence in his physical safety exceeded his self-assurance as a legal craftsman. Before being named to the Lago Agrio bench in 2008, he had served as a local prosecutor, but he lacked expertise in civil procedure. As a judge, he turned to a longtime colleague for assistance: attorney Alberto Guerra. Guerra understood the business of the Lago court, including the Chevron case, because he was the first judge to oversee the pollution suit in 2003. (Guerra opened the trial standing in front of the vivid mural of Amazonian Lady Justice.) By 2004, Guerra had rotated off *Aguinda II,* and in May 2008, his career took an unfortunate turn when the national Judicial Council dismissed him from the bench. The council determined he had shown bias by expressing skepticism to other public officials about the legitimacy of the suit against Chevron. Guerra ascribed his ouster to having accused two of his successors as judge on the pollution case of taking kickbacks from court-appointed experts in the Chevron case. The Lago Agrio court rarely had a dull moment.

Whatever the reason for Guerra's removal, he was out of a government job and looking for income. His friend Zambrano had a taxpayer-funded salary but a competence deficit. So they made an arrangement: "I would help him by writing writs and rulings, which Mr. Zambrano had to issue as judge in civil cases," Guerra said years later in a sworn statement. Zambrano agreed to pay Guerra $1,000 a month. "I was Mr. Zambrano's ghostwriter," Guerra said, "and I wrote the great majority of the rulings issued in civil cases assigned to Mr. Zambrano, including the Chevron case." Guerra said he did not draft the ultimate 188-page judgment against Chevron, however. Instead, he served only as an editor, "making around twenty changes to improve its structure and make it seem more like a judgment." Zambrano made no public reference to Guerra's role, which constituted misconduct even under Ecuador's flexible judicial norms.

Even with Guerra's revisions, the February 2011 judgment against Chevron made for a meandering, disjointed read. As a preliminary matter, it acknowledged Donziger's "disrespectful statements" about the Ecuadorian judiciary. Contrary to what Chevron claimed, however, the judgment concluded that "no pressure has been effectively exerted on this court" by the American plaintiffs' lawyer. Where Judge Kaplan in New York suspected criminal conspiracy, the Ecuadorian judiciary perceived harmless impertinence. Donziger's obnoxious conduct would be "disregarded."

Echoing the Patton Boggs argument, the ruling had much harsher words for Chevron. Beyond their relentless objections, the company's attorneys had dissembled: There had been the "false" security threat Chevron cited to get the Guanta inspection canceled. And the judgment cited "misconduct" by Diego Borja, the former Chevron contractor who arranged the sting of Judge Nuñez. The oil company's attacks on the integrity of the court "have been constant throughout the process and have even been publicly repeated by the spokespersons of the defendant company, reaching the ears of the judge." In fact, the ruling asserted, "There is no evidence of any substantial lack of solemnity or violation of the guarantees of due process." Yes, Calmbacher, the plaintiffs' technical consultant, had disowned his analyses. And yes, Cabrera, the court-appointed expert, allegedly colluded with the plaintiffs. But, in the final analysis, these complications barely registered. "What an expert does or does not say," the ruling explained, "does not bind the judge's hands." To avoid confusion, the opinion purported to exclude all of the work of Calmbacher and Cabrera. In one fell swoop, the court brushed aside potentially fatal credibility problems.

With similar insouciance, the ruling breezed past Chevron's objection that Texaco could not have violated Ecuadorian environmental standards, because such standards didn't exist in the 1970s and 1980s. The judgment noted that broader mandates were on the books: The Hydrocarbon Law of 1971 called for "protection of flora and fauna and other natural resources." The Ecuadorian state failed to pursue enforcement, but that did not release Texaco from its obligations. A lack of regulation "cannot be understood as an implicit authorization" to pollute. Moreover, the government's decision to grant Texaco a release from pollution liability in exchange for the company's partial cleanup did not bind private individuals: "There is no legal reason to extend such representation to all citizens and deprive them of rights that are in themselves inviolate." After 1990, Petroecuador may have added to the contamination, but the national oil company's negligence did not exonerate Texaco.

How much contamination was there? In a weirdly offhand manner, the ruling offered some examples: 10 percent of the soil samples showed total petroleum hydrocarbons exceeding five thousand parts per million. At least fourteen samples showed dangerous levels of benzene, a constituent of TPH and a powerful carcinogen. Ten samples revealed potentially hazardous amounts of toluene, which can damage the nervous system. More than one hundred samples contained carcinogenic chromium, about which the ruling asserted, "Any amount bigger than one found in any natural form in the environment should be removed because of the dangerousness that it presents."

Chevron pointed to water samples showing bacterial contamination traceable to human or animal sewage. Surely, the company argued, an alternative source of pollution that could have caused health risks deserved judicial attention. This argument did not impress Zambrano. "Even when it has been proved that there is a possibility that any of these contaminating agents (coliforms or fertilizers) may also be a potential cause of any of the damage proved," the ruling stated, "this possibility does not alter the actual fact proved in the file that several agents used and/or produced during hydrocarbon exploitation can be found in the environment."

The plaintiffs lacked medical records proving specific cancer cases. The epidemiological studies Donziger cited didn't show a causal relationship between oil and illness. But the court swept that aside, too. Taken together, the studies and other evidence "suggest a connection between the risk of having cancer and living in an area having petroleum exploitation," according to the ruling. "It is inevitable to notice what these signs indicate." At another point, though, the decision stated, "This court has not considered the conclusions presented by the experts in their reports because they contradict each other, despite the fact that they refer to the same reality." These clashing assertions could not be coherently reconciled. Either the author of the judgment did or did not rely on technical evidence.

An American judge would not recognize the Lago Agrio decision as one based on conventional legal reasoning or rigorous scientific evidence. The Ecuadorian ruling included certain emblems of erudition—passing references, for instance, to case law from France, Australia, Britain, and the United States. But substantively, intuition carried the day. Page after page recounted testimony by ordinary men and women who had attended judicial inspections of the rain forest well sites. During one such encounter, the Cofán leader Emergildo Criollo had translated from the tribe's native language into Spanish for a woman named Romelia Mendua. "With the arrival of Texaco," Mendua said, "there was pollution of big and small rivers. That's why we suffered a lot." Texaco, she added, "killed animals that we used to eat. That's why we currently do not have enough food. Children also remain small. We also suffer from unknown illnesses with the arrival of the Texaco Company." The ruling acknowledged that such "declarations are not reliable and incontrovertible proof that effects to these citizens' health really exist. However they cannot be denied value, since we can observe an impressive coincidence between the facts described by all of these declarations, without there existing any testimony or declaration against it."

In the face of such logic, Chevron had no recourse. The court assessed damages of $5.4 billion for remediating soil to a level of no more than 1,000 TPH and another $600 million for groundwater cleanup. The derivation of these dollar figures was not explained in any detail. Other awards included $1.4 billion for community health services, $200 million for restoring native animal species, and $100 million for "community rebuilding and ethnic reaffirmation." The ruling did not specify which communities or which ethnicities. The punitive doubling of the $9 billion total reflected the "antisocial nature of the misconduct" and "the defendant's attitude during the case." All of this money would flow into a trust administered by the Lago Agrio–based activist group the Frente, which would receive 10 percent of the total—$1.82 billion—as compensation for its services. How Pablo Fajardo, Luís Yanza, and the other Frente leaders would spend nearly $2 billion, why they deserved the monumental windfall, and how much of the largesse they would share with Donziger—these and many other questions remained unanswered.

Chapter Twenty

POLLUTION

To visit the Cofán village at Dureno one drives for thirty minutes along a twisting road out of Lago Agrio to a compound where the tribe operates a canoe-building business in several interconnected sheds on a landing above the Aguarico River. Workers fashion water-tight boats from strips of fiberglass, using industrial-strength adhesives. Tribal leader Emergildo Criollo noted that one of his sons worked in the shop. "We make the best canoes," Criollo explained in Spanish, "not just for the Cofán, but all the people in the area."

On the drive to this spot in the spring of 2011, Criollo told me the story of the arrival by helicopter of Texaco explorers, the rice and cheese handed out by company men, the drilling for oil, the poisoning of rivers, and the death of his first two sons. We boarded a narrow twenty-foot canoe for the trip down the muddy Aguarico and around a bend to the Cofán hamlet. For twenty-five minutes, the breeze provided welcome relief from the late-morning heat. Lush greenery framed the waterway and insulated us from the oil zone. Gone were the chemical fumes of the Indian boat shop and the smell of petroleum so common throughout the region. Except for the snarling outboard motor, the rain forest seemed at peace.

My canoe ride to the Cofán encampment was reminiscent of

travels depicted in *Crude* and on *60 Minutes*. Similar river commutes appeared in newspaper and magazine articles describing the battle against Chevron. In one slight variation, I was the first journalist to make the river jaunt after the $19 billion verdict. I may have been imagining it, but Criollo and my other local hosts exhibited a measure of confidence absent from earlier accounts. "We have won," he told me. "When are they starting the cleanup?"

The Cofán leader made the trip standing in the canoe, a vinyl satchel filled with court papers slung over his shoulder. He wore dark slacks, a short-sleeved shirt, and polished black shoes. "We are here," he announced, as the boat's prow nestled into a rocky, unmarked beach. Accompanied by a welcoming committee of mangy dogs, we clambered up the riverbank to the dirt-path entrance to the village. A couple hundred people lived in wooden houses, some built on stilts, spread around a central clearing. Next to the clearing stood several concrete communal buildings, one of them a schoolhouse with broken benches. The structures lacked indoor plumbing. Small gas generators provided electricity for televisions and hot plates. In nearby fields, the villagers grew banana, yucca, and cacao. They hunted, but with rifles, not the blowguns of Criollo's youth. Jaguars skulked near the village, he said, and occasionally snatched chickens.

Asked to point out his home, Criollo said that he and his wife had opted some years ago for the relative comfort of a house in Lago Agrio. He said he sometimes received consulting fees and reimbursement of expenses for his work on the legal case. He still came to the village frequently, and he moved comfortably among the people he represented.

For my exclusive benefit, an open-air artisan market materialized. Criollo sat down in the shade as women wearing colorful blouses displayed necklaces, earrings, and purses made from brown and orange beads. The women had straight, jet-black hair and wore bright crimson nail polish. For $25, I obtained a bagful of delicate trinkets. Criollo got up, indicating that my visit would now continue.

We walked a short distance to examine a new water-filtration unit. "Trudie came to our village, and she paid for these," Criollo said. More precisely, the Rainforest Foundation that Trudie Styler and Sting cofounded collaborated with the United Nations to fund a clean-water project at the Cofán village. Elevated on a two-story wooden tower, the tank bore its manufacturer's name, Rotoplas, and a label identifying it as *"Plastico/Anti-Bacterias."*

"It didn't work at first," Criollo said, because no one had taken responsibility for maintaining the large black plastic container that collected rainwater and filtered it through layers of sand and quartz. So he assigned specific families to look after the equipment. Five tanks were set up, and two were operational, each supplying enough water for twelve people. Criollo had been told that five more were on the way, but he was not sure when they would arrive. In the meantime, most people were still drinking from the streams, which he said remained contaminated. Some families boiled the stream water.

Criollo introduced me to Eduardo Chapal, the schoolteacher. Chapal wore a necklace of crocodile teeth over a yellow Washington, D.C., tourist T-shirt. The teacher expressed concern that fewer and fewer children were learning the tribe's native language. Spanish was fine for those who wished to know it, he said. Like Criollo, he spoke Spanish. But "if our language changes, you cannot say you are Cofán anymore." An even bigger worry, Chapal said, was unemployment. The Cofán needed jobs to generate cash for consumer goods.

That's where the lawsuit came in, Criollo interjected. "We do not want money to get rich," he said. "We want to clean up the environment, which is a big project." Remediation would be "good for the people because it would provide jobs for many years." The village leader looked to the litigation, not the local or national leg-islature, to finance public works.

The plaintiffs' "toxic tour"—a term used matter-of-factly in Lago Agrio—took me to the homes and fields of numerous residents of the northeastern Oriente. My guide for some of the expedition was Donald Moncayo, an employee of the Frente who lived with his wife and infant daughter in a tiny run-down house near Lago Agrio. A mestizo, Moncayo was born in the area in 1973 and worked on a farm as a young man. Some of his schoolmates and friends got jobs with oil companies or subcontractors. "I was one of the naïve people, too," he said one day over a lunch of arroz con pollo. "I did not think about the causes and effects in our lives. I did not think about what man can do to nature or what corporations can do to the people."

A stint as a volunteer with the Frente changed that. He greatly admired Pablo Fajardo. The Frente sent Moncayo to a leadership academy to learn how to organize. Now, as part of his paid job, he escorted outsiders on visits to the region. Money Steven Donziger raised in the United States, Moncayo said, provided for his educa-tion and now for his modest salary. "Steven," he added, "is a very good man. We all respect him."

Moncayo's political awakening caused him to reevaluate his parents' premature deaths, which he came to blame on the oil in-dustry. "My dad died when I was eight years old," he said. "They killed him with alcohol." His mother died five years later, in 1986. She washed clothes all day in a stream. "The produced water from the oil operations made her sick," Moncayo said. One day, she had a seizure. Her family took her to the hospital. She died soon after, leaving an adolescent Donald and four siblings orphaned.

He introduced me to poor campesinos. Some, like José Antonio

Bricerio Castillo, the elderly farmer who had salved aching joints with warm petroleum, held mixed views about the oil industry. Bricerio balanced the advantages of road construction against the ills of contamination. Others were unambiguously bitter. Marlene Parades Cabrera, thirty-three, stood outside her house on a scrubby hill as she described how her mother-in-law, father-in-law, and brother-in-law had all died of cancer in the past year. The extended family grew sugarcane and raised farm animals. Now her eleven-year-old son, Willington, one of five children, had stomach problems. Doctors in Quito had removed his appendix, but the illness persisted. She feared he, too, suffered from cancer. "Cancer," I discovered, was the all-purpose diagnosis for serious illness. As a puppy, a piglet, and a toddler boy circled her legs, all vying for attention, Parades noted that her husband had pancreatic cancer. She blamed the oil pollution. "A lot of companies leave waste, not just one company," she said. "We don't know which one is which."

In the community of Patria Nueve, Moncayo ushered me into the two-room home of Santos Darwin Calero Pardo. The thirty-one-year-old husband, father, and former oil company security guard reclined in a hammock. Once a vigorous 196-pound man, Calero now weighed 112 pounds. He shook hands weakly, sweating and wheezing.

Calero could substantiate his diagnosis. His barefoot wife displayed medical records from a clinic in Quito where doctors had said Santos had stomach cancer. Pharmacy bills indicated hundreds of dollars a month spent on "natural treatments." Neighbors helped defray the costs. In a raspy whisper, Calero blamed "the oil company" and the government for his sickness. "They don't give anything to the affected," he said. "Look at me. I am nothing. I count only on God."

Sitting nearby, Calero's mother said that her husband had died of stomach cancer several years earlier. Doctors said it was a kidney ailment, she noted, but the family knew it was cancer, attributable to the waste oil spread on the roads in the 1970s and 1980s.

I asked Calero's mother what kind of contacts she had had with Texaco and Petroecuador over the years.

She snorted derisively. "They don't speak to us," she said. "We didn't know about the oil contamination, but it was all around us, under our feet."

Did oil bring any benefits?

"Personally, I don't see anything better from the oil," she said. "Someone makes money. Not me." Her son died several months later.

As the February 2011 ruling detailed, no shortage of human misery existed in proximity to the petroleum business in the Oriente. Many of the unfortunate understandably connected the suffering to the industry, even if they had little scientific evidence of a link. As far as Donald Moncayo of the Frente was concerned, any doubt about causation ought to be resolved against the oil company. The Lago Agrio court decision had adopted the same presumption.

Moncayo said that a visit to Sacha 53 would help me understand the situation. He referred to the site as "Chevron's pride and joy," because the panel of court-appointed experts had concluded in 2006 that, despite the presence of contamination at the site, they could not hold the company culpable. As the Frente's Toyota pickup pulled up to Sacha 53, Moncayo practically jumped from the front passenger seat, eager to show me around. "These are the hidden pits," he declared, "the ones covered over before the 1994 remediation process even began. Aerial military photos showed us these hidden pits. There are five hundred pits like this."

We pulled on yellow rubber boots and marched single-file through forest and underbrush. "No one talks about these,"

Moncayo continued. "Did Texaco show you this? No, of course not. For Texaco, these pits are remedied, and this is imaginary."

In a wooded area, he showed me a swimming pool–sized patch where no trees stood, only tall grass and broad-leafed ferns. "That's the hidden pit," he said, "covered over with a thin layer of dirt." We moved forward, and the ground grew spongy. A half-buried truck tire poked out of the muck. A rusted oil barrel stood nearby. They looked like theatrical props.

Moncayo plunged a two-handled awl into the soil, twisted it violently back and forth, and brought up a plug of petroleum-infused dirt from a few feet beneath the surface. He thrust the plug under my nose. It smelled like oil. "This is the 'clean' pit, okay?" he said, sounding angry. "This is Chevron's remediation. And for this the judge found them guilty. We seek justice for this atrocity." He paused. "I wish Judge Kaplan could take a toxic tour. Then he would see the real Chevron. He can come first with Chevron people, and then I will take him here. It will change his mind."

I promised that if I ever met Kaplan I would pass along the invitation.

Moncayo laughed joylessly.

As we drove away, a larger four-wheel-drive vehicle crossed our path. "That's Jim Craig with the Chevron toxic tour," Moncayo said. "Jim Craig will tell you lies tomorrow."

I had already met Craig earlier that week. A former wire service reporter with Reuters and Bloomberg News, he had left journalism for corporate crisis management and now worked for Chevron. Craig divided his time between a family in Lima, Peru, his childhood home in Connecticut, and Chevron-related assignments in Ecuador. He spoke Spanish fluently. In Ecuador, he traveled with armed former soldiers and policemen who provided security for Chevron. Craig told me he was one of the company employees beheaded in effigy during the 2009 demonstration in Lago Agrio. He interpreted that, reasonably enough, as a threat.

Craig took me to a central "pit farm" in the Sacha fields operated by Petroecuador and the Venezuelan national oil company, known by the initials PDVSA. American producers haven't operated in Ecuador for many years. Rather than dig waste pits next to operating oil wells, the Ecuadorian-Venezuelan venture trucked waste to one location, which resembled a graveyard for giants, each buried pit marked by a soil mound and a small wooden cross indicating the well from which its contents had come. Craig stressed that scores of fresh Petroecuador pits, brimming with drilling muds and waste petroleum, were unlined. "The technology," he said, "hasn't changed one bit."

What about the produced water?

He acknowledged that Petroecuador and its foreign partners from Venezuela, Spain, and China had adopted reinjection methods that buried most of the salty produced water back into emptied oil reservoirs. "But that change was completed only five years ago," he said. "Until then, the state of the art in Ecuador was the way Texaco handled produced water in the 1970s."

We drove along roads bordered by pipelines, whose hot liquid contents caused steam to rise after each downpour. Children splashed in streams next to their mothers washing clothes, the pipelines snaking around them and overhead. Gas flares fired above the tree line.

" 'Amazon Chernobyl'?" Craig asked at one point. "For the last hour, is that what you've seen?"

No, it did not look like lifeless, radioactive Chernobyl (which I knew only from photographs). The Oriente pulsed with people, vehicles, and farm animals. Evidence of commerce and industry was everywhere. It resembled a rain forest version of Gulf Coast Texas in the unregulated era of Buckskin Joe Cullinan. It was not the worst or poorest place I had ever seen. It was, at the same time, no place I'd want to live.

Craig's driver pulled into the Sacha 53 site. We examined the pits that the neutral panel had deemed adequately remediated. Once the experts reached that conclusion, Craig said, the plaintiffs "suddenly wanted to stop the judicial inspection process and bring in their corrupt 'global expert.'"

Didn't the panel find contamination at Sacha 53, which they attributed to an oil spill?

Yes, Craig said. "But it wasn't clear whose oil spill that was, and Texaco wasn't given responsibility for cleaning that up in the Remediation Action Plan."

Were there hundreds of hidden pits, as the plaintiffs alleged?

"That's a myth," Craig said. "They see shadows on an aerial map and talk about 'hidden pits.' There are no hidden pits. There might be oil on the ground at Sacha 53. There's certainly oil on the ground in other places. But there's no way to say that it's Texaco's oil." He even suggested that in recent years, the Frente had tried to incriminate the company by spreading new oil at some of the sites Texaco remediated.

Craig had two modes. In one, he discounted any evidence of contamination. Rogue oil from the Texaco era, he said, by now would have degraded into asphalt, and wasn't dangerous. "You have a chunk of asphalt in a swimming pool, you could still go swimming," he added. "I wouldn't eat it, but it's not going to do any harm at the bottom of the pool." Even in liquid form, waste oil from pits or spills couldn't move very much, he argued, because of the impermeability of the region's dense clay soil.

His other mode was more measured, if not exactly empathetic: "You have poor people. I assume if they say they are sick, they are in fact sick. Fine. But the idea that this is all the fault of the evil oil company is just not true. In fact, it is a fraud. Texaco did what it was asked to do, and it did not leave behind dangers to health. Oil drilling is a dirty business. It is going to create a mess. But the Ecuadorians were in charge. Texaco didn't sneak in one night and start drilling in the Oriente."

What about the water?

"I do not want to bathe in these streams," Craig admitted. "I do not want to drink from these streams. I do not want to live next to an oil drilling operation with a natural gas flare going all the time. But this is the deal that Ecuador made to join the modern world." Texaco signed contracts with a national government responsible for protecting the interests of indigenous tribe members and migrant farmers. "Texaco invested hundreds of millions of dollars that Ecuador did not have and brought business expertise that Ecuador did not have. Ecuador got billions of dollars in taxes, royalties, and profits. That was the deal."

Contaminated streams and rivers were part of the deal?

Craig said that the plaintiffs exaggerated the petroleum contamination. Local agricultural practices and the dumping of raw municipal sewage into streams and rivers had tainted water supplies with hazardous levels of fecal bacteria. He took me to a spot not far from the center of Lago Agrio where gray untreated sewage flowed into the muddy brown Orienco River, which snaked through town and then joined the Aguarico. "This is the same kind of water that finds its way to San Carlos, where the plaintiffs did their famous study finding a supposed cancer cluster," Craig said.

As we stood on a small bridge overlooking the stinking intersection of filthy streams, area residents came out of their homes and made cell phone calls. Within minutes, a man drove up in a Chevrolet SUV and identified himself as David Pinzón, the president of the neighborhood association. He pointed to a weather-beaten street sign that said, BIEN VENIDOS AL BARRIO SAN VALENTIN. Without asking who we were, Pinzón launched into a description of how he had tried for years to get the sewage treated and the stream cleaned up. No one in the local or national government seemed to care.

"All of the waste from all of those houses goes into this stream," he explained, gesturing as we walked for several blocks. Making matters worse, a slaughterhouse nearby dumped its cuttings into the water, he said. Despite all of these disgusting contents, people drew their drinking water just a little ways downstream. "We have rashes, stomach problems, children's noses itch," he said. Pinzón took off a shoe and pulled down his sock to display a partly bandaged infection running from his ankle to his knee. He attributed the ugly condition to polluted water.

We were walking on an unpaved side street, past crumbling concrete homes. "I could show you oil contamination," Pinzón said. There had been a series of Petroecuador spills near Pablo Fajardo's hometown of Shushufindi. "It happens regularly," Pinzón said, as if describing a local weather pattern.

Not long after I had returned to New York, some sixteen thousand people in Shushufindi lost access to publicly supplied drinking water because of the leakage of reddish-brown fluids from Petroecuador drilling-waste pits into the Shushufindi River. *El Universo* reported that the town's mayor declared a "state of emergency." At a public meeting, municipal officials in Shushufindi demanded that the state-owned company improve its notoriously poor performance. After all, one council member said, "this is not the first time this has happened."

Chapter Twenty-one

RETRIBUTION

In December 2011, less than a year after the Lago Agrio verdict, Marco Calvopina, Petroecuador's general manager, announced that the national oil company would launch a $70 million program to clean up pollution in the Amazon, including some areas involved in the Chevron case. Calvopina did not say whether the $70 million represented new money or double-counted funds associated with past Petroecuador remediation announcements. "The pollution is in areas assigned to us, and we've got the obligation to clean them up," he told reporters. "It's like if someone throws garbage in front of your house. At some point you have to clean it up." He did not explain why Petroecuador was recognizing its obligation sixteen years after the initial remediation assignments were made in the mid-1990s. Nor did he address fresh contamination of the sort that ruined the drinking-water supply in Shushufindi.

Donziger, who previously had lobbied against remediation by Petroecuador, fearing that it would undercut the Lago Agrio lawsuit, now took a different public stance, or at least his spokeswoman, Karen Hinton, did. She told the Dow Jones News Service that the plaintiffs welcomed any cleanup. Hinton called

$70 million "modest compared to the magnitude of the harm Chevron left in Ecuador."

The company's Hew Pate expressed more enthusiasm, if for self-serving reasons. "The Ecuadorian government deserves credit for taking positive steps to help the people and environment of the Oriente and to break the cycle of corruption and misinformation caused by the fraudulent case against Chevron," Pate said. He stressed that the $70 million figure "stands in contrast to the multibillion-dollar claim fabricated by American plaintiffs' lawyers to extort money from Chevron."

Intriguingly, Pate hinted that if the Correa government shut down the Lago litigation, the company would discuss helping with further cleanup. "Chevron," he said, "would welcome a constructive dialogue with the government of Ecuador."

Since arriving at Chevron, Pate had assumed that the corporation would lose in court in Lago Agrio. "The writing is on the wall," he told colleagues as early as 2009. He maintained his predecessor Charles James's strategy of fighting the suit, but mainly so that after an anticipated defeat, the company could demonstrate to courts in other countries that it had been denied due process. Pate thought that the best hope for ending the legal quagmire in the Oriente was circumventing Donziger. Toward that end, Chevron had sued the government of Ecuador in 2009 before the Permanent Court of Arbitration in The Hague, Netherlands. The arbitration court has jurisdiction over certain international contracts and treaties. Chevron complained that, as a former investor in Ecuador (via Texaco), its rights had been violated under an agreement between Washington and Quito known as the Bilateral Investment Treaty. Chevron asked the arbitration court to order the Correa administration to enforce the 1998 liability release and end the Lago Agrio lawsuit. As an alternative, the company demanded that the Quito government "indemnify" Chevron, meaning the government would pay any verdict against the company. If it could not snuff out the pollution case altogether, Chevron wanted to create an unmistakable incentive for Correa to cut a deal with the company. Chevron implied that it would consider making a modest, voluntary contribution to a cleanup initiative, as long as Donziger and the Frente were excluded.

Far removed from the populist politics of Ecuador, the Hague panel began issuing preliminary pronouncements indicating sympathy for Chevron's position. When Pate appeared at the periodic arbitration proceedings, he reiterated the company's offer of "constructive dialogue" with the Correa administration. All through 2010 and 2011, though, Ecuador's representatives failed to respond to his overtures. Finding no negotiating partner in Quito, Chevron escalated hostilities against Donziger in New York.

The company's counterattack took a toll. At first, the private detectives tailing Donziger around Manhattan had made for entertaining conversation. Although Donziger had driven off many former colleagues, he retained a following among environmentalists impressed by his defiance of Chevron. "I have tremendous professional respect for Steven," Michael Brune told me. In 2010, the former head of the Rainforest Action Network had become executive director of the larger and more mainstream Sierra Club. "He may have made a few mistakes, some missteps, but he is the driving force behind what's probably the most important environmental lawsuit in the world." Brune chose his words carefully, seeking to express personal support while also insulating the Sierra Club from Donziger's radioactive reputation.

As time wore on, Donziger became increasingly isolated. Mainstream environmental leaders like Brune might tentatively answer a journalist's questions, but they did not take any meaningful action in Donziger's defense. Donziger's invitations to speak at colleges and law schools diminished to a trickle. The filmmaker Joe

Berlinger, feeling burned by his unanticipated role in the RICO case, steered clear of Donziger. "I guess I had to ask myself whether Steven showed me the whole story in Ecuador," Berlinger told me.

The novelty and intrigue related to Chevron's surveillance in New York wore off. Donziger worried that the spying would frighten his wife and young son. Laura told him she wished the entire case would just go away—the oil company, the Indians, all of it. (When I asked, a company spokesman did not deny that private eyes were monitoring Donziger.) Laura interpreted the spying as a harbinger of something much worse to come. She asked her husband whether he was going to jail. What did the company have on him?

Donziger tried to reassure her. Criminal prosecution, he said, was out of the question. Chevron was just trying to scare him. Eventually, it would all blow over. In truth, his wife's anxiety haunted Donziger. He distracted himself by hounding Hinton to put out anti-Chevron press releases, even when they had nothing new to say.

Chevron made life increasingly difficult for Donziger's dwindling cohort of backers, as well. The company had named the Stratus environmental consulting firm as a codefendant in the racketeering suit against Donziger. As a result, Stratus was forced to hire expensive lawyers and endure harsh public questions about its reputation. Stressing Stratus's role in the Cabrera charade, Chevron launched an online campaign attacking the firm's reliability. The pressure grew so great that Stratus, which depended heavily on public-sector clients, told its attorneys to explore what it would take to get Chevron to back off. In private negotiations, the oil company indicated that in exchange for a cease-fire, Stratus would have to turn on Donziger and disavow all of its scientific work for the plaintiffs.

Burford Capital, the hedge fund that had invested in Donziger's operation, faced a similar dilemma. The financiers discovered that the oil company was warning major corporate law firms to shun

Burford. That kind of threat from one of the largest multinationals in the world brings results. Without ties to big law firms, Burford would wither. The hedge fund soon buckled, telling Donziger
that it would not invest any additional money in the case. In a letter
dated September 29, 2011, Burford accused the plaintiffs' lawyer of
hiding his relationship with Cabrera. "In order to secure desper-
ately needed funding," Burford said, Donziger carried out a "multi-
month scheme to deceive and defraud." Further distancing itself
from the case, Burford said it sold most of its interest in plaintiffs'
recovery to another investor, whom it refused to identify.

Judge Kaplan, meanwhile, encouraged Chevron to move ahead
with its racketeering suit. In September 2011, the federal appeals
court in New York told Kaplan he had overstepped his authority
by purporting to block enforcement of the judgment all around
the globe. This rap on the knuckles embarrassed Kaplan, but it did
not deter him. The appellate court didn't question his underlying
findings about Donziger's apparent misconduct, and it declined
Donziger's request to remove Kaplan from the case because of
his unmistakable aversion to the plaintiffs' attorney. Kaplan proceeded to issue a string of interim rulings inviting Chevron to use
his courtroom to prove that Donziger exploited the Ecuadorian
judicial system and extorted the American corporation.

Events in Ecuador provided the oil company with additional
evidence for this endeavor. In February 2012, the country's Judicial Council ousted Judge Zambrano, the man who signed the
$19 billion verdict. The disciplinary body cited allegations by the
National Organized Crime Prevention Unit that, in other cases,
Zambrano had unlawfully coddled convicted drug traffickers. The
firing brought to four out of six the proportion of judges in the
case forced off the bench in disgrace, a dismissal rate of 67 percent.

The oil pollution suit was not unique. Ecuador's judiciary had a
well-earned reputation for corruption and chaos. This was a reputation, of course, that Texaco played down when it convinced the

federal courts in New York to send the case to Ecuador in the 1990s, over Donziger's objections. In its 2011 index on judicial sleaze, the nonprofit organization Transparency International ranked Ecuador 120th out of 183 countries. New Zealand enjoyed the top spot for judicial integrity. The United States ranked 24th, just in front of France. Albania, Lesotho, and Vietnam all came in ahead of Ecuador, which tied with Kazakhstan.

Chapter Twenty-two

CORRUPTION

In January 2013, Chevron brought forward the most startling claim in two decades of startling claims by the opposing sides in the Amazon pollution case: Before being forced off the bench, former judge Zambrano had allowed the plaintiffs' lawyers to compose large portions of the February 2011 judgment issued in his name. He did this, according to the company, in exchange for a proposed $500,000 bribe from the plaintiffs.

If true, this contention took Donziger's ghostwriting exploits to new depths and erased his historic environmental victory. Other misconduct by Donziger's team made the surrealistic-sounding allegation plausible. Under duress during his deposition, Donziger had confessed that his paid experts at Stratus had covertly drafted the Cabrera report. Now Chevron asserted it had proof that, like Cabrera, Zambrano secretly permitted plaintiffs' representatives—specific names weren't named—to do his work.

The accusation came from a knowledgeable, if highly compromised, source: former judge Alberto Guerra, who had acknowledged that for years he served as Zambrano's secret paid draftsman on a range of cases. Guerra possessed ample evidence of his clandestine work for Zambrano. Stored on his computer, he had numerous files containing hundreds of pages of rulings he had written but which Zambrano issued as his own. The ghostwriting went beyond the Chevron case to encompass all manner of legal disputes that came before the Lago Agrio court. Guerra also retained calendars with contemporaneous notations of payments Zambrano made to him. Guerra even had a bank deposit slip showing that on one occasion Zambrano personally made a direct deposit of $300 into Guerra's account at Banco Pichincha in Quito. Shipping records backed up Guerra's claim that he and Zambrano sometimes exchanged drafts of court materials by an overnight delivery service.

Guerra described his dealings with Zambrano in a detailed sworn declaration procured by Chevron and filed with the federal court in New York. In late 2009, he said, "Mr. Zambrano asked me to attempt, through friends of mine, to get in touch with the attorneys for Chevron in order to negotiate an agreement by which the company would pay Mr. Zambrano and me for issuing the final judgment in Chevron's favor." This marked an expansion of the earlier Zambrano-Guerra collaboration. "Mr. Zambrano told me that Chevron would have much more money than the plaintiffs for this agreement, and therefore we could get a better deal and greater profits for ourselves," Guerra recounted.

He took Zambrano's proposal to Chevron's Ecuadorian lawyers, but they abruptly turned him down. The company, the lawyers said, would not buy a verdict.

So, with Zambrano's approval, Guerra said, he turned to the plaintiffs. The corrupt judges found Donziger's team more receptive. Donziger and Fajardo agreed, as a first step, to pay Guerra $1,000 a month for interim rulings that would speed the case toward a big award against Chevron. During one meeting at a Quito restaurant called Honey & Honey, Guerra recounted, "Mr. Donziger thanked me for my work as ghostwriter in this case and for helping steer the case in favor of the plaintiffs." The former judge said that his payments "were given to me by Mr. Fajardo in cash or were deposited into my savings account at Banco Pichincha." Guerra produced records of two of these direct deposits which indicated they were made by a Frente employee. "Mr. Zambrano and I agreed that I would write the court rulings in favor of the plaintiffs," Guerra added. "Sometimes I would write a court decision in favor of Chevron to avoid suspicion."

Assuming Guerra's claims were true, it was nothing short of astounding that he and Zambrano thought they would get away with this scam, especially since they had already revealed their appetite for graft to Chevron's Ecuadorian lawyers. Rather than immediately blow the whistle on Guerra and Zambrano, the company and its local attorneys drafted contemporaneous affidavits describing the judges' illicit proposal and then sat back to see how the situation would play out. Chevron eventually filed the affidavits and Guerra's declaration with the federal court in New York.

Guerra's account incorporated anecdotal specifics that enhanced its trustworthiness. In late 2010, with a final judgment in the offing, the former judge said he attended another meeting at Honey & Honey with Fajardo and Donziger. Guerra told the plaintiffs' lawyers that Zambrano would allow them to draft the final judgment for a bribe of $500,000, which Zambrano and Guerra would split. Donziger indicated interest, according to Guerra. But "Mr. Donziger replied that at that moment they did not have that sum of money to pay us." The plaintiffs' team agreed to provide the half-million dollars once they received their eventual recovery from Chevron. Guerra and Zambrano accepted these terms.

"In late January or early February of 2011, approximately two weeks before the trial court in the Chevron case issued the judgment, Mr. Zambrano gave me a draft of the judgment so that I could revise it," Guerra said. "It was through him that I found out that the attorneys for the plaintiffs had written the judgment and had delivered it to him." Using a laptop provided by Fajardo, Guerra did his light edit and returned the draft to Zambrano. "Based on what Mr. Zambrano told me," Guerra added, "it is my understanding that the plaintiffs' attorneys made changes to the judgment up until the very last minute before it was published."

This eleventh-hour fiddling closely resembled the plaintiffs' compulsive tinkering with Cabrera's report until just before the court-appointed expert submitted his pre-scripted damage analysis in 2008.

The plaintiffs had their judgment, which was promptly upheld on appeal in Ecuador. But Donziger and Fajardo didn't have the money from the verdict, so there was no bounty to be shared with Zambrano and Guerra. About a year later, Zambrano joined Guerra in the ranks of ex-judges driven from the Lago Agrio courthouse for misconduct, although not the alleged misconduct related to the Chevron case, which hadn't yet come to light.

Then, with a greed bordering on mania, Zambrano and Guerra decided to switch sides yet again, according to Guerra. They attempted to sell their loyalty one more time to Chevron. Guerra said that Zambrano authorized him "to begin talks with Chevron's representatives to reveal the truth regarding the drafting of the judgment."

Determined to discredit the February 2011 verdict, the oil company at this point agreed to negotiate with Guerra. It offered him an attractive financial package for his cooperation, beginning with $38,000 up front, a payment described as compensation for his cell phones, hard drives, and other records. The company also paid to move Guerra and his family of four from Ecuador to an undisclosed location in the United States. Chevron said it would provide the Guerras with $12,000 a month for two years to cover housing and other living expenses. Guerra's total take in cash would come to $326,000. On top of that, Chevron threw in health insurance and a promise to pay his legal fees—a truly gold-plated, corporate witness-protection program.

Zambrano intended to accept a similar deal with the oil company, according to Guerra. Then, to Chevron's frustration, Zambrano had a last-minute "change of heart." Zambrano would not explain his reasons for spurning Chevron.

It's fair to ask why Guerra deserves to be believed. The triple-crossing defrocked judge had a significant financial incentive to say whatever Chevron wanted.

In some ways, his bizarre story echoed that of Diego Borja, the slippery former company contractor who teamed up with a convicted American drug trafficker to videotape their attempts to incriminate another ex-judge in the case. Both men belonged to a cohort of entrepreneurial, ethically challenged Ecuadorians who saw the Chevron controversy as an opportunity for a quick score. As with Borja, Chevron handed cash to Guerra for information intended to undermine an expensive judgment against the company. And as with Borja, the company arranged for its snitch and his family to escape Ecuador and settle into a comfortable, anonymous existence in the United States. Chevron would not tell me where it had squirreled away either informant.

Aware of Guerra's patent fallibility, Chevron lawyer Randy Mastro went on Fox Business Channel to bolster his witness. The former prosecutor compared Guerra to an organized-crime "turncoat" who received government protection for ratting out fellow gangsters. Mastro suggested that to convict a clever crime boss—in his telling, that would be Donziger—the feds typically have to rely on moles no less sketchy than Guerra. Chevron had recruited the tainted jurist just as the FBI would woo a Mafia stool pigeon.

Despite the impurity of Guerra's motives and Chevron's ample inducements to get him to sing, the fallen judge's story more or less held together. Ghostwriting had become an established practice for Donziger and his team. They got away with it with Cabrera—for a while, anyway—and might well have thought they could do so again with Zambrano. From its trove of Donziger e-mail, Chevron extracted messages in which Fajardo appeared to refer to Zambrano and Guerra as "the puppet" and "the puppeteer," code language of the sort the plaintiffs' lawyers had used in earlier communication about Cabrera. Fajardo believed that Guerra pulled Zambrano's strings. Guerra said the plaintiffs paid him to do so, as they had paid Cabrera.

Chevron's forensic analysis provided another reason to take Guerra seriously. The company hired linguistic experts who demonstrated that about a third of the judgment's 188 pages contained verbatim passages from internal memoranda written by the plaintiffs' team but never filed with the court in Lago Agrio. The memos used wording different from that of the briefs and other documents the plaintiffs had filed. One memo explained the plaintiffs' position on why, as a matter of corporate law, Chevron could be held liable for the conduct of a Texaco subsidiary many years before Chevron acquired Texaco. Gibson Dunn found the memos on Donziger's computer hard drive. Beyond its reliance on the unfiled plaintiffs' memos, the Zambrano judgment also cited distinctively coded scientific data from the plaintiffs' internal files which similarly had never been officially provided to the court.

Even in the face of this damning evidence, Donziger refused to give an inch. His Manhattan apartment became a bunker, his mood increasingly volatile. He insisted to anyone who would listen that in complicated lawsuits in both the United States and other countries, litigants routinely provided judges with off-the-record information that found its way verbatim into rulings. Chevron and Gibson Dunn "are taking something that is customary and acting like just because it's happening in Ecuador under a different legal system that it's sinister, and it's not," he told one interviewer.

Donzigers's contention was preposterous on its face. No self-respecting jurist in any modern legal system accepts covert memos from a party and slips the material, unattributed, into his judgment. Donziger's suggestion that Ecuador's judiciary was being held to a higher standard was actually an implied insult to those Ecuadorian judges and attorneys who did follow the rule of law.

In Lago Agrio, the author or authors of the ruling that appeared under Judge Zambrano's name could not have obtained either the plaintiffs' private memos or their coded testing data from any source other than the plaintiffs themselves, Chevron contended. People in the plaintiffs' camp, at a minimum, helped cobble together the judgment, according to the company. The most reasonable inference was that Zambrano, like Cabrera before him, had served as little more than a cipher.

Chapter Twenty-three

TRIAL

"Mr. Zambrano, welcome to New York." The greeting from Chevron's lead attorney, Randy Mastro, could not have been more enthusiastic or less sincere. Chevron had called Zambrano in the fall of 2013 as a "hostile witness" in the company's racketeering suit against Donziger and his clients in U.S. District Court in Lower Manhattan. Mastro intended to shred the fallen Ecuadorian judge's unlikely account of how he wrote the February 2011 Lago Agrio judgment.

Given that Chevron had already branded Zambrano a bribe-seeking co-conspirator in Donziger's corrupt enterprise, Mastro had doubted the Ecuadorian would show up at all. But a lot about this case defied easy explanation, and for whatever reason, here was Zambrano on the witness stand in Judge Kaplan's chilly twenty-first-floor courtroom. What transpired over the following three days can only be described as bizarre.

Accustomed to an equatorial climate, Zambrano began his appearance sipping hot tea from the courthouse cafeteria and wearing a long charcoal-colored coat over his dress shirt and tie. By the second day, he had added a gray scarf, black gloves, and a red knit

Angry Birds hat. The eyes of the Angry Bird appeared just above Zambrano's own, so he appeared to glare at Mastro with four furious eyes.

"You are the author of the Lago Agrio–Chevron judgment?" the Gibson Dunn lawyer asked.

Zambrano paused for long seconds before answering. "*Sí*," he finally said, followed by a translator's rendition into English: "I worked many hours, many days, including several weekends."

Had anyone helped him?

"No one has helped me to write the judgment. I was the one who exclusively drafted it."

Mastro announced that he would ask the witness a series of questions about the ruling. The original Spanish text had been placed in front of Zambrano. Judge Kaplan ordered him not to look at it. Apparently confused, Zambrano began to leaf through the document anyway. Kaplan leapt from his black-padded chair and, looming over the witness, told him sharply to put down the ruling. Nervous whispers swept through the crowded spectators' section; federal judges rarely, if ever, engaged in such dramatics. Mastro demanded that Zambrano obey Kaplan. The flummoxed courtroom translator struggled to keep up.

Once things settled down, Zambrano did not fare well on Mastro's closed-book exam. The Ecuadorian didn't know what TPH stood for, even though the acronym for total petroleum hydrocarbons appeared no fewer than thirty-five times in the ruling. He couldn't recall the chemical substance the judgment described as "the most powerful carcinogenic agent" associated with oil contamination (benzene). He guessed wrong when asked which scientific study the judgment called the "statistical data of highest importance." And he could not name the Ecuadorian jurisprudential theory the decision relied on to link TPH pollution to human harm ("sufficient causation").

The judgment, Mastro noted, included erudite citations of French, Australian, British, and American legal doctrines. Did Zambrano speak or read French or English?

Zambrano admitted he did not. He claimed that his eighteen-year-old secretary, who also did not know any languages other than Spanish, had found the foreign legal materials for him. "The young woman who would help me type the judgment was the one going on the Internet," Zambrano testified. She "chose the Spanish [translation] option" on legal websites. "That is how I would become aware or informed of the subject I was interested in. She would print them so I could read them later."

This description of a high school–educated typist who happened to be a wizard researcher of international law did not ring true, and Zambrano's testimony got less plausible from there. Mastro asked how so many technical passages spread over numerous pages of "his" judgment matched verbatim passages from internal memos written by the plaintiffs but never formally filed with the court. Zambrano answered that documents related to the case occasionally were slipped under his office door. The ex-judge said he "verified" the content of these mystery documents by comparing them to the formal record. "This was relevant information," he said, "that as I read it, I realized could be of use in my decision." So, in it went—no questions asked.

Zambrano's account seemed ludicrous on its face. This was not how a legitimate judge behaved, whether in Ecuador, the United States, or anywhere else. He conceded that his fellow former judge Alberto Guerra secretly drafted orders for him in late 2010 and 2011. Evidence at the RICO trial showed that Guerra's computer contained nine draft orders later issued by Zambrano in the Chevron case. Zambrano also confirmed that on one occasion he gave a cash-strapped Guerra a loan of $300. But Zambrano insisted that other than that one time, he didn't pay his colleague for ghostwriting. He couldn't explain Guerra's datebook notations showing a series of such payments. Zambrano also flatly denied dispatching Guerra to seek a $500,000 bribe from the plaintiffs or telling Guerra that the plaintiffs composed the February 2011 judgment.

Zambrano contradicted himself frequently—so often that Kaplan remarked at one point that the witness undercut his version of events in "absolutely irreconcilable ways." Zambrano insisted, for example, that the entire judgment was written on a brand-new computer kept in his courthouse office. But a variety of records introduced into evidence showed that he did not receive the machine in question until more than a month after he said he began dictating the ruling. After completing the most important project of his career, Zambrano testified, he hadn't saved a single piece of paper or computer file that would corroborate his authorship of the judgment. He said he threw away all of his notes and all of the impressive Internet research supposedly printed out by his precocious assistant.

Zambrano's career path since issuance of the Lago Agrio verdict raised additional questions. He confirmed that a year after he made international headlines in the Chevron case, Ecuador's Judicial Council removed him from office because he released an accused drug trafficker who, in the council's words, "was arrested in flagrante delicto for illegal possession of narcotics and psychotropic drugs." The disciplinary body didn't explicitly accuse Zambrano of taking a bribe but found him guilty of acting "with malice, manifest negligence or inexcusable error." Despite this humiliation, Zambrano testified that he was once again gainfully employed—by the Ecuadorian government. In the spring of 2013, a state-controlled oil refinery hired him as a legal adviser. The Correa administration, which vociferously condemned Chevron's refusal to pay the Lago Agrio judgment, thus rewarded the disgraced judge whose signature shifted culpability for the rain forest pollution to the American corporation.

When it was his turn on the stand, Guerra portrayed himself

as a criminal now willing to confess just about anything. Dressed conventionally in a dark business suit, he described his judicial career in the 1990s and 2000s as an extended opportunity to sell influence. "While I was a judge, the payment of bribes to judges in exchange for a desired result was commonplace," he said in a sworn declaration accompanying his live testimony. "I occasionally accepted bribes from litigants in exchange for issuing favorable rulings." In this milieu, Guerra explained, it seemed unremarkable that he and Zambrano would seek to profit by throwing the Chevron case. Guerra described his misdeeds as nothing more or less than the way judicial business got done in Ecuador.

The main purpose of Chevron's interrogation of the former Ecuadorian judges—indeed the aim of the entire RICO suit against Donziger—was to discredit Ecuador's legal system and negate the $19 billion Lago Agrio judgment. Donziger's clients couldn't enforce the verdict in Ecuador, because the company lacked physical assets there. Chevron's Section 1782 campaign in U.S. federal courts had soured the American judiciary on the goings-on in Lago Agrio, making it unlikely that the verdict would ever get enforced in Chevron's home country. That, however, was not the end of the story. The possibility, however remote, of sharing in a multibillion-dollar payoff enticed a new collection of adventurous lawyers to agree to join forces with Donziger and his clients. Operating on spec, three groups of attorneys of diverse nationalities filed enforcement actions in Canada, Brazil, and Argentina—countries where Chevron had hard assets worth billions of dollars.

Courts in Argentina and Brazil reacted warily to the enforcement suits. Chevron played a prominent role in the Latin American countries, which depended heavily on outside capital to develop oil and natural gas reserves on which they had wagered their economic futures. The company's money and technical expertise would be sorely missed if it pulled out of either country over the Ecuadorian dispute. In March 2013, the chief executive of YPF, the Argentine state-owned oil company, published a stern open letter warning the Lago Agrio plaintiffs that their collection efforts were "absolutely detrimental to Argentina and could have a negative effect on investment." Given YPF's status as a powerful arm of the national government, this statement could not go unnoticed in Argentina's highest judicial chambers. Subsequently, YPF announced that it would move ahead with a multibillion-dollar project with Chevron, and Argentina's top court cleared away a legal impediment to that deal. These seemed like signals that Argentina didn't wish to adjudicate the Ecuadorians' claims against Chevron. The Brazilian judiciary remained mute in the face of the enforcement action there, while judges in Canada moved at an only slightly less glacial pace as they considered convoluted procedural issues preliminary to getting to the merits of the Lago Agrio judgment.

In the United States, Donziger had had to scramble to fend off Chevron's attempt to destroy his reputation. By early 2013, the last of the Burford money had been spent. Jim Tyrrell and Patton Boggs would have to write off millions of dollars of billable hours. Tyrrell fumed privately, blaming Donziger and swearing that Patton Boggs would do as little as possible to assist the troublesome New York attorney. John Keker, a nationally known white-collar defense lawyer based in San Francisco whom Donziger had hired to represent him personally against Chevron's racketeering suit, bailed out altogether. Keker told Judge Kaplan in May 2013 that he was withdrawing from the case because Donziger owed him $1.4 million and couldn't pay. Keker took the opportunity to castigate the RICO case as a "Dickensian farce." Kaplan fired back in writing that Donziger and his defense attorney had proved just as prolific and splenetic in their filings as Chevron.

Donziger complained in a June 2013 filing that he would have to contend with Gibson Dunn on his own, or pro se. He noted self-pityingly that he had "never litigated a civil case in federal court." Overlooking his earlier attempt to get Chevron's attorneys criminally prosecuted in Ecuador, he lectured Kaplan that in an adversarial system of justice, "facts and evidence thereof are supposed to determine outcomes, not whether one side has been able to pick off persons defending the interests of the other." Keker, of course, hadn't been "picked off." He had quit.

Despite his protestations of helplessness, Donziger remained as intrepid as ever. Court filings show that in the spring of 2013, he traveled to England, where he hosted an "executive breakfast" at the Arts Club in London. His purpose there was to recruit new investors to replace Burford. In a testament to his persuasive skills, London-based Woodsford Litigation Funding agreed to invest $2.5 million in the case in exchange for a confidential share of any proceeds. Even within his own family, Donziger exerted himself to raise funds. State court records from Florida showed that as he battled Chevron, Donziger was suing the lawyer overseeing a family trust fund. Donziger won this fight in Florida and with it assets worth $1.9 million.

Donziger's status as a pro se litigant in the RICO case did not last very long. On the eve of trial, a new battery of four American lawyers materialized in New York to defend him. He had enlisted them through an informal network of politically left-leaning attorneys that also helped him assemble a volunteer research squad of a dozen recent law school graduates and young activists. The whole crew camped out in a three-bedroom loft apartment Donziger rented in the Tribeca neighborhood near the courthouse. The place had the cheerful, disheveled ambiance of an urban commune.

"I consider it a privilege to represent Steven Donziger," Richard Friedman told me just before the RICO trial started. A gracious professional based in Seattle, Friedman could not have been more different from his rambunctious client. Friedman specialized in suing insurance companies for bad faith—and had made a lot of money. He served as president of the Inner Circle of Advocates, an invitation-only group of a hundred of the most accomplished trial lawyers in the United States. "Steven has changed the way people think about the relationship between multinational corporations and developing countries," Friedman said. Zoe Littlepage, a pharmaceutical class-action attorney from Houston whom Friedman persuaded to help defend Donziger, said she feared that if Chevron succeeded, large corporations would use RICO to go after her and other members of the plaintiffs' bar. As for Donziger, she was less admiring than Friedman. "It's not illegal to be a jackass," she told me. "It's not a violation of RICO to be abusive to the people around you." Chevron, of course, was accusing Donziger of far more than being an obnoxious boss.

Twenty years after he had accompanied the first group of traditionally adorned indigenous Ecuadorian plaintiffs to the federal court on Foley Square, Donziger returned to face trial himself. He and his fresh phalanx of lawyers were greeted by a small contingent of protesters assembled by Amazon Watch. The demonstrators, chanting in Spanish, waved the Ecuadorian flag and multicolored banners condemning Chevron. The company's lawyers arrived in a convoy of bulky black SUVs: twenty-five men and women dressed in muted shades of gray and navy blue. Though less photogenic, the Gibson Dunn delegation were confident they'd assembled overwhelming evidence that Donziger's victory in Lago Agrio had been rotten to the core.

Over six weeks of trial, a parade of live witnesses, bolstered by reams of exhibits and deposition transcripts, illustrated that nearly everyone who had ever worked for or with Donziger now considered him a fraud. Charles Calmbacher, the former technical adviser, called him "a perfidious thief." Dave Russell, who tried in vain to get Donziger to stop using his $6 billion cleanup estimate, recounted that he had said as early as December 2004 that "Texaco may be right when they indicate that the remediation is performing as designed." Jeff Shinder, a New York commercial lawyer who agreed in 2010 to help Donziger, only to quit almost immediately on ethical grounds, testified that he felt "physically ill" upon discovering the chicanery surrounding the Cabrera report. "I wanted no part of it," Shinder said.

One assignment Shinder backed out of was justifying the conduct of the Stratus consulting firm. Stratus's principals had stopped defending themselves months before the RICO trial began. Chevron agreed to dismiss Stratus as a defendant in exchange for the consultants' capitulation. Doug Beltman, the Ph.D. remediation expert who had condemned Chevron on *60 Minutes*, reversed himself in a humiliating sworn declaration: "The Cabrera damages assessment," he said, "is tainted and not supported by reliable scientific bases, and I disavow it." Beltman confessed that he allowed Donziger to manipulate evidence. Stratus had abandoned proper research methods and sold out its reputation. "I deeply regret," Beltman added, "that I allowed myself and my company to be used in the Lago Agrio litigation in the way that we were." Stratus eventually fired Beltman, leaving Donziger without any reputable American scientific expert standing behind him.

The trial proved frustrating to Donziger. At the last moment, Chevron dropped any demand for money damages, asking Judge Kaplan only for an order prohibiting Donziger and the plaintiffs from profiting from their ill-gotten judgment. This meant that Kaplan would try the suit without a jury. To Donziger's aggravation, a civil suit for "equitable relief" doesn't come with a Seventh Amendment right to a jury. His hope of inciting lay hostility toward the big oil company suddenly crumbled. Making matters worse, if the company prevailed, it could still ask Kaplan to force Donziger to reimburse it for its reasonable legal fees, a component of equitable relief not considered to be damages. Based on Gibson Dunn's lavish staffing, Chevron's legal expenses for the RICO case would easily reach into the tens of millions of dollars—amounts that, in any event, Donziger didn't have. Personal bankruptcy loomed as a very real possibility.

Donziger's exasperation was obvious when I met him about a week into the trial. Over the years, our relationship had had its ups and downs. He cooperated with a cover story I wrote about him for *Bloomberg Businessweek* in March 2011 entitled "Amazon Crusader. Chevron Pest. Fraud?" We continued to meet for interviews, and he facilitated my first reporting trip to Ecuador that year. As my ambitions turned toward writing this book, however, Donziger pulled back, ultimately cutting off direct communication. In 2012, when I made a second excursion to Ecuador, he obstructed my access to people in Lago Agrio, directing his clients to cancel previously scheduled interviews. Although he never explained his hostility, I suspected that he feared that as I learned more about the case, my view of him would darken. Also, he resented that someone else would write a book about "his" story.

On a Friday when Kaplan was not holding court, Donziger proposed that we meet near his apartment on the Upper West Side. Chris Gowen, a lawyer and Democratic Party activist who had replaced Karen Hinton as Donziger's public relations person, explained that his mercurial client wanted to make sure I understood their trial strategy. When I arrived at a bistro on Broadway, Donziger seemed tired and downcast. Theoretically helping to represent himself, he lacked the courtroom skills to do his cause much good. His one turn trying to cross-examine a Chevron witness did not go well and wasn't repeated. During court sessions, he occupied himself by fiddling with an Apple laptop computer and scribbling notes on a yellow legal pad. At the restaurant on Broadway, Donziger ordered an iced tea and asked what questions I had.

I'd been asking questions for many months without getting any answers, I responded. Why the change?

Donziger glared at me. Then he blurted that I hadn't been writing about the trial—an exceedingly odd statement, as I'd written more than any other journalist. Gowen seemed as perplexed as I was. Donziger then leaned over the small bar table and extended his index finger toward my face. Why, he demanded, was I "covering up" for Chevron?

"That's ridiculous," I said. I would leave, I added, if he was trying to intimidate me. Donziger started shouting about my role in a cover-up, so I got up and left. A few steps outside the restaurant, I realized he was following me, still bellowing. Gowen trailed behind us, begging Donziger to stop. I turned to face them.

"You are a biased journalist!" Donziger yelled. "You are a biased journalist!" He loomed over me (at six-four, Donziger was eight inches taller than me), his index finger again in my face. "I am going to expose you! You are a biased journalist! You are going to be exposed!"

I recalled the carefully orchestrated scene from *Crude* where Donziger berated the Chevron lawyer—*"abogado Tek-ZAH-ko corrupto!"*—for the benefit of American filmmakers and Ecuadorian journalists. While eerily similar in its cadences, his performance along upper Broadway seemed less rehearsed. Seven years after the movie, Donziger fully embodied the hotheaded character he had played in the documentary. Life imitated art.

My next thought was a question: What would I do if Donziger actually poked me? To paraphrase his description of the *Crude* episode, he'd gotten so close I could smell his breath.

Fortunately, after a few more loud threats, Donziger turned and stalked off toward his apartment on 104th Street. I'd never gotten a word out. I turned to Gowen, who had watched the encounter, mouth agape. "This," Gowen said, "is why everyone hates Steve."

*   *   *

Amazingly, some people still admired Donziger, or at least admired the idea of him. Trudie Styler attended the RICO trial a couple of times to show her support. Donziger greeted her with a European-style air kiss on each cheek. One afternoon, Sting accompanied his wife. Dressed in all black with stiletto heels, Styler watched the action intently. Sting, in a gray T-shirt, tweed trousers, and well-worn brown dress shoes lacking laces (yet still looking incredibly glamorous), appeared to wish he was anywhere else in the world but that courtroom. "This is all a sideshow," Sting told me in the hallway during a break. "A lot of lawyers arguing in New York while people are still suffering in the rain forest." The musician had a point.

When Donziger finally took the stand in his own defense, he portrayed himself as a victim of the sideshow, targeted because of his "commitment to constantly push back even as we face from Chevron what I believe could be the most well-funded corporate retaliation campaign in history." In the face of Mastro's withering cross-examination, he spoke with pride. "I have no apologies," he said. Any missteps were "inconsequential errors." In response to the allegation that he conspired with Guerra to bribe Zambrano, Donziger seemed offended. "I would never do that," he said. "Let me be very clear."

He was less definitive when confronted with circumstantial evidence that some kind of ghostwriting plot occurred. Mastro introduced the e-mail exchanges in which Fajardo kept Donziger apprised of dealings with the crooked Ecuadorian jurists, referring to Zambrano as "the puppet" and Guerra as "the puppeteer." In September 2009, Fajardo told Donziger, "The puppeteer is pulling the string and the puppet is returning the package." About a week later, according to a bank deposit slip Chevron's investigators located, an employee of the plaintiffs' Ecuadorian legal team deposited $1,000 into Guerra's account. The next month, Fajardo alerted Donziger: "The puppeteer won't move his puppet until the audience [pays] him something." Days later, $1,000 was withdrawn from the plaintiffs' Ecuadorian account.

Mastro demanded that Donziger explain these communications: "'The puppet will finish the matter tomorrow,'—do you recall that, Mr. Donziger?"

Donziger brushed off the code language as "nicknames, jokes, that kind of stuff."

"The puppeteer," Mastro insisted, that was Guerra?

"That's not my recollection," Donziger said.

"The puppet was Judge Zambrano?"

"I have no recollection." Donziger had no explanation, either, for the judgment's verbatim repetition of extended passages from the plaintiffs' unfiled memos. He vaguely asserted that there were possible reasons for such a coincidence, but he never actually identified them. In written testimony that accompanied his courtroom appearance, he offered this carefully crafted assertion: "I did not write the judgment in the *Aguinda* case in Ecuador. I have no knowledge that anybody on the legal team of the plaintiffs wrote the judgment in this case, or wrote any part of the judgment." This non-denial denial left open the possibility that Pablo Fajardo and other Ecuadorian members of the plaintiffs' team drafted parts of the judgment but didn't explicitly tell Donziger when or how they did it.

Chapter Twenty-four

CONCLUSIONS

Grounded in ancient British common law and honed over centuries of courtroom experience, the American judicial system promises—and sometimes provides—a forum in which powerful institutions can be called to account by those of modest means. A criminal defendant, if he has an effective lawyer, can cross-examine the police and win exoneration based on a single lay juror's "reasonable doubt." Ordinary individuals—again, assuming they find the right attorney—can challenge the conduct of a global corporation. Steven Donziger, first in the United States and later in Ecuador (into which he helped import American-style class-action procedures), sought to harness the leveling ethos of the law to repair human and ecological damage from unregulated oil development.

Network television shows, glossy magazines, and a celebrated filmmaker heralded Donziger as a pioneer. He boasted of inventing a new "business model" for legal insurgency, one that married hedge-fund financing and leftist politics. In reality, though, litigation is not guerrilla warfare. Donziger's choice of the courtroom, even one in Lago Agrio, subjected him to the strictures of lawyerly behavior. He believed his foe violated those limitations, so he could violate them, too. He went further and further, until he drew the skeptical attention of the U.S. judiciary thousands of miles away. He alienated his closest comrades and lost his ethical bearings. The poignancy of his clients' misfortune could not save him.

Activists lead protests, draft legislation, galvanize popular opinion, and cut political deals. In the extreme, a principled activist may employ civil disobedience and risk prison to dramatize his cause. A lawyer invoking the authority of courts enjoys less latitude. If he wishes to maintain credibility, he cannot pressure or bribe witnesses the way a lobbyist woos lawmakers with campaign dollars. A lawyer shouldn't try to intimidate judges as an old-time ward boss browbeat members of the city council. A lawyer may not secretly act as ventriloquist to a dummy judge the way speechwriters put words in politicians' mouths.

Different rules apply to the practice of law, and rightly so. Law is an alternative to brute political combat. In politics, raw might—as exercised by voting blocs, shouting demonstrators, and/or maneuvering financiers—often prevails. Invoking legal process brings into play constraints that Donziger declined to observe. That Chevron also pushed the boundaries—allying itself with the Ecuadorian military, for example, and attempting to bribe a journalist to spy on the plaintiffs' legal team—did not validate Donziger's excesses. He debased the very idea of seeking truth by means of a trial based on facts. Without a sturdy verdict, he had nothing—perhaps less than nothing: His cynicism about the obligation to demonstrate harm by means of hard, defensible scientific evidence undercut the contention that empirical proof could overcome the oil company's greater wealth and influence. He allowed Chevron to suggest that the entire conflict amounted to a duplicitous money grab, rather than a means to address the legitimate grievances of the Oriente population.

In the beginning, Donziger set out to seek justice and make a name for himself as a legal firebrand, goals that were not mutually exclusive. Over time, though, drunk on the attention of journalists and Hollywood stars, he succumbed to hubris, a temptation as old as Greek mythology and as intoxicating as seeing your image on television. Lines blurred. He convinced himself that in Lago Agrio the only way to beat a multinational oil company was, in Malcolm X's phrase, "by any means necessary." In the short term, the strategy worked. Donziger blackmailed a vulnerable Ecuadorian judge. He spoon-fed conclusions to a supposedly disinterested court expert. When the terms of the final judgment were put up for sale, Donziger's team allegedly made an offer.

But a dirty win in Ecuador did not get any oil cleaned up or any sick children treated. Fighting to keep his lawsuit alive until the next week, the next month, the next year, Donziger lost sight of the endgame—that, lacking a means to enforce a judgment in Ecuador, he would have to take any verdict on the road, exposing it to the scrutiny of judges in other countries. He lost sight of the childhood lesson that two wrongs don't make a right. He did not anticipate that Chevron would hold him up as an example: a warning to other plaintiffs' lawyers, a severed head on a pike. He also did not foresee that his showboating for Joseph Berlinger's camera would provide a federal judge with ample basis to put his character on trial.

Donziger did damage to more than just his case and his reputation. He drew a cloud of doubt over ambitious transnational human-rights suits more generally. His innovative business model proved a failure because of his reckless management and lack of a moral compass.

He had help, of course, in discrediting humanitarian class actions. Cristóbal Bonifaz humiliated himself in the spurious spin-off suit in San Francisco, as did the lawyers who brought sham actions against Dole in Nicaragua and the United States. Rather than create a body of precedent that would embolden other activist attorneys to bring mass suits seeking to challenge American-based multinationals, Donziger did the opposite: He offered Gibson Dunn an opportunity to execute its kill-the-messenger playbook.

Randy Mastro and his partners are already using the Ecuador case in pitches to potential new corporate clients enmeshed in controversy overseas. Gibson Dunn could trademark the strategy as the Donziger Defense.

In April 2013, the U.S. Supreme Court erected a formal impediment to American lawyers seeking to prove human-rights violations by multinational corporations outside of the United States. The justices unanimously ruled that a group of Nigerian plaintiffs who accused Royal Dutch Shell of complicity in oppressing them could not sue in American courts. The decision, which did not explicitly apply to *Aguinda,* severely limited the sweep of the Alien Tort Statute, the ambiguous 1789 law under which the Ecuador suit had originally been filed. In another unanimous ruling eight months later, a victory for the German carmaker Daimler, the Supreme Court raised the bar for lawyers seeking to sue foreign-based multinationals in the United States over alleged abuses in third countries.

It would go too far to say that Donziger's actions bore directly on the Supreme Court's curtailment of U.S. human-rights jurisdiction. But it's entirely fair to speculate that the discomfiting echoes of the Ecuadorian litigation contributed to the background noise discouraging at least some of the justices from inviting more such suits. The demise of the Lago Agrio case and the Supreme Court's door-slamming decision on the Alien Tort Statute illustrate a broader deterioration of the class action, which had reached its apogee in the 1990s. "The class action," a Supreme Court majority declared in yet another ruling, in a commercial case in 2013, "is an exception to the usual rule that litigation is conducted by and on behalf of the individual named plaintiff only." The space for that exception was shrinking rapidly.

A number of factors contributed to the Supreme Court's growing distrust of class actions. In various recent decisions, the justices have noted the practical difficulty of showing that large numbers of putative victims suffered similar injuries as a result of a defendant's actions. Practical experience with class actions has revealed troubling anomalies. The settlement of massive suits concerning asbestos-related illnesses channeled money to severely ill pipe fitters, but also to claimants whose symptoms were slight or even nonexistent. Shareholder class actions alleging management fraud have often produced lavish contingency fees for the attorneys who filed them but only a pittance for each class member. In certain consumer cases, lawyers have walked away with millions, having won only discount coupons allowing their clients to buy more of the very products or services they complained about.

Nothing has done more to weaken the reputation of the class action as a legal tool than the tendency of celebrated plaintiffs' lawyers to overstep ethical lines. Dickie Scruggs became one of the richest men in Mississippi by suing the asbestos-products industry in the 1980s and cigarette manufacturers in the 1990s. Then in 2008 and 2009, he twice pled guilty in connection with judicial-bribery investigations and was sentenced to seven years in federal prison. Boardroom scourge Mel Weiss of New York made a fortune representing masses of shareholders claiming deceit by top corporate executives. In 2008, Weiss pled guilty to paying illegal kickbacks to straw-man clients to generate cases that otherwise wouldn't have existed; he, too, spent time behind bars. After a long career representing union pension funds and other institutional investors that sued big companies, Bill Lerach of San Diego forged a $7.2 billion class-action settlement related to the collapse of Enron, a company undone by very real fraud. Then, like Weiss, he pled guilty to kickback allegations, went to prison, and provided his critics with invaluable evidence of the base motives and methods of the big-time plaintiffs' bar.

The list, sadly, goes on and on: self-described vindicators of "the little guy" who, despite their contingency-fee riches, egregiously overreach. Unchecked pride in smiting corporate supremacy, combined with repeated pecuniary windfalls, leads all too many lawyers astray. It is not clear as of this writing whether Donziger's conduct in Ecuador will subject him to criminal charges. But he's a shoo-in for the plaintiffs' lawyer Hall of Infamy: a gallery of rogues who have undercut the idea of disciplining corporations by means of litigation. Donziger forged a new business model to be avoided, not emulated.

Donziger's misdeeds do not, however, exonerate the oil companies or the government of Ecuador. This is a tale with no shortage of knaves and villains.

Texaco had the initial and best opportunity in the 1970s and 1980s to avert the entire *Aguinda* calamity by doing business in Ecuador in a more honorable manner: lining its waste pits and re-injecting produced water. Having instead lived down to Ecuador's negligible environmental standards, the company encountered another chance to do the right thing and, not incidentally, limit its exposure to costly litigation. It could have organized and led a more thorough cleanup in the 1990s. Yes, the company convinced Ecuador to let it walk away after an inadequate partial remediation. But the more responsible path would have led to cleaning up all of the waste pits and spills, with the Ecuadorian government matching whatever amount Texaco spent to get the job done. Texaco chose a more shortsighted approach, and a series of lackadaisical administrations in Quito played along. The Cofán and their neighbors suffered.

After all that, Texaco still could have settled the first iteration of *Aguinda* for a manageable sum that might have underwritten a timely remediation. When originally filed in 1993 in New York, the pollution suit justifiably targeted Texaco. The company at that point had just departed Ecuador and could be implicated in nearly all of the then-evident contamination. In recognition of its failure to oversee Texaco, the Ecuadorian government also deserved to be named a defendant, even though Petroecuador had not yet demonstrated fully its capacity for carelessness. Rather than figure out a compromise with the plaintiffs, however, Texaco, and later Chevron, used reams of legal filings to paper over the misfortune in Ecuador. The corporate strategy of deflecting the dispute from federal court in New York to the rain forest forum in Lago Agrio produced unintended and expensive consequences. The American oil executives got what they asked for in terms of jurisdiction and legal norms. We should shed no tears on their behalf.

As for the actual owners of Chevron, its shareholders, they would not still be paying Gibson Dunn's sizable fees if the company had demonstrated more foresight. Gibson Dunn's compensation alone, estimated conservatively at more than $400 million over several years, would have gone a long way toward cleaning up contamination in the Oriente. From a strictly corporate point of view, consider all of the hours Chevron executives could have devoted to developing new business if they had not spent so much time skirmishing with Donziger over decades-old events in Lago Agrio.

While publicly it has not shown remorse over the Oriente, Chevron's board of directors has expressed concern about the company's recent environmental performance elsewhere. In spring of 2013, the board trimmed bonuses and stock awards for several top executives as punishment for a series of incidents since 2011. These mishaps included seepage from a deepwater project off the coast of Brazil, the explosion of a drilling rig in Nigeria that resulted in two deaths, and a huge fire at a Northern California refinery after a corroded pipe ruptured.

Despite these events, the board said it retained full confidence in management. One reason for this forbearance was that in terms of market capitalization, Chevron, at more than $230 billion, surpassed its perennial rival Royal Dutch Shell in early 2013. That made Chevron the number two oil producer worldwide, behind only ExxonMobil. As measured by stock performance alone during this period, Chevron ranked number one in the industry. In the boardroom, much is forgiven when top executives produce numbers of this sort.

Many observers describe the Oriente pollution case as a conflict between the giant American oil producer (evil or abused, depending on one's perspective) and the plaintiffs (innocent or manipulative). In fact, the dispute is more complicated. The country of Ecuador and its government-owned oil company bear heavy responsibility for what transpired in the jungle.

In the 1960s, Ecuador invited Texaco to explore and invest. The company did not sneak into the Oriente. In the 1970s and 1980s, the Quito government and various Ecuadorian business interests collected most of the revenue from Oriente oil—all according to contract. In the 1990s, Petroecuador formally accepted the duty of cleaning up two-thirds of the former Texaco well sites. Rather than protect the poor people who lived near its operations, the state-owned oil company emulated Texaco's worst tendencies. The populist Rafael Correa, easily reelected president in 2013, continued to rail against American corporations but failed to use his nation's still-flowing oil proceeds to clean up the rain forest. Petroecuador's belated promises of remediation rang false, as illustrated by the continuing contamination in Shushufindi.

Safely ensconced for a third term, Correa has encouraged new producers—Andes Petroleum and PetroOriental—to expand their activities in oil fields overlapping with and adjacent to those of the former Texaco concession. Andes Petroleum and PetroOriental employ Ecuadorian engineers and laborers, but they are wholly owned by China National Petroleum Corporation and China Petro-chemical Corporation, also known as SINOPEC. Ecuadorians are watching the gauges at the Lago Agrio Storage and Transfer Station in Sucumbíos and doing seismic mapping and test drilling in Orellana and Pastaza Provinces. But the neatly dressed executives who occasionally arrive by helicopter are Chinese. In early 2013, the Correa government dispatched representatives to Beijing in hopes of convincing the Chinese to bid on vast, still-untouched parts of the Amazon farther to the south. The Ecuadorian delegation met SINOPEC representatives in a Hilton hotel in the Chinese capital to pitch million-acre contracts. Correa's solicitude toward the Chinese doesn't stem from cultural sympathy or long-standing strategic ties. The Chinese are scouring Latin America and Africa for natural resources to feed a voracious domestic economy. They have tremendous influence in Ecuador, and an inside track in the bidding on unexplored jungle oil fields, because the Correa government owes China more than $11 billion from past loans. Ecuador has no way to pay those debts anytime soon.

Indigenous groups have protested Correa's expansion of foreign oil development. "They have not consulted us, and we're here to tell the big investors that they don't have our permission to exploit our land," Narcisa Mashienta of the Shuar tribe told reporters in 2013. Correa's oil minister, Andrés Donso Fabara, dismissed such objections as naïve and self-interested. He accused the rural protesters of pursuing "a political agenda," as if that were somehow improper. The tribes, he said, "are not thinking about development or about fighting against poverty."

The dynamics of the oil debate in Ecuador thus remain depressingly consistent, with nominally populist Quito politicians as condescending toward the rural populace as any military junta official or U.S. oil executive ever was. Unlike American energy companies, however, SINOPEC is not in danger of facing environmental law-suits filed by lawyers in Beijing. The Communist government will see to that.

Petroecuador, meanwhile, has continued to demonstrate that ecological standards in the Oriente remain dismal. In June 2013, the state-owned producer acknowledged that a major pipeline break had caused a spill of some ten thousand barrels of crude. A portion of the oil flowed into the Napo River. Officials in Quito were forced to inform authorities in Peru that escaped crude could make its way across the Ecuadorian border via the Amazon's intricate network of waterways.

Epilogue

"This case is extraordinary," Judge Kaplan wrote. "The facts are many and sometimes complex. They include things that normally come only out of Hollywood." Kaplan's ruling in *Chevron v. Donziger,* dated March 4, 2014, ran to 485 pages annotated by 1,842 footnotes. At sixty-nine, Kaplan had served on the federal bench for almost twenty years. *Chevron v. Donziger,* while surely not his last major piece of judicial work, had the heft of a career-capping manifesto.

Kaplan marveled at the evidence he'd seen: "coded emails among Donziger and his colleagues describing their private interactions with and machinations directed at judges and a court-appointed expert, their payments to a supposedly neutral expert out of a secret account, a lawyer who invited a film crew to innumerable private strategy meetings and even to ex parte meetings with judges, an Ecuadorian judge who claims to have written the multibillion-dollar decisions but was so inexperienced and uncomfortable with civil cases that he had someone else (a former judge who had been removed from the bench) draft some civil decisions for him, an eighteen-year-old typist who supposedly did Internet research in American, English, and French law for the same judge, who knew only Spanish, and much more."

As striking as the litany of transgressions was Kaplan's

measured tone—one that occasionally had eluded him during earlier stages of the case. "Donziger," the judge acknowledged, "began his involvement in this controversy with a desire to improve conditions in the area in which his Ecuadorian clients live. To be sure, he sought also to do well for himself while doing good for others, but there was nothing wrong with that." This was a dispensation Chevron never granted Donziger, whom the company and its lawyer at Gibson Dunn implied had the heart and ambitions of a gangster.

"In the end, however," Kaplan continued, Donziger and the Ecuadorian lawyers he led "corrupted the Lago Agrio case." They fabricated evidence. They coerced a judge to appoint a supposedly impartial "global" damages expert whom Donziger handpicked and paid to "totally play ball" with the Lago Agrio plaintiffs. Donziger secretly paid a Colorado consulting firm to write the expert's report and falsely presented the report as legitimate, independent work. Then the plaintiffs' team told half-truths or worse to U.S. courts to prevent exposure of their wrongdoing. Ultimately, Kaplan said, the plaintiffs' lawyers "wrote the Lago Agrio court's judgment themselves and promised $500,000 to the Ecuadorian judge to rule in their favor and sign their judgment."

Corporate lawyers and lobbyists had been eagerly awaiting Kaplan's ruling. "Those of us who've followed the case can't say we're surprised by how it came out," Darren McKinney told me. McKinney monitors mass litigation for the American Tort Reform Association, a corporate-funded lobbying group in Washington. He promoted *Chevron v. Donziger* as a model, saying, "We hope it will encourage other defendant companies that have been victimized by fraudulent lawsuits to fight back with RICO suits of their own."

Kaplan could have made broad pronouncements playing to the corporate audience, signaling that he saw his opinion as a template for combatting plaintiffs-lawyer trickery. But he didn't. He didn't generalize from the *Aguinda* litigation, and he didn't draw a bright jurisprudential line to distinguish worthy human-rights suits from corporate shakedowns. On the other hand, Kaplan did say that wherever that line might lie, Donziger crossed it. "If ever there were a case warranting equitable relief with respect to a judgment procured by fraud," the judge wrote, "this is it."

By "equitable relief" Kaplan meant that his order—technically known as an injunction—would bar Donziger and his clients from enforcing the Ecuadorian judgment in any court in the United States. With regard to courts in other countries, Kaplan bowed to the Second Circuit's earlier-stated skepticism of preemptive world-wide injunctions. "This court does not grant an injunction barring enforcement of the Lago Agrio judgment anywhere in the world," he said. If a judge in Canada or Argentina saw fit to punish Chevron, Kaplan conceded, he couldn't do anything about it. Instead he prohibited Donziger and his clients, the defendants in *Chevron v. Donziger*, "from profiting in any way from the egregious fraud that occurred." Any penalty imposed on Chevron in the form of money damages could not flow into the pockets of the Lago Agrio plaintiffs and their attorneys.

On one level, the injunction seemed ambiguous: If the plaintiffs could not benefit monetarily, how would a foreign judge enforce the Ecuadorian judgment? On another level, though, Kaplan's practical intent couldn't have been clearer. By branding Donziger a racketeer and the Lago Agrio judgment a fraud, he aimed to persuade any self-respecting judge, no matter where he sat, to repudiate the Ecuadorian verdict long before reaching the question of damages or other remedies.

While Kaplan was presiding over the *Chevron v. Donziger* trial in the fall of 2013, Ecuador's Supreme Court had halved the judgment amount from $19 billion to $9.5 billion. Kaplan's ruling, assuming it were upheld in the United States and respected by courts else-where, made the dollar figure irrelevant. Chevron planned to use the RICO findings as a basis for arguing that wherever Donziger might try to enforce the Ecuadorian judgment, it was worthless.

Donziger's supporters railed against Kaplan. "Corporate impunity is the theme of our days," Sting's wife, Trudie Styler, protested in a mournful *Huffington Post* article the day after the decision.

Kaplan, however, conceded the existence of industrial contamination in the Oriente. "On that assumption," he wrote, "Texaco and perhaps even Chevron—though it never drilled for oil in Ecuador—might bear some responsibility." That went beyond anything Chevron would admit.

"Improvement of the conditions for the residents of the Oriente appears to be both desirable and overdue," Kaplan continued. "But [Donziger's] effort to change the subject to the Oriente, understandable as a tactic, misses the point of this case." Even if Donziger had a just cause, and the judge expressed "no opinion on that," the lawyer was "not entitled to corrupt the process" to achieve his goal. "Justice is not served by inflicting injustice."

Kaplan derided what he called Donziger's "'this-is-the-way-it-is-done-in-Ecuador' excuses" as "a remarkable insult to the people of Ecuador." Donziger's misconduct, he wrote, "would be offensive to the laws of any nation that aspires to the rule of law, including Ecuador."

Donziger fully expected this defeat. Six weeks earlier, he had announced he'd hired an up-and-coming Washington attorney named Deepak Gupta to represent him on appeal. The opportunity to oppose Chevron in a fight over the rain forest still exerted a powerful gravitational pull on left-leaning activists. Gupta, a thirty-six-year-old former lawyer at Public Citizen, Ralph Nader's consumer watchdog group, called the engagement "the ultimate David v. Goliath case."

In his response to Kaplan, Donziger played on the theme of bullying by an American corporation and a powerful federal judge. "This is an appalling decision resulting from a deeply flawed proceeding that overturns a unanimous ruling by Ecuador's Supreme Court," he said. He accused Kaplan of allowing "his implacable hostility toward me, my Ecuadorian clients, and their country [to] infect his view of the case." Gupta had plausible grounds on which to base an appeal, but Kaplan's low opinion of Donziger was not one of them. The Second Circuit had repeatedly refused to remove Kaplan from the case, and his exhaustive ruling didn't have the earmarks of bias. A more promising basis for appeal would be an attack on the propriety and sweep of Kaplan's injunction.

What happens to a lawyer who is branded an outlaw by a federal judge in the course of a private lawsuit? Kaplan's civil-law conclusions weren't the equivalent of a criminal verdict based on a jury's determination of guilt beyond a reasonable doubt. The Manhattan U.S. Attorney's Office could read the opinion as a (very detailed) memo recommending prosecution, but that seemed unlikely. A number of Kaplan's key findings, while emphatic, were based on inferences from hotly contested testimony. Much of the suspect activity took place years earlier in faraway Ecuador, where critical witnesses would resist cooperating with a U.S. prosecution. And prosecutors would confront the far more daunting beyond-a-reasonable-doubt criminal burden of proof, as compared to the more-likely-than-not civil standard Chevron had met.

That didn't mean, however, that Donziger was entirely off the hook. In his ruling, Kaplan went out of his way to refer to Donziger's membership in the New York bar. "His conduct, whether in the United States or in Ecuador," the judge wrote, "was subject in every respect to the New York rules governing the conduct of lawyers." In case bar disciplinary authorities missed his point, Kaplan helpfully provided a footnote citing relevant provisions of the New York Rules of Professional Conduct. Unlike prosecutors, bar investigators don't have to prove infractions beyond a reasonable doubt.

Potential professional discipline wasn't the only consequence Donziger could face. Chevron invoked a provision of the RICO statute that allows a victorious plaintiff to seek reimbursement of its legal expenses. The company asked for $32 million, a request Kaplan had under advisement as of this writing. And Chevron wasn't the only party that could sue Donziger. The Philadelphia class-action lawyer Joe Kohn had already taken preliminary steps for a suit against Donziger seeking to recover the millions of dollars Kohn's firm had invested in the case.

As always, Donziger seemed to relish the prospect of endless legal struggle. The particulars didn't distract him. Kaplan's decision, he asserted, "is full of vitriol," when in fact the ruling was solidly grounded in a copious factual record. The judge, Donziger added, "ignores the overwhelming evidence that Chevron committed environmental crimes and fraud in Ecuador," even though Kaplan granted that there may have been wrongdoing in the rain forest. Finally, Donziger insisted, "this ruling is a far cry from what Chevron wanted"—a statement that betrayed what can only be understood as a refusal to accept reality. Whatever its wisdom, Judge Kaplan's decision was exactly what Chevron wanted.

Acknowledgments

This book began with a profile of Steven Donziger for *Bloomberg Businessweek*. My thanks to the magazine's editor, Josh Tyrangiel, for putting the article on the cover and indulging my continuing fascination with the story. Thanks also to Josh's then boss, Norman Pearlstine, who, as it happens, gave me my start at the *Wall Street Journal* longer ago than either of us would like to admit. On three book projects, literary agent Stuart Krichevsky has provided sound advice and ready friendship. I hope our Mediterranean lunches continue for many years. At Crown, executive editor Roger Scholl once again offered excellent guidance. Laurence Barrett, well into his sixth decade as a writer and editor, read chapter drafts with an eagle eye. Last and most important on the home team, there is Julie Cohen, whose love, friendship, and humor sustain me every day. Beau the dachshund, asleep on my lap, shares my admiration for Julie.

During my reporting in Lago Agrio, Quito, New York, San Ramon, and points beyond, a number of people were especially generous with their time: Mitch Anderson, Luis Alberto Aráuz, Christopher Bogart, José Antonio Bricerio Castillo, Jim Craig, Emergildo Criollo, Servio Curipoma, Chris Gidez, Karen Hinton, Chris Jochnick, Judith Kimerling, Randy Mastro, Donald Moncayo, Hew Pate, Kent Robertson, John Sanbrailo, Giovanni Rosanía

Schiavone, Doug Southgate, James Tyrrell, Rob Wasserstrom, and Andrew Woods. Steven Donziger spoke to me at length for the initial magazine profile and in the months thereafter. When my attention turned to this book, however, he cut off communication and discouraged certain other people from cooperating. He never explained his decision. Fortunately, a plentiful public record and a wide array of other sources, including people who know Donziger well, yielded ample raw material.

Source Notes

In many instances, I have indicated sources in the book's text. I offer the following notes as elaboration and as an aid in tracking down relevant articles and books.

Chapter One: Surveillance

As with scene play throughout in the book, the opening vignette of Steven Donziger in New York is based on a combination of interviews and written sources, in this instance press releases Donziger issued via Karen Hinton, which described the alleged Chevron surveillance. Where I describe people's thoughts, I rely on first-person accounts, descriptions provided by others with personal knowledge of the given situation, and/or written accounts gathered from court records or other sources.

Chapter Two: Pressure

The Quito courtroom scene appears in Joe Berlinger's 2009 documentary film, *Crude: The Real Price of Oil*. Additional relevant material comes from Berlinger's raw footage, or outtakes, which Chevron obtained via discovery and included in public court filings. You can find the court material by using the website pacer.gov and searching the docket of the company's civil-racketeering lawsuit, *Chevron Corp. v. Steven R. Donziger*, Case No. 11 Civ. 0691, in the Southern District of New York. The quotes from Donziger's diary-style notes are also drawn from court filings in *Chevron v. Donziger*.

Chapter Three: Arrival

Emergildo Criollo's description of Cofán history and interaction with Texaco comes from my interview with him in Ecuador. Allen Gerlach's *Indians, Oil, and Politics: A Recent History of Ecuador* (2003) contains useful background material on the industry's impact on the rain forest.

Chapter Four: Production

I did research on Texaco's exploration and drilling in Ecuador in Chevron's corporate archives in San Ramon. Tom Petzinger's excellent *Oil & Honor: The Texaco-Pennzoil Wars* (1987) provided additional history on Texaco. I also relied on Judith Kimerling's monograph, *Amazon Crude* (1991), and her scholarly articles, especially "Indigenous Peoples and the Oil Frontier in Amazonia," her book-length 2006 piece for the *NYU Journal of International Law and Politics*. Other useful background on Ecuadorian oil, colonization of the rain forest, and related topics came from Gerlach's *Indians, Oil, and Politics,* David Martz's *Politics and Petroleum in Ecuador* (1987) and David Schodt's *Ecuador: An Andean Enigma* (1987). Sven Wunder's *Oil Wealth and the Fate of the Forest* (2003) clarified the roles of agriculture and petroleum activities in deforestation. I interviewed José Antonio Bricerio Castillo, Giovanni Rosanía Schiavone, and Luis Alberto Aráuz in Ecuador. The Shields memo and other internal Texaco correspondence come from discovery documents obtained by the *Aguinda* plaintiffs, which they made public by means of federal court filings, including counterclaims in *Chevron v. Donziger.*

Chapter Five: Litigation

The records of the original 1993 lawsuit in *Maria Aguinda v. Texaco Inc.,* Case No. 93 Civ. 7527, in the Southern District of New York are publicly available. The *New York Times* provided helpful coverage, such as James Brooke, "Oil and Tourism Don't Mix, Inciting Amazon Battle," September 26, 1993, and Agis Salpukas, "Ecuadorian Indians Suing Texaco," November 4, 1993. Some of Donziger's articles from his time as a reporter in the 1980s are available online, including those I quote from: "Nicaragua, U.S. to Talk, Despite Tension," United Press International, November 15, 1984; "Raids of Villages Add to Nicaragua Suffering," *Houston Chronicle,* March 14, 1985; and "Americans in Nicaragua Vent Anger: Fate of Rebel Suppliers Should Teach U.S. Lesson, They Say," *Orlando Sentinel,* October 12, 1986. Donziger's early work crafting narratives for the media is illustrated by Bill Disessa, "Cuban Inmate Middleman Was Chosen for Role Because He Spoke the Best English," *Houston Chronicle,* November 30, 1987. The *Harvard Crimson* noticed his tendency to spark conflict as a law student: Jonathan M. Berlin, "Flyers Allege Ethical Violations: Charge Law Record Allows Activist to Bias Coverage," November 1, 1990. The *New York Times* noticed, too: "A Class Sends a Message to Harvard Law School," November 21, 1990. The *Los Angeles Times,* among other major outlets, covered Donziger's mission to Iraq: Sam Fullwood III and Nick B. Williams Jr., "170,000 Iraqi Children Face Death, Health Study Finds," May 21, 1991. Donziger's reference to taking inspiration from the photos of Humphrey and RFK in his grandfather's office can be found in Clifford Krauss, "An Avenger, on the Defensive," *New York Times,* July 31, 2013.

Useful background on Cristóbal Bonifaz and his family can be found in Paul Braverman, "Tilting at Texaco," *American Lawyer,* November 2001. As noted in the text, Judith Kimerling described her original research in the influential *Amazon Crude* (1991). I supplement her economic analysis with figures compiled by Douglas Southgate in "National Interests, Multinational Actors, and Petroleum Development in the Ecuadorian Amazon," *Whitehead Journal of Diplomacy and International Relations,* Winter/Spring 2011, and Allen Gerlach in *Indians, Oil, and Politics: A Recent History of Ecuador* (2003). Kimerling recounted her interaction with Bonifaz, including their correspondence, in the scholarly articles mentioned earlier. Donziger's comments about his early work as a criminal defense attorney and his decision to join the Bonifaz team come from a proposal he drafted in 2006 for a planned memoir that never came to fruition. His musings about asymmetrical legal warfare were quoted in Michael Goldhaber's first-rate profile, "Overexposed," *American Lawyer,* April 2010. I am in Kimerling's debt for the anecdote about how the U.S. Agency for International Development inadvertently helped promote the *Aguinda* suit in New York in 1993.

Chapter Six: Remediation

Donziger discussed the early *Aguinda* litigation strategy in "Rainforest Chernobyl: Litigating Indigenous Rights and the Environment in Latin America," *American University Washington College of Law Human Rights Brief,* Winter 2004. The Joseph Kohn quotes come from *Crude* outtakes. Kimerling's massively footnoted 2006 NYU *Journal of International Law and Politics* article provided helpful references to J. Donald Annett's 1991 letter to the Natural Resources Defense Council, Warren Gillies's 1992 speech to Petroecuador employees, and Wilma Subra's comments on Texaco's remediation of the Oriente oil fields. Chevron included in its court filings the grateful 1997 letter from Hugo Gerardo Camacho Naranjo to Texaco.

Chapter Seven: Jurisdiction

Judge Broderick made his ambivalent preliminary ruling in *Aguinda v. Texaco Inc.*, Case No. 93 Civ. 7527, 1994 WL 142006 (S.D.N.Y., April 11, 1994). Judge Rakoff's article is "Moral Qualms About Environmental Prosecutions," *New York Law Journal*, July 11, 1991. Judith Kimerling provided the November 1995 correspondence with the Capuchin missionary. Rakoff initially dismissed the suit in *Aguinda v. Texaco Inc.*, 945 F. Supp. 625 (S.D.N.Y., 1996). The U.S. Court of Appeals for the Second Circuit recounted the Ecuadorian government's shifting positions on the case, and its own oversight of Rakoff's rulings, in *Aguinda v. Texaco Inc.*, 303 F. 3d 470 (2d Cir. 2002). Diana Jean Schemo wrote the *Times* dispatch, "Ecuadorians Want Texaco to Clear Toxic Residue," February 1, 1998. Rakoff's dismissal ruling can be found at *Aguinda v. Texaco Inc.*, 142 F. Supp. 625 (S.D.N.Y., 2001). In her 2006 NYU law review article, Kimerling documented Donziger's campaign to embarrass Texaco in connection with its job-discrimination litigation and, subsequently, its merger with Chevron. The *Times* described the Chevron-Texaco combination, including Wall Street's reaction, in Neela Banerjee and Mary Williams Walsh, "1 New Oil Company, 2 Corporate Cultures," October 17, 2000.

Chapter Eight: *Justicia!*

Robert Worth reported the scene of the Ecuadorians visiting Manhattan in "Just Tourists on Broadway, But Barefoot and Craving Roast Monkey," *New York Times*, March 12, 2002. The opening of the trial in *Aguinda v. Chevron Corp.* in Lago Agrio received widespread media coverage. Some of the best images of the protests and proceedings can be found in photographer Lou Dematteis's 2007 book, *Crude Reflections: Oil, Ruin, and Resistance in the Amazon Rainforest,* which also features an essay by Sting and Trudie Styler. Judge Alberto Guerra recounted his thoughts about the beginning of the trial in his sworn declaration in *Chevron v. Donziger.* Bianca Jagger's participation in the case was reported by the Inter Press Service in "Ecuador: Bianca Jagger Backs Lawsuit Against ChevronTexaco," October 10, 2003, and "Bianca Jagger Promotes Lawsuit Against Chevron-Texaco in Ecuador," Associated Press, October 10, 2003.

The 2001 study of San Carlos by Miguel San Sebastián and colleagues is called "Exposures and Cancer Incidence Near Oil Fields in the Amazon Basin of Ecuador," *Occupational & Environmental Medicine.* The follow-up study, also led by San Sebastián, can be found at "Outcomes of Pregnancy Among Women Living in Proximity of Oil Fields in the Amazon Basin of Ecuador," *International Journal of Occupational and Environmental Health* (2002). Evidence of Donziger's successful promotion of the Lago

Agrio trial can be found in Brooke Masters, "Case in Ecuador Viewed as Key Pollution Fight," *Washington Post,* May 6, 2003, and Marc Lifsher, "Chevron Would Face $5 Billion Tab for Amazon Cleanup, Expert Says," *Wall Street Journal,* October 30, 2003 (which contains David Russell's comparison of the Oriente to Chernobyl).

Chapter Nine: Inspection

Donziger adopted the Chernobyl metaphor in, among other articles and statements, his 2004 piece for the American University *Human Rights Brief,* "Rainforest Chernobyl: Litigating Indigenous Rights and the Environment in Latin America." Bianca Jagger followed suit in Tamara Grippi, "Jagger to Address ChevronTexaco Shareholders," *Tri-Valley Herald,* April 27, 2004. My account of the judicial inspections draws on interviews with David Russell, Charles Calmbacher, and other participants. Quotations from citizen attendees at the inspections come from the 188-page February 14, 2011, ruling in *Aguinda v. Chevron Corp.* by the trial court in Lago Agrio. To describe Texaco's drilling and waste-disposal practices in the 1970s and 1980s, I relied on court filings and interviews with current and former oil industry employees. The *New York Times* nicely described one inspection in Brian Ellsworth, "Court Goes to Oil Fields in Ecuador Pollution Suit," August 27, 2004. The face-off between Pablo Fajardo and Adolfo Callejas appears in *Crude.* For my portrait of Fajardo, I relied on interviews and several published profiles, including William Langewiesche's extensive "Jungle Law," *Vanity Fair,* May 2007.

Examples of Chevron-sponsored critiques of the San Sebastián research on cancer in the Oriente include: Alejandro Arana and Felix Arellano, "Cancer Incidence Near Oilfields in the Amazon Basin of Ecuador Revisited," *Occupational & Environmental Medicine* (2007), and Michael Kelsh, Libby Morimoto, and Edmund Lau, "Cancer Mortality and Oil Production in the Amazon Region of Ecuador, 1990–2005," *International Archives of Occupational and Environmental Health* (2008). *Bloomberg Businessweek,* when it was still known as *BusinessWeek,* provided helpful background on Charles James: "A Chat with Justice's Charles James," August 2, 2001, and "Sorry, Bill. Charles James Is No Softie," August 3, 2001. The Guanta episode was described in detail in various court filings and Donziger's personal notes. I also relied on interviews. The various inspections of the Sacha 53 well site were included in court filings. Donziger chronicled his team's reaction to Sacha 53 and the decision to seek a "global expert" in his notes.

Chapter Ten: Lobbying

The vivid scene of Donziger coaching Emergildo Criollo in Houston appears in the documentary *Crude*. The Chevron annual shareholders meeting was described by Rick Jurgens in "Activists Face Off With Chevron CEO," *Contra Costa Times*, April 26, 2006. For my description of Charles James, I relied on David Baker's profile, "Charles James Defends Chevron Around the World," *San Francisco Chronicle*, May 26, 2009; Michael Goldhaber's Q&A, "Oil's Well That Ends Well: Parting Shots from Chevron's Charles James," *Corporate Counsel*, March 1, 2010; and an autobiographical speech James delivered before the Directors Roundtable in fall 2007.

Donziger recounted his private dealings with Judge German Yáñez and Frente leader Luís Yanza in his personal notes, where he also described his unsuccessful attempt to persuade female Frente interns to seduce Yáñez.

Chapter Eleven: Publicity

Donziger described in the notes his thoughts about and dealings with Rafael Correa and his advisers. Berlinger captured the scene of Donziger at Correa's inauguration. Fernando Reyes recalled his encounters with Donziger in a sworn declaration filed with the federal court in New York. In his notes, Donziger confirmed his covert dealings with Reyes and with Richard Cabrera. Berlinger's *Crude* outtakes include extensive footage of the March 3, 2007, meeting at which Donziger's team told Cabrera of their plans for his supposedly independent analysis. Berlinger recounted his early dealings with Donziger in a promotional essay the filmmaker wrote in 2009 about *Crude*. Donziger's "they don't know shit" and "smoke and mirrors" comments appear in the documentary outtakes. Berlinger also memorialized Correa's helicopter trip to the oil fields, as well as Trudie Styler's visit to some of the same places. The transcript of the December 2007 CNN *Heroes* show is available online.

Chapter Twelve: Relationships

For my description of Donziger's relationship with his wife, I drew on Donziger's personal notes and my interviews with people who know them. Donziger's introspection about his career, personal life, and related matters can be found in his notes and in his abortive 2006 book proposal. Berlinger recorded Donziger's interaction with attorney Joseph Kohn in Philadelphia. Donziger described in his notes the inconclusive settlement talks he and Kohn conducted with Chevron's outside attorney Tim Cullen.

Chapter Thirteen: Fiasco
Cristóbal Bonifaz's disgrace in federal court in San Francisco can be found in the public record of *Gonzalez v. Texaco Inc.,* Case No. 06-Civ-02820, in the Northern District of California, particularly in Judge William Alsup's August 3, 2007, "Order Granting Motions for Summary Judgment and Terminating Sanctions." See also: David Bario, "Oil Slick: Chevron Wins Sanctions Against a Plaintiffs' Lawyer," *American Lawyer,* March 2008. My description of Servio Curipoma and his family history relied on interviews in Ecuador and New York, as well as background in the Dematteis book *Crude Reflections: Oil, Ruin, and Resistance in the Amazon Rainforest.*

Chapter Fourteen: Authorship
The scene of Donziger conferring with Luís Yanza and Atossa Soltani appeared in outtakes from *Crude.* The scene of Richard Cabrera presiding over field inspections appeared in the documentary itself. David Russell's correspondence with Donziger can be found in the court files for *Chevron v. Donziger.* Donziger's e-mail exchanges with Stratus are likewise found in the court record. For the description of the 2009 Sundance premiere of *Crude,* I relied on various websites, including those of Indiewire and CBS News (e.g. "Sting's Message at Sundance," CBS, February 11, 2009), and Manohla Dargis, "In the Snows of Sundance, A Marked Chill in the Air," *New York Times,* January 22, 2009. The 2009 *60 Minutes* segment is available online, as is Martha Hamilton's insightful critique, "How *60 Minutes* Missed on Chevron," *Columbia Journalism Review,* April 2010.

Chapter Fifteen: Entrapment
My reporting for "Amazon Crusader. Corporate Pest. Fraud?" *Bloomberg Businessweek,* March 2011, informed my analysis of Chevron's strategy. Mary Cuddehe described her engagement with Chevron's private-eye firm, Kroll, in "A Spy in the Jungle," *The Atlantic,* August 2, 2010. Chevron narrated the Diego Borja episode in a series of press releases in 2009, as well as court filings. The Borja tapes remain available online on the company's website. The *Los Angeles Times* offered a concise evaluation of the Borja recordings in a September 5, 2009, house editorial, "Chevron's Legal Fireworks." The *New York Times* covered the controversy in Simon Romero and Clifford Krauss, "Chevron Offers Evidence of Bribery Scheme in Ecuador Lawsuit," August 31, 2009, and Krauss's follow-up, "Revelation Undermines Chevron Case in Ecuador," October 29, 2009.

Chapter Sixteen: Cleansing
American Lawyer celebrated Gibson, Dunn & Crutcher in "Game Changers," January 2010. David Hechler, "The Kill Step," *Corporate Counsel,* October 2009, provided helpful background on the firm and the Dole case. My description of Gibson Dunn's detective work in the Chevron case is based primarily on interviews. The firm's website, gibsondunn.com, has biographical information about Randy Mastro and the Transnational Litigation Group. Mastro has been the topic of lively local press coverage for many years, including Douglas Feiden, "Rudy Aide Mastro's Quitting," *Daily News,* June 29, 1998, and Dan Barry, "Top Giuliani Aide Is Leaving City Hall, *New York Times,* June 29, 1998.

Chapter Seventeen: Outtakes
Dave Itzkoff followed the Berlinger–First Amendment saga for the *New York Times*: "Judge Rules That Filmmaker Must Give Footage to Chevron," May 6, 2010; "Media Companies File Brief on Behalf of Filmmaker in Chevron Case," June 2, 2010; and "Court Rejects Claim of Journalist's Privilege for Documentary Filmmaker," January 14, 2011. Julio Prieto's fearful e-mail in March 2010 and Joe Kohn's increasingly anxious correspondence in 2009 and 2010 can be found in court filings in *Chevron v. Donziger*. Records of Russell DeLeon's financing of the *Aguinda* lawsuit likewise come from court filings. Roger Parloff wrote an informative piece on Donziger's adventures in litigation finance: "Have You Got a Piece of This Lawsuit?" *Fortune,* May 2011. Useful biographical background on James Tyrrell can be found in Anthony DePalma, *City of Dust: Illness, Arrogance, and 9/11* (2011). The marathon Donziger deposition is part of the court record in *Chevron v. Donziger*.

Chapter Eighteen: Racketeering
The parties made all of the relevant filings and rulings in the Ecuadorian court in Lago Agrio available (originals and translations) in the court records of *Chevron v. Donziger*. I obtained official transcripts of the hearings before Judge Kaplan from the parties.

Chapter Nineteen: Decision
Former judge Zambrano discussed his work habits and experience in Hugh Bronstein, "Ecuador Judge Works Marathon Hours on Chevron Case," Reuters, January 31, 2011. Former judge Guerra described his collaboration with Zambrano in a sworn declaration filed by the company in *Chevron v. Donziger*. The excerpts from the February 14, 2011, Lago Agrio ruling are taken directly from an official translation of the judgment.

Chapter Twenty: Pollution
My descriptions of the Cofán village and the two versions of the "toxic tour" were drawn from firsthand reporting and interviews.

Chapter Twenty-one: Retribution
During one of my reporting trips to Ecuador, I observed the Petroecuador spill and cleanup. Petroecuador's remediation announcement was described by Victor Gomez in "Ecuador Will Clean Up Areas in $18 bln Chevron Case," Reuters, December 14, 2011. My accounts of Hew Pate's thinking about the Ecuador case, Donziger's reaction to the company surveillance, and Burford Capital's withdrawal from financing the *Aguinda* suit were based on interviews. The Burford letter became public in a Chevron court filing in federal court in New York.

Chapter Twenty-two: Corruption
As noted in the text, I relied on Guerra's declaration and the heavily documented Chevron forensic analysis of the February 14, 2011, judgment—all available in the federal court record in New York—to reach my conclusions about the ruling's authorship. See also my articles for Businessweek .com: "Payoffs to Ex-Judge Are Latest Twist in Chevron Case," January 28, 2013; "Lawyer Denies Court Payoffs in Chevron Pollution Case," April 4, 2013; and "Judicial Mayhem in Chevron's Pollution Case," April 5, 2013. Donziger's description of the legal goings-on in Lago Agrio as unremarkable and customary came from Steven Mufson's *Washington Post* article, "How Patton Boggs Got Mired in an Epic Legal Battle with Chevron over Jungle Oil Pits," June 29, 2013.

Chapter Twenty-three: Trial
This chapter is based on federal court proceedings I observed, court transcripts and documents, and interviews indicated in the text.

Chapter Twenty-four: Conclusions
For my description of recent Chevron developments, both financial successes and environmental failures, I relied on coverage by the *Wall Street Journal*, including: Daniel Gilbert and Joann S. Lublin, "Chevron Cuts Executive Pay," March 28, 2013, and Liam Denning, "Chevron, Shell and Big Oil's Big Divide," March 20, 2013. The Ecuadorian oil-investor road show was described by Jonathan Kaiman in "Ecuador Courts Chinese Oil Bids for Amazonian Land," *Guardian*, March 26, 2013.

Epilogue

In addition to Judge Kaplan's March 4, 2014, ruling, I relied on the following: Jan Wolfe, "Donziger Taps Gupta Beck as Chevron Appeal Looms," *The Litigation Daily,* January 23, 2014; Paul M. Barrett, "Chevron's RICO Victory Provides a Model for Other Companies," *Bloomberg Businessweek,* March 4, 2014; and Trudie Styler, "Seeking Justice in Ecuador," *Huffington Post,* March 5, 2014.

Bibliography

Judicial Rulings
The following court decisions chart the major developments in the controversy over oil pollution in the Oriente:

The federal trial court in New York dismissed the original *Aguinda v. Texaco Inc.* in 2001 in an opinion found at 142 F. Supp. 2d 534 (S.D.N.Y.). Judge Jed Rakoff ruled that the suit belonged, if anywhere, in Ecuador.

The U.S. Court of Appeals for the Second Circuit affirmed Rakoff's ruling in 2002 at 303 F. 3d 470 (2d Cir.).

The Ecuadorian trial court ruled for the plaintiffs in *Aguinda v. Chevron Corp.*, February 14, 2011, at 8:37 a.m. (English translation at http://www.theamazonpost.com/wp-content/uploads/2011-02-14 Lago Agrio Judgment PDF).

Ruling for Chevron in its civil-racketeering suit against Donziger, Judge Lewis Kaplan offered his view of the case in *Chevron Corp. v. Donziger*, 1:11-cv-00691-LAK-JCF, Document 1874, filed 3/4/14.

Articles
Donziger's legal war against Chevron has received voluminous coverage in newspapers, periodicals, and academic publications since the early 1990s. These are the most informative of the in-depth articles, beginning, immodestly, with the one that led to this book:

Barrett, Paul M., "Amazon Crusader. Corporate Pest. Fraud?" *Bloomberg Businessweek*, March 2011.

————, "Chevron Looks to Its Home Court for a Comeback Win," *Bloomberg Businessweek,* July 2011.

————, "Chevron's Lawyers at Gibson Dunn Get Tough in Ecuador Pollution Case," *Bloomberg Businessweek,* April 2013.

Braverman, Paul, "Tilting at Texaco," *American Lawyer,* October, 2001.

Goldhaber, Michael D., "Overexposed," *American Lawyer,* April 2011.

————, "Closing In on Truth and Justice in the Chevron-Ecuador Case," *Litigation Daily,* February 2013.

Hamilton, Martha, "How *60 Minutes* Missed on Chevron," *Columbia Journalism Review,* April 2010.

Kane, Joe, "Moi Goes to Washington," *The New Yorker,* May 1994.

Keefe, Patrick Radden, "Reversal of Fortune," *The New Yorker,* January 2012.

Kimerling, Judith, "Indigenous Peoples and the Oil Frontier in Amazonia: The Case of Ecuador, ChevronTexaco, and *Aguinda v. Texaco,*" *New York University Journal of International Law and Politics,* November 2006.

————, "Transnational Operations, Bi-National Injustice: Indigenous Amazonian Peoples and Ecuador, ChevronTexaco, and *Aguinda v. Texaco,*" *L'Observateur Des Nations Unies,* 2008.

Kolker, Carlyn, "Jungle Warfare," *American Lawyer,* November 2006.

Krauss, Clifford, "An Avenger, on the Defensive: Lawyer Who Beat Chevron in Ecuador Faces a Trial of His Own," *New York Times,* July 2013.

Langewiesche, William, "Jungle Law," *Vanity Fair,* May 2007.

Maas, Peter, "Slick," *Outside,* March 2007.

Mufson, Steven, "How Patton Boggs Got Mired in an Epic Legal Battle with Chevron over Jungle Oil Pits," *Washington Post,* June 2013.

Parloff, Roger, "Evidence of Fraud Mounts in Ecuadorian Suit Against Chevron," *Fortune,* December 2010.

————, "Have You Got a Piece of This Lawsuit?" *Fortune,* May 2011.

————, "Chevron Seeks to Sue Patton Boggs for Fraud and Deceit," *Fortune,* May 2013.

Press, Eyal, "Texaco on Trial," *The Nation,* May 1999.

Smith, Michael, and Karen Gullo, "Texaco Toxic Past Haunts Chevron as Judgment Looms," *Bloomberg News,* December 2008.

Southgate, Douglas, "National Interests, Multinational Assets, and Petroleum Developments in the Ecuadorian Amazon," *Whitehead Journal of Diplomacy and International Relations,* Winter/Spring 2011.

Wasserstrom, Robert, and Douglas Southgate, "Deforestation, Agrarian Reform, and Oil Development in Ecuador, 1964–1994," *Natural Resources,* March 2013.

Books

Aráuz, Luis Alberto, *Derecho Petrolero Ecuatoriano,* Quito: Comité de Empresa de los Trabajadores de Petroproducción, 2009.

Bower, Tom, *Oil: Money, Politics, and Power in the 21st Century,* New York: Grand Central, 2009.

De La Torre, Carlos, and Steve Striffler, eds., *The Ecuador Reader: History, Culture, Politics,* Durham, N.C.: Duke University, 2008.

Dematteis, Lou, and Kayana Szymczak, *Crude Reflections: Oil, Ruin, and Resistance in the Amazon Rainforest,* San Francisco: City Lights, 2007

Fretes-Cibils, Vincente, Marcelo M. Giugale, and José Roberto Lopéz-Cálix, eds., *Ecuador: An Economic and Social Agenda in the New Millenium,* Washington, D.C.: The World Bank, 2003

Gerlach, Allen, *Indians, Oil, and Politics: A Recent History of Ecuador,* Wilmington, Del.: Scholarly Resources, 2003.

Hofmeister, John, *Why We Hate the Oil Companies: Straight Talk from an Energy Insider,* New York: Palgrave MacMillan, 2010.

Hurtado, Osvaldo, *Portrait of a Nation: Culture and Progress in Ecuador,* Lanham, Md.: Madison, 2010.

Kane, Joe, *Savages,* New York: Knopf, 1995.

Kimerling, Judith, *Amazon Crude,* New York: Natural Resources Defense Council, 1991.

Maas, Peter, *Crude World: The Violent Twilight of Oil,* New York: Knopf, 2009.

Martz, David D., *Politics and Petroleum in Ecuador,* New Brunswick, N.J.: Transaction, 1987.

Petzinger, Thomas, *Oil & Honor: The Texaco-Pennzoil Wars,* New York: Putnam, 1987.

Sampson, Anthony, *The Seven Sisters: The Great Oil Companies and the World They Shaped,* London: Hodder & Stoughton, 1975.

Schodt, David W., *Ecuador: An Andean Enigma*, Boulder, Colo.: Westview, 1987.

Wunder, Sven, *Oil Wealth and the Fate of the Forest: A Comparative Study of Eight Tropical Countries*, London: Routledge, 2003.

Yergin, Daniel, *The Prize: The Epic Quest for Oil, Money & Power*, New York: Free Press, 1991.

Index